The HEART Has Its REASONS

The
HEART
Has Its
REASONS

a novel

KERRY BLAIR

Covenant Communications, Inc.

Published by Covenant Communications, Inc.
American Fork, Utah

Printed in the United States of America
First Printing: June 1999

06 05 04 03 02 01 00 99   10 9 8 7 6 5 4 3 2 1

ISBN 1-57734-479-0

CHAPTER 1

"Romance is a poor substitute for reason," Andi Reynolds said calmly as she backed her car from the driveway of her suburban home. "Especially when eternity's at stake." She glanced at her sister's skeptical face and smiled. "Sterling may not be as dashing as the heroes in those silly novels you read, Clytie, but he's everything a woman could want in an eternal companion."

"I bet your marriage would just *seem* eternal because he's so boring," Clytie retorted. "And, anyway, you don't love him."

"Of course I do."

"No, you don't. You love that checklist-for-choosing-an-eternal-companion of yours, and Sterling just happens to fit the qualifications."

"Perfectly."

Perfectly, Clytie repeated to herself. *Mr. and Mrs. Perfect.*

In just a few days, if the world continued on its present course, Elder Sterling Channing would return from his mission, and Ariadne Reynolds would announce her engagement to him. Everyone who knew them would declare it the perfect match. Everyone, that is, but her younger sister. Though only sixteen years old and scarcely three and a half feet tall, Clytie was prepared to enlist God's help in altering the world's course if it would keep her older sister from making the biggest mistake of her eternal life. Sterling might well be Mr. Perfect, but he was still perfectly wrong for Andi.

"But you don't really love him," Clytie repeated. "You're just afraid to test the limits of your narrow little comfort zone."

Andi couldn't help but laugh. "Where did you hear such silly psychobabble?"

"On a TV talk show," Clytie admitted reluctantly. "But it's true."

"Does Dad know you watch that stuff?"

"It's educational."

"Only if you're studying to become a deviant."

Clytie widened her already large aqua eyes and asked sweetly, "Is a deviant someone like Sterling?"

"No," Andi responded with a hint of a smile. "It's nothing like Sterling. He's perfect." Her smile changed to a frown of annoyance at the long line of traffic that stretched before them down Center Street. "And please don't keep on about him," she said, steering clear of a bright orange pylon as the traffic slowed to a standstill. She reached for an unopened airmail envelope on the dashboard.

"A letter from Elder Perfect," Clytie observed. "It must be Monday." For the last two years, neither rain nor sleet nor llama bite had deterred Sterling's weekly missives from Peru. He was reliable—Clytie would grant him that—but from what she had read of his letters, he wrote more of what you'd expect to hear from Paul (if you were a Corinthian) than what you'd hope to hear (if you were a girl) from your prospective eternal companion.

When the car in front of them moved forward, Andi handed the letter to Clytie. "Go ahead and open it for me."

"Are you sure? What if it's the proposal you've been waiting for?"

"I'm not expecting a proposal," Andi said. "Everything between us is already understood." Still, her heart beat a little faster as her sister's tiny fingers slipped under the flap. After all, this was the last letter Sterling had written from the mission field. Maybe he could finally tell her how he felt now that he was coming home. She glanced at Clytie hopefully. "Well, what does it say?"

Clytie scanned the single sheet of neat penmanship with a little shrug. "I think he may have written a new section for the Doctrine and Covenants."

"What?" Andi asked, trying to understand Clytie and simultaneously determine which lane would take her through the heavy traffic and onto Brown Road.

"Well, maybe it's an essay on the first Article of Faith," Clytie continued. "Anyway, it's all about faith, repentance, and enduring to the end." She glanced at her sister's profile and wondered if the frown was due to Sterling's indifferent letter or all the cars backed up in front of HoHoKam Stadium. "You weren't expecting a proposal . . . ," she began.

"No, of course not."

"Then you won't be disappointed when you read this." Clytie suppressed a smile as she folded the letter carefully and returned it to the dashboard. Then she craned her neck to try to see out the window. "What's going on here?"

"Mass confusion," Andi replied. Somewhere along the way, she had chosen the wrong lane and was now, of all things, in a line waiting to park at the baseball stadium for a spring training game. Why, she wondered, did the stupid Cubs have to come all the way to Arizona to snarl up traffic? Andi wished they'd go back to Chicago and take all these people with them.

Her fingers tightened on the steering wheel in frustration as a turquoise-vested parking attendant approached the car. As it was, she had only thirty minutes to drop Clytie off at school and make it to her job at the Phoenix Zoo. Her green eyes narrowed as she scanned the lot for an exit. "Clytie, do you see a way out of here?"

"No."

"Not that you're looking," Andi noted impatiently as she rolled down the window. Her younger sister's attention was clearly focused on HoHoKam's main gate where a gaggle of excited people—mostly women—pushed and squealed in competition to be nearer . . . who? She turned finally to the attendant and frowned to see his curious eyes locked on little Clytie.

You've never seen a dwarf? she wanted to say. *Sorry we don't have postcards to send your friends.* She cast him her most withering look and muttered, "I hate baseball."

"Like it or not, lady, it's five bucks to park here."

"I don't want to park," Andi informed him indignantly, wishing now she had one of her charges from the Tropics Trail at the zoo along. This gangly kid wouldn't stare so hard at Clytie if there were a crocodile in the back seat.

As the next driver in line leaned on his horn, the young man leaned forward anxiously. "Howland's pitching today," he offered optimistically, as if that would somehow influence her to grab a hot dog and rush to the nearest seat.

"Is that him?" Clytie asked eagerly. A blue ball cap was all that was visible of the tall, young southpaw above a sea of ecstatic fans.

"Yeah, that's him. If you hurry, maybe you can get an autograph."

Clytie raised a stubby arm to sweep the long blonde hair back from her eyes as she tried to see the ballplayer's face. "Have you ever met him? What does he look like?"

"She doesn't care," Andi interjected. "As I was trying to say, we're not here for the game. We ended up here by mistake. Well, actually, it was more as a result of poor traffic planning on the city's part but . . ." As a cacophony of horns drowned out her words, Andi looked from the harried attendant toward the far side of the lot—and only exit—and reluctantly pulled open the change tray beneath the radio. Glowering at the young man, she fished out three crumpled bills and eight quarters. "Oh, here!" she said, thrusting the money through the open window. "Now can we go?"

The youth pocketed the parking fee and waved them on. "Enjoy the game!" he called. "That Howland's really something."

"Do you believe this?" Andi asked as she swerved around a program vendor near the front gate and bumped over a curb. "That guy didn't listen to a word I said."

"Hmmm?" Clytie had turned in her seat to stare backwards toward the crowd. As she watched, the center of attention raised his face for a moment to gaze up into the cloudless sky. "Oh," she gasped. "He's so cute! Andi, let's park and go over for a minute."

"To gawk at some egotistical jock? You've got to be kidding."

"It would be fun."

"Be reasonable, Clytie. You need to get to school, and I need to get to work."

"Can't you ever do anything that isn't reasonable?"

Andi smiled fondly at her diminutive little sister and slowed the car. She'd do anything to make Clytie happy. Every day she watched the struggle her little sister faced as a teenage dwarf in a Barbie-doll obsessed world. Then she glanced over her shoulder at the ever-growing throng surrounding the celebrity pitcher and pressed the accelerator. She'd do anything, that is, but allow her to be trampled by a crowd of idiotic athlete-worshippers. "Turn around, Clytie," she said. "I absolutely guarantee you're not missing anything here."

"How do you know? You didn't see him." Still, Clytie settled back into the seat obediently. After a few minutes she asked quietly, "Andi, don't you ever wonder if *you're* missing something?"

"No. Like what?"

"Excitement? Suspense?" She paused meaningfully. "Romance?"

"If this is about Sterling again, I don't want to hear it." Andi steered clear of an incoming delivery truck and offered a quick prayer of thanksgiving to finally be back on a city street. Of course, she reflected, she was also five dollars poorer and fifteen minutes late. Maybe she should write letters of complaint to the Cubs and the city and forward copies to the local newspaper. Composing them in her mind, she began to feel better already.

"Just don't say you'll marry Sterling until . . ."

Andi forgot the letters and took advantage of a stop signal to examine her sister's earnest face. "Until what, Clytie?"

"Until . . ." Clytie's cheeks colored as she faltered for an explanation. *Until Heavenly Father answered her prayer and sent Andi's soulmate?* She'd known all along that it would be wicked to ask God to dispose of Mr. Wrong—even for a good cause—but there was surely nothing amiss in asking for the timely appearance of Mr. Right. She'd petitioned faithfully for weeks now, and with Sterling practically on the plane home, the time for Mr. Right's appearance had pretty much come down to now or never. Had it been too much to ask for divine intervention to deliver at least one new candidate for a prospective brother-in-law?

Clytie gazed out the window pensively and caught her breath at the sight of a sky so clear and blue it was miraculous in itself. She said softly, "Until the day you're absolutely positive there's no one else."

Andi, Clytie saw by her sister's quick smile, was confident that that day had already passed. But Clytie believed she knew better. With her perfect faith, and the Lord's perfect timing, the world's course could be expected to change at any minute. Today, she saw contentedly, was a day custom made for miracles.

CHAPTER 2

Greg blew a small, pink bubble as he released the ball and hoped for a miracle. Divine intervention might be the only thing that could keep his pitches in the park, and him on the mound for a third season. As the bat made contact and the ball went soaring, he popped the bubble between his teeth and wondered what March weather was like in Pittsville, PA. After yet another pre-season game in which his performance had ranged from bad to abysmal, his bags were practically packed for a trip down to the farm team. *Pittsville.* Greg liked the sound of it. His life had been headed for Pittsville since his brother's death, anyway.

He turned reluctantly to watch the ball spin across the cloudless sky toward left field. *So much for a miracle,* he thought. *That ball's outta here.* He glanced toward the Cubs' dugout as the rookie tagged third base on his run home. *It and me both.*

As Greg waited the eternity it seemed to take the manager to signal the bullpen and jog out to the mound, the southpaw's blue eyes rose to the stands. Here and there a group cheered on the Padres, but the majority of the 12,000 fans were sullen. Not that he could blame them. They'd invested ten bucks and a Monday afternoon to see what Greg Howland, currently the biggest draw in baseball, had to offer. It wasn't much.

He pulled the brim of his hat further down over his face as Biderman slapped the embroidered "C" on his broad chest and extended his hand for the ball. "Hit the showers early, kid," he growled, "and see if you can pull it back together next time."

Yeah, Greg thought, wincing at the scattered catcalls that punctuated his jog across the field toward the bench. *Pull it back together, kid.* But what was "it"? He'd give anything to pull together the mysterious void in his supposedly charmed life. The problem was, at only twenty-four, he already *had* everything you're supposed to need to be happy: talent, fame, and money enough for a couple of lifetimes. He paused at the top of the dugout and looked sheepishly at the day's honorary batboy, who rolled his wheelchair forward as his idol descended the stairs. Heck, he even had his health.

Greg glanced at the All-Star magazine on the young boy's lap and frowned at his own face smiling up from the cover. *That's me, all right,* he thought ruefully. *Poster boy for the American Dream.* He looked quickly away and made a beeline for the locker room.

"You were just great today, Mr. Howland!" the batboy called after him.

Greg ignored the snickers from his teammates on the bench as he paused at the clubhouse door then turned back to kneel in the dirt at the boy's side. "Thanks," he said quietly, "but you're the one who's been great. Are you having fun?"

"Yeah! I'll never ever forget I met you. Thanks for the autographed ball and your picture and everything."

Greg nodded mutely. Seeing a child's eyes light up over something as inherently worthless as his name scribbled on a scrap of paper never ceased to humble and thrill him. Mostly, it was what kept him showing up at the ballparks, although since Jim's death, it had stuck him with Zeke Martoni as well. Greg patted the little boy's shoulder and tried to dismiss the painful thought. Avoidance was the only game plan he'd come up with in long days of deliberation since Jim's funeral. He'd ignore his pain—and his publicist—long enough for both to, somehow, disappear. He mustered a thin smile. "It was a pleasure to meet you. Enjoy the rest of the game."

Finally alone in the locker room, Greg pulled the striped jersey over his head and tossed it toward a bin. If he hurried, he might be able to leave the clubhouse before a trainer showed up to ice down his arm and suggest yet another course of conditioning routines.

Greg dressed quickly, slammed his locker door shut, and turned to leave. But a dark form seemed to have materialized from the shadows and now blocked the aisle. *Speak of the devil.*

"Hey, Grego," the man hailed him. "Good to see ya, kid." He was trim and attractive, a full-sized ad for an Arizona dude ranch in narrow-legged Levis, snakeskin boots, and checked cowboy shirt. Greg wondered for a moment where the man had left his Stetson, then decided the omission was by design, to avoid covering the wavy black hair that had been oiled and combed to perfection.

Greg exhaled a shallow sigh of apprehension as he leaned back against the steel locker and propped one leg up on the bench, hoping to display to his visitor more casualness than he felt. "What are you doing here, Zeke? I thought you were in Chicago squeezing blood out of turnips."

The middle-aged man smiled as he stepped nearer. "Glad you got outta there early, kid, so's we can talk in private."

Recoiling at the familiar smell of liquor and expensive cigars, Greg crossed his arms firmly across his chest. "What do you want this time?"

"That's not very sociable, Grego, after I came all this way to see my favorite client." The smile widened, revealing a gleaming row of capped teeth. "The way I read the papers, kid, you could use a friend."

Probably, Greg thought, *but that doesn't tell me what* you're *doing here.*

In a previous century, Zeke Martoni might have peddled snake oil from the back of a traveling cart, one county ahead of the law. In this incarnation, he was the publicist representing Greg. The young athlete leaned his sandy blond head against his locker door and wondered what sin he might have committed in a former life to stick him with Zeke in this one. Realistically, even Greg had to admit it likely had less to do with karma than coincidence.

Just over a year before, Zeke had been on a routine, if scurrilous, business excursion through eastern Iowa when his car broke down on the interstate and had to be towed into Greg's tiny hometown. It was after hours at the auto shop, for the owner at least, but Zeke managed to track him to the tavern where locals often gathered to hear the latest exploits of Roy Howland's younger son, the up and coming darling of the sports world.

Zeke had listened casually at first, then avidly, buying Roy one drink after another. By nightfall, he was ensconced in the Howlands' shabby kitchen, across the table from Greg and Jim. The Cubs' newest phenomenon had returned to Peosta for his mother's birthday and was, by this time, feeling even more sorry about his visit than usual. He'd brought her his Rookie of the Year award and watched silently as Roy waved it grandly in front of Zeke.

It was clear to Greg that his father considered Martoni a godsend, but he eyed the glib pitchman doubtfully. He suspected that God had never taken much of a hand in anything this man was up to.

"Fame is like a roller coaster," Zeke told them, "and our kid won't be at the top very long. Before you know it, it's the fast track straight down. It'll make ya sick."

Greg had smelled the stale beer on Zeke's breath and felt sick already.

But Zeke warmed to his metaphor. "You're right up there, Grego, sitting in the first car. You need me to milk this thing for ya now, while we still can." He leaned back with a meaningful wink at Greg's dad.

"What'd I tell ya?" Roy turned to ask his wife. Sadie had retreated quietly to the sink, her birthday forgotten. "Is this great, or what? My kid's gonna be famous."

"I just want to play baseball," Greg said cautiously. "I don't want to be famous." He didn't, in fact, want to be noticed at all. Hence the dark glasses he wore almost everywhere, even in his mother's kitchen. He glanced apprehensively at his father's puffy face. Especially in his mother's kitchen. "Trenzle's my agent," he continued, leaning unconsciously toward Jim for support. "I don't need a publicist."

"Trenzle!" His father spat out the name like an epithet. "What'd he ever do except cost us a bundle?" Roy motioned to Zeke, his actions exaggerated and his deep voice slurred from the effects of agitation and booze. "Ever'body said the kid coulda gone pro at eighteen, but this bum Trenzle talked him into goin' to some idiot school. Four years down a rat hole."

Jim finally glanced up from the chipped, plastic tabletop, his long fingers massaging his forehead. "Look, Dad—"

Greg pushed back his chair before his brother could finish. "I've got to go. It's a long drive back to Chicago."

"Tonight?" Sadie asked. "You're leaving tonight, Greg?" A plate slipped from her thin hands into the water as she turned from the sink. "But you just got here."

"He ain't goin' nowhere 'til we settle this." Roy slapped a greasy palm on the table and swiped the remnants of the cake to the floor.

Greg stood a head taller than his father and was much stronger. His hands knotted reflexively. Then, from the corner of his eye, he saw his mother shrink back against the counter, color draining from her face as surely as dirty water trickled from the rag she squeezed to her chest. Greg drew in a slow breath and stretched his fingers out, one at a time. Then he bent to scoop the largest pieces of cake back onto the foam tray and slid it back on the table, away from his father.

Zeke watched with interest, his own fingers smoothing the already impeccable hair at his temples. As his eyes passed from Roy's heavy face to the red half-moons Greg's nails had left in the palms of his hands, he smiled.

"Greg . . . ," Jim began.

The young pitcher studied the pained expression on his brother's face with concern. He could see that Jim was suffering from another one of his headaches. Casting a troubled glance at his mother, Greg sighed, "Look, fine, okay? What's a stupid shoe deal going to hurt me, anyway?" He wiped the sticky pink frosting onto his pants and clasped Jim's shoulder as he spoke to Zeke. "Work something out if you want to, Martoni, and let my brother see it. I'll do it when I can." Crossing the room to Sadie's side, he pecked her cheek on his way out the door. "Happy birthday, Ma."

Less than a year later, Jim was dead and Greg was a reluctant superstar, on and off the field. When he wasn't pitching baseballs, he was pitching products and Zeke was pitching him. It seemed to Greg that his name was always in a headline, usually linked with an actress or model he'd never heard of, let alone spent a night with. The celebrity ballplayer couldn't walk into a supermarket without sunglasses and a hat to hide his famous face. Even glasses couldn't hide the embarrassment he felt checking out the tabloids. Any day now, he expected to read of his abduction by space aliens. Not that that would be a bad thing. He'd cheerfully inhabit Jupiter for a little solitude. Privacy is all he'd wanted, and mostly what he hadn't received, during these past few weeks following Jim's death.

Now, face to face with the smug author of his brother's betrayal and his own so-called success, Greg crossed his arms more firmly and said, "You could have called."

"They're still digging cars out of snow banks in Chicago, Grego, and it's bikini weather here," Zeke pointed out. "Besides, I've been leaving you messages. You don't call me back."

"You know what they say, no news is good news."

"That's not what I hear." Zeke's faux smile disappeared as his black eyes narrowed. "I hear you've lost your arm."

"Maybe, but don't lose any sleep over me, Zeke. You've made your million."

"Sure, but I've got overhead and three exes, Grego." He relaxed onto the bench and motioned for Greg to do the same, frowning when the young pitcher remained standing. "But this isn't about me," he continued smoothly, masking his irritation. "It's you I'm thinking of. I'm worried about ya, kid."

"I'm fine."

Zeke's slim fingers stroked his sideburns in a gesture Greg had seen many times. It reminded him of a sleek cat preening to congratulate itself on cornering a mouse. "It was tough luck, Jimmy dying that way." He appeared pleased when the younger man turned away, and his voice dropped to a purr. "His wife and kids doing okay?"

"Yeah, I guess," Greg said shortly.

"Your folks?"

"They're okay."

"You still feeling bad about this?"

A response caught in Greg's throat, threatening to choke him. He swallowed hard; the knot remained. Slowly, he turned toward Zeke. The thought of Jim's dealings with this man and, subsequently, his own, weakened his knees and he sank onto the bench. He repeated "I'm fine," but there was no conviction.

Looking carefully over his shoulder to assure himself they were alone, Zeke reached for a snap at the top of his shirt pocket, then extracted an envelope from which he removed a small cellophane packet. "I brought you a little something, kid. It's a present, say. You don't have to hurt this way anymore. This'll make you forget all your problems—even forget Jimmy for a while. You'll feel great and you'll throw great, guaranteed."

It took a few seconds for the pouch of white powder in Zeke's outstretched hand to register with Greg's brain. When it did, he jumped to his feet. "Have you lost your mind?"

Zeke smiled reassuringly as he held it up and moved it closer. "It's the best stuff money can buy, Grego. Give it a try, just once, and see if it doesn't change everything. It'll make you the best pitcher on the planet."

More like the stupidest. Greg grabbed his duffel and backed around the man's knees toward the exit. "I ought to get rid of you right now, Martoni."

"But you won't, kid," Zeke chuckled. "You won't." His job security lay in a black metal box back in Chicago and they both knew it. He pocketed the drug and watched Greg leave, his eyes narrowing to slits. It was only a matter of time. With everything to lose, Howland wouldn't go far.

CHAPTER 3

"All around and all above," Andi hummed softly as she went about her afternoon tasks, the frustrations of the morning almost forgotten in the lush serenity of the Tropics Trail at the zoo. *"Bear this witness: God is love."*

Who could doubt it in this micro-world of sun-dappled trees populated by lemurs, ocelots, and some of the most amazing birds on earth? Certainly Andi couldn't imagine a nicer day, a more benevolent Creator, or, when she thought about it, a more perfect life. Counting her blessings could well fill the afternoon. For one, she had an ideal job and loved every minute of the twenty hours she put in here in addition to her classes at Arizona State University; two, she had a wonderful family; and three, her missionary would return home this Friday.

Temple marriage was the next major step in Andi's carefully charted pathway toward perfection. As a Beehive, she'd dutifully sat down to plan her life and list the qualities she would want in an eternal companion. By the time she was a Laurel, she was well on course and had already realized she needn't look further than the front of the chapel for marriage material. There, Sterling Channing presided each week behind the sacrament table. Perhaps he wasn't the most romantic or exciting priest in the stake, but he was probably the most spiritual and certainly the most responsible. And despite what Clytie might think, romance was a poor substitute for reason when eternity was at stake.

She smiled up at the toucan in the aviary and tipped her head to match his. "Hello there," she said, reaching into a small pail attached to her belt for a slice of fresh fruit. "Would you like a snack?"

"Can he fly?" a thin voice inquired from behind her.

Andi turned her smile toward an elderly woman who leaned around her to peer curiously up at the bird. "Why, certainly he could, if there were more room in the exhibit for it."

The woman shook her head sadly. "Poor little thing."

"Oh, no! He's very happy here," Andi assured her. "He's better fed and much safer than he would be anywhere in the wild."

The woman regarded her with a twinkle in her eye. "Are you telling me, dear, that you think being secure in a cage is the same thing as being happy?"

"Well, in this case, yes." Andi's smile faded as the woman patted her arm then moved away. She seemed, Andi thought, to pity her now as well. "You're happy, aren't you?" she asked the bird as she turned back to slip pineapple between the narrow bars. "You're not missing anything in there, you know."

How do you know? Andi paused at the echo of her sister's words and considered the aviary. It was tall, but not very wide, and though the surrounding trees lent the illusion of life in a jungle setting, the animal was definitely caged. She studied the toucan's sleek ebony feathers and colorful beak for signs of distress, but he was obviously healthy and alert. "Really," she decided finally, "you are one lucky little bird." She added another small piece of fruit to the dish, frowning slightly when the bird hopped away to perch on a higher branch. "Life isn't meant to be exciting or romantic," she explained.

The feathered creature's bright black eyes looked steadily away, and Andi almost sighed at his apparent disappointment in the news. Then she tossed back her mane of curls and laughed at herself. How silly could she be? She didn't need to justify herself to the zoo animals. "Well, I'm happy," she told the toucan as she moved on to the next aviary. "Perfectly happy, thank you."

Greg adjusted his sunglasses as he approached a bridged lagoon that marked the entrance to the Phoenix Zoo. He wished he knew what he was doing here. After all, the *Do the Zoo!* billboard he had passed on his drive to anywhere that was away from Zeke wasn't a direct order. Why had it seemed like one? This was probably a bad idea. He wished he had gone back to his room instead. As much as he disliked being indoors (even domed stadiums made him nervous), he disliked crowds even more.

As a boisterous school group approached, Greg turned quickly away to lean over the metal rail. This was exactly why he almost never had the urge to sightsee. There was too great a possibility of becoming a sideshow himself. He pretended to study the turtles that had hoisted themselves on a moss-covered log to bask in the warm afternoon sun and found himself envying them their serene camaraderie amid the noisy activity of wild ducks with whom they shared a watery home.

A preschool gathered along the far bank, and Greg watched the dozen little kids reach into grease-spotted sacks of popcorn, eager to offer remnants of their snack to ducks equally eager to receive them. He smiled to acknowledge the universal attraction between little kids and ducks. Back home, he was often persuaded by Jim's two little boys to grab a bag of bread and head out for a quick visit to a nearby pond.

It was at that pond, Greg reflected now, that he had first faced death. He was three or four at the time, young enough that he never knew how he had slipped from the solid security of the bank into the swirling confusion of the pool of water. But he had never forgotten the muddy water that filled his nose and mouth, and he remembered, too, an eerie disquiet, a dark tunnel, and the sheer panic that gripped him when he could find no top, or bottom, to the numbing cold. Most vividly, he remembered Jim's strong, nine-year-old arms coming around him, pulling him out of the blackness, back into the light.

Greg's smile thinned and disappeared. Twenty years later he'd been unable to return the heroics. Instead, he'd sat helplessly at Jim's bedside and watched his only brother, and best friend, slip into blackness forever. Since that last starless night eight weeks ago when he had left the hospital alone, Greg had stopped counting the number of times he felt overwhelmed by despair.

There's gotta be a way to get through this, he told himself, raking a hand through his thick, sandy hair as he stared, unseeing, into the water below. *Other people must have noticed that life is pointless, but everybody doesn't take up with a Zeke, or end up as bitter as my dad. What do they see that I'm missing?*

Greg's eyes traced the intricate patterns on the turtles' shells as he mentally reviewed the only survival plan he'd received. It had come from Lupe, a kindly Hispanic waitress at the hotel restaurant and the closest thing Greg had to a friend in Arizona, or anyplace else for that matter. Since the middle of February, she'd fed him a steady diet of pancakes and platitudes, advising "*tenga paciencia*—be patient" and "*habla con Dios*—talk with God."

Her advice to pray had been as foreign as her language. Greg had never prayed. He didn't know how to pray. He even admitted that he didn't know who, or what, he believed in to pray to. But Lupe had calmly covered his pancakes with syrup and his protests with an assurance that "prayer is a matter of believing in God long enough to give Him a chance to prove that He believes in you."

Even if there is a God, Greg thought, clenching his jaw to swallow the hot tears that ran down the back of his throat, *why should He care about me?* He blinked rapidly. He wouldn't cry, and he certainly couldn't pray here, on the bridge to some park in the middle of the desert.

You aren't the first man to seek God in a desert.

Although it caused him to glance up, Greg knew the voice was in his head. Or was it in his heart? Wherever it was, it was quiet, calm, and, as always, sure of itself. It was a voice he had heard before and ordinarily followed, but never named.

Pray, the voice prompted. *Ask, and it shall be given you. Seek, and ye shall find.*

Talk about an offer too good to refuse. The little trust, hope, and purpose Greg had managed to find in life had seemed to die with his brother. He had nothing left to lose by accepting this anonymous dare, so Greg Howland clasped his hands self-consciously over the smooth metal rod, closed his eyes, and uttered his first, simple prayer.

God, if you are there, please help me. I don't know what I need, even, but I need something. Something to believe in. Something to hang on to. Something. Please, God, show me what it is.

Moments passed as Greg waited quietly, almost hopefully. When he finally opened his eyes, the scene was essentially the same. The tired, popcorn-less preschoolers trooped toward a waiting van while the ducks glided effortlessly across the pond and the sunbaked turtles blinked and stretched, oblivious to the man on the bridge and the rest of the world. Greg's eyes swept the horizon. There were no angels, burning bushes, or heavenly manifestations of any sort in evidence, which was, of course, pretty much as he expected.

Laughter from a point beyond the bridge broke his reverie, and he quickly passed the back of a thumb along the bottom rim of his glasses, angry with himself for expecting a miracle from a universe with nothing to offer. "Take a good look," he said to the turtles. "You'll probably never see anyone else so stupid in your lives."

Peace, be still.

Greg paused, then dismissed the voice impatiently. Hearing things was the very least of his problems.

"See you later, alligators," Andi promised as she passed their swampy exhibit on her way to the front of the zoo. "I'll be back with supper before you know it." She glanced at her watch and bumped her walk up to a jog. She was supposed to relieve Les at the safari train ten minutes ago. The annoying delay at the baseball stadium this morning had thrown off her entire day's schedule.

Inside the gate, Greg picked up a map and plopped on a wide-brimmed, touristy hat before a single glance could be directed his way. It was apparently disguise enough. He had remained safely incognito for ten minutes now. He congratulated himself on this new record as he studied the map. The African Trail was just to his left. He could see the sienna-spotted heads and necks of giraffes from where he stood. Lions, tigers, and zebras would be along that path, he noted. Ahead was the Tropics Trail. It was mostly birds, and therefore likely to be less popular than the rest of the zoo. Besides, he liked birds.

As he considered, he noticed the hurried approach of a slender young woman. The Tropics were forgotten as Greg admired the red and gold halo of curls bouncing past on the way to the safari train. Reaching her destination, she propped one arm against the zebra-striped tram as she chatted with the driver. She wore knee-length khaki shorts and a crisp, white cotton blouse, colorfully embroidered with the zoo emblem. Her legs and arms were a golden tan from days in the Arizona sun and her face . . . Greg couldn't see her face. He moved closer for a better view.

From a vantage point just outside the gift shop, he could see the light sprinkling of freckles across her nose. When she smiled, which was often, he smiled with her, admiring her dimples and straight white teeth. Certainly she wasn't the most beautiful girl he had ever seen, but there was something about her that was tremendously attractive. So, when the driver left the train and she swung up to take his place, Greg practically bowled over half a dozen people to get in line for a ticket.

On the first tour around the park, he barely noticed the animals from his seat in the fourth car, but thoroughly enjoyed the ride nonetheless. By the third trip, Greg had picked up quite a lot of zoo trivia, along with a not-so-trivial interest in a certain redheaded zoo employee. On the fourth tour, when the train paused near Harmony Farm to let off passengers, he moved to the row directly behind her seat. Riding back to the station, he found himself wanting to touch her hair to see if it was as soft and warm as it looked and to gaze into her eyes to see if they were brown or the blue he imagined. Greg could also smell her perfume, a light, spicy fragrance that reminded him, for some reason, of picnics and apple pie.

Finally, he told himself that enough was enough and got off the train. It was late afternoon and he had been on the hard seats for more than two hours. He'd either introduce himself to the main attraction here or go home. But despite his best intentions, three minutes later Greg was in the ticket line once again.

"You can buy a zoo membership for $50," the now-familiar voice said from just behind his right ear, "then the train rides are free. In your case, it could save you a fortune."

He turned quickly and looked down at her. She was smaller than she had appeared on the high seat, and her eyes were emerald green. Framed with bronze lashes, they were the clearest, most beautiful eyes Greg had ever seen. Right now they were dancing, which he took as a good sign. "I, uh, I've enjoyed the tours," he began lamely.

"So I gathered. Sometimes people with little children ride around twice, but you're the first able-bodied man I've seen go four times and line up for a fifth. You must really like the train."

Greg nodded sheepishly, suddenly unable to find his voice under the irregular, insistent rhythm of his heart. He'd read novels where this kind of thing happened, but he hadn't believed them.

"Well, enjoy your visit," Andi said, "and on behalf of the zoo, thanks for your support!" With a little wave, she swung around a canopy support pole and started up the path toward the Tropics.

"Just a minute!"

Andi paused in front of a tall, wrought-iron aviary to gaze back at him curiously. He had tripped, apparently over his own feet, and fallen into the pole. Perhaps he wasn't as able-bodied as he looked, despite all those muscles.

Recovering quickly, Greg closed the distance between them in a couple of strides, then stared over her shoulder into the foliage while he waited for his tongue to catch up. "Kookaburra bird!" he declared triumphantly when it did, a moment later. He pointed confidently to the feathered denizen of the cage. "It's a native of Australia; also called a Laughing Jack because it makes a trilling noise that sounds like laughter."

Andi smiled and tilted her head, spilling curls over her shoulder. "At least you weren't sleeping through my tours."

Her hair color reminded Greg of new pennies and everyone knows how lucky it is to find a new penny. He grinned. "I didn't miss a word. You're a great guide. Aren't you driving the next train?"

"No, I was filling in while Les took lunch and handled a school tour. He knows the spiel lots better than I do. You'll love him."

Greg doubted that. "What do you do?"

"Well, right now I promised to meet some alligators for supper."

"No, really."

"Yes, really. The alligators and crocodiles are all hungry. Excuse me."

Greg couldn't bear to excuse her. He fell into step as she moved away from the cage to make room for a young couple with a stroller. "What do you feed alligators?"

"Oh, nosey tourists, mostly."

For some odd reason, Andi regretted the sudden disappearance of his grin. She smiled up at him. "Sorry, that's an old joke. Really, our gators eat fish from their lake and a specially mixed supplement." She winked at her own reflection in his glasses. "And don't even ask what's in the mix if you plan to eat anytime soon."

"I love alligators!" Greg said, realizing instantly how foolish it sounded. No wonder the kookaburra bird was laughing.

"You do? Then it's too bad you couldn't see them from the zoo train." Andi's smile was broader now, but Greg didn't care if she laughed in his face. The deepening of those adorable dimples was worth a little humiliation.

Unfortunately, she lowered her face to look at her watch. "It was nice talking to you, but I really have to go. You wouldn't believe how cranky those crocs get when they're hungry."

"I could come along," Greg suggested, "and help you with the feeding."

Andi shook her head slowly. "I'm sorry, but only zoo employees are allowed in the food prep areas." She tried to get a better look at the face beneath the ridiculous hat and dark shades. She'd admired his athletic build from the tram's rearview mirror and had been intensely aware of his proximity on the way back from the Children's Zoo. Looking up at him, she had to admit that she liked the little cleft in his chin and that shy, lopsided grin. He might even be handsome, she thought, if she could see more than her own reflection in his glasses. Andi peered closer at that reflection, surprised at the look on her face. What was she thinking? She'd spent the last two years waiting for Sterling. What could have possessed her to approach this stranger in the first place, let alone to spend the last few minutes clearly admiring him? "Sorry," she repeated firmly.

"That's okay, it's getting late. I was about to call it a day anyway."

His evident disappointment gave her pause. "You still have time to look around," she suggested. "We don't close for another forty minutes or so."

"I better save some excitement for next time."

"Well, at least walk through the Forest of Uco. You can't see it from the train. It's Phoenix's version of a tropical rain forest." He obviously wasn't impressed. "It's really fun," she persisted. "Everyone loves the spectacled bears." Andi pointed to a fork in the path, indicating a route opposite from the one she would take. "Just go up that hill and take a left at the elephants. It isn't far."

"Okay," he said, reluctant to disagree. "Thanks for your help." Greg watched until she disappeared around the bend, then folded his map and stuffed it in a back pocket. He wasn't interested in fake rain forests or bears, spectacled or otherwise.

On the way to the exit he bought some bottled water and paused to drink it in the shade of an information display. As he disinterestedly reviewed programs offered by the zoo, Greg had a sudden inspiration. He found the community relations office and went inside. When the zoo director walked him to his car twenty minutes later, Greg was whistling—an avocation he hadn't pursued since Jim's death. The tune *"See You Later, Alligator"* made him almost lighthearted. Maybe the billboard's recommendation to "Do the Zoo" hadn't been such a bad idea after all. In fact, the more he thought about it, it might have been the best advice he'd received in a long time.

CHAPTER 4

Wednesday's sun had barely crested the Superstition Mountains to the east when Greg arrived back at the Phoenix Zoo. He crossed the bridge as the first rays stained the red rock formations of Papago Park a deep vermilion. The animals were awake, stretching sinewy muscles, and calling out in dozens of foreign tongues for morning room service. Once in the front office, Greg gave his own excellent, if unwitting, impersonation of a Sumatran tiger as he paced restlessly between the door and window.

He hadn't pitched in Tuesday's game, so he'd been able to use the bench time productively, thinking of . . . He mentally kicked himself again for not asking her name. But she'd be here any minute, and they'd have a couple of hours alone to get acquainted. Alone, that is, except for the alligators. Greg congratulated himself again on his ingenuity and scooped up a donut and Styrofoam cup of juice on his next pass by the secretary's desk.

Carol looked up nervously. "Are you sure I can't make you some coffee, Mr. Howland?"

"No thanks. I'm fine."

"It's no trouble."

"No, really," Greg insisted. "Juice is great."

She cast him a clearly admiring look. "I'm glad I'm not an athlete like you. I couldn't get by without four cups a day."

Greg smiled politely though his abstinence had less to do with training than the smell of the stuff. Taking a bite from the donut, he consulted his watch for the second time that minute.

Across the room, the zoo director did the same, with obvious dismay. "I'm sorry, Mr. Howland," Fred Waverly said, hoisting his hefty frame from behind the large, cluttered desk. "The keeper should be here any minute." He looked anxiously from Greg to the wall clock. "But you're a busy man, we can't keep you waiting. I'll take you to the exhibit myself."

"No!" Greg said quickly. "Uh, no thanks." He slid contritely into the first chair he saw, behind the door. "I'm early. I don't mind waiting." He was immensely relieved when the door swung open and the girl from the train breezed in.

"Hi, Carol," she greeted the secretary. "What's up? Stu said to come in here before going over to the gators."

Carol giggled and motioned for her to turn around. "You have a very special guest today."

"A guest?"

The pitcher rose and extended his hand. "Hi. I'm Greg Howland."

"Andi Reynolds," she responded slowly. His name was vaguely familiar, his face a little more so. "Do I know you?" She frowned, trying to remember. "Are you the guy with the straw hat and sunglasses—from the train Monday?"

Greg nodded, reluctant to release her hand. It was small and soft and warm, not at all the kind of hand you'd expect to find feeding alligators. "That's me."

Andi extracted her fingers as she studied his face. He might be handsome, she mused, if you admired boyish good looks. She still liked the cleft in his chin and loved the color of his eyes. She knew she shouldn't stare, but couldn't seem to look away, either. He was smiling, clearly pleased, but there was something clouding the incredible blueness, making his eyes seem uncertain, or sad, or both.

The zoo director came quickly to her side. "I'm glad you're here, Andi. We've kept Mr. Howland waiting too long already."

"Waiting for what?"

"For a tour of the swamp," Greg said. "I'm here to meet my alligators."

"Your alligators?"

"I adopted a few. You didn't believe me when I said I love alligators?" Andi shook her head slowly.

"Mr. Howland made a very generous contribution to the Zooper Parents program," Mr. Waverly informed her.

Greg grinned. "Surely you've heard of it? You kick in the money for a year's worth of food and become some lucky critter's adoptive parent."

"And you adopted an alligator?"

"Seven, I think."

"All seven?"

Greg was enjoying this. "And the five crocodiles. I'd never cross a crocodile. I believed you when you said they get cranky when they're hungry." He grinned again as he indicated the director. "Mr. Waverly here was kind enough to invite me in this morning to meet all my scaly little adoptees in person."

The zoo executive beamed at the recognition.

Andi blinked. *Who is this guy?* Carol and Mr. Waverly were obviously impressed, but why not? She didn't know what it cost to feed a dozen aquatic reptiles for a year, but it must cost a lot, and hefty donations were always welcome in a nonprofit organization like the Phoenix Zoo.

She regarded Greg closely. He was probably harmless, she decided, just eccentric. She could humor him for an hour or so to make the boss happy. "Well then, Mr. Howland, if you'll come with me, we'll go meet your alligators." She smiled. "Sorry we can't take the train."

"Do you want to?" Waverly asked Greg quickly. "You certainly may, if you'd like."

Greg winked at Andi. "Thanks, but I've spent enough time on the train tour. I think I'm able-bodied enough to make it to the swamp on foot."

"Take my cart. I insist," the zoo director said, extending his hand to shake Greg's. "It's been a real pleasure to meet you, Mr. Howland. An honor. If there is anything we can do to make your visit more pleasant, don't hesitate to ask. The zoo doesn't open until nine and no one here will disturb you. Andi, bring Mr. Howland back to the office when you're through so I can take him out the private exit. We don't want him inconvenienced in any way."

"I will," she said, trying to hide her continuing amazement. Waverly hadn't been this impressed by the governor's recent tour. *Who is this guy?* "This way, Mr. Howland."

"Please call me Greg," he said, following her from the office into the cool desert morning.

The day promised to be clear and beautiful. The newly minted sun shone through light puffs of cloud to reflect glints of silver and pink in the granite rock formations that encircled the zoo. Greg breathed deeply as he climbed into the small electric cart with Andi at the wheel. It was the kind of day that used to make him glad to be alive. With this vibrant girl beside him, he almost believed he could feel that way again. At the very least, he hoped to enjoy this one morning with her, after arranging it so carefully. It was definitely the most money he'd spent for a first date, and likely more than he would spend on all the dates he'd ever have, combined.

As Andi steered the cart up the asphalt path, Greg forced himself to relax into the plastic cushions and turned toward her. "May I call you Andi?"

She assented, her abundant curls swinging from a ponytail threaded through the back of a baseball-style cap. She waved at a pair of grounds crewmen who turned their way and was puzzled by their gaping stares. She forgot them, however, when Greg spoke again.

"Andi's an unusual name. Is it short for something?"

"Sort of. My name's Ariadne but my little brother couldn't say it. His best attempts came out Andi."

Greg didn't think he could say it either. *Ariadne?* He opted, under the condition of an already thickening tongue, not to try.

Andi swung the cart expertly around a corner and slowed to give Greg a chance to admire a rare albino peacock in full array atop a nearby fence. "My name is Greek," she explained, speeding up again. "My father teaches Hellenic studies at the university. He wanted to name all of us in Greek, but my mother drew the line after me. Everyone else was given a regular-style first name with Dad's Greek stuck in the middle."

"Everyone else?"

"There are six of us kids."

Greg nodded slowly as he tried to engage his brain in the conversation. Throwing killer fastballs was a cinch. It was small talk that he'd never master. He struggled to keep the conversation going. "What does it mean?"

"What do you think it means to have six kids?" She smiled as his fair skin colored beneath his tan.

"No, I mean Ari—your name. What does it mean in Greek?"

It was Andi's turn to blush. She turned her face away as she braked to a stop in front of the ringtailed lemurs. "It means 'divine.'"

Silently, Greg agreed.

"Hi, Les!" Andi called to a keeper clearing brush from the exhibit. "I got your note this morning. Congratulate your brother for me."

"Is Friday okay, then?" Les looked up at her and did a quick double take upon seeing Greg. "Oh, gosh!"

Andi turned from him to her seatmate suspiciously. Her eyes lingered on Greg's masculine profile longer than she intended, and she averted them quickly. "Friday? Um, I don't know, Les. I'm almost sure I have an appointment Friday." She could feel Greg's eyes on her and couldn't think. She frowned in consternation. Well, it couldn't be anything too important, she reasoned, or she'd remember. "Okay, Les," she said finally. "Friday's fine."

The pitcher forgot he was avoiding recognition as he stared frankly at the tall, lanky young man whom he assumed Andi was making a date with. *You have nothing to be jealous of,* he told himself firmly. *You just met this girl. They may be engaged, for all you know.* But Andi didn't wear a ring. He'd noticed that on Monday. Greg started from his thoughts when he realized the young man was talking to him. "I'm sorry," he apologized. "What did you say?"

Les dropped his rake and moved forward eagerly. "I said that it's great to see you here, Mr. Howland. Everybody's talking about it."

"Uh, thanks," Greg mumbled, looking sideways at Andi. She was regarding him with a mixture of curiosity and annoyance, and he didn't know what more to say.

Finally noting his discomfort, and remembering Mr. Waverly's admonition, Andi restarted the cart. "See you, Les." When they were on their way again, she glanced at Greg. "Purina Gator Chow must cost more than I thought. You're quite a celebrity around here."

Obviously, Greg thought, *this girl doesn't watch TV, read* People, *or eat* Wheaties. He studied the view from his side of the cart, reluctant to tell her that he was quite a celebrity almost everywhere. She clearly didn't know who he was, but, after all, who was he? He *felt* like an awkward teenager on his first date. Before he could decide how best to enlighten her, she pulled up to the alligator habitat and slid gracefully from her seat.

"So, do you want to get to know your reptiles, or what?"

Greg jumped from the cart eagerly, grateful for the distraction. He'd tell her later, maybe, if she asked.

CHAPTER 5

The alligator food prep area consisted of a small, concrete room on the shore of a fish-hatchery-lake-turned-zoo-swamp. Andi swung a pail into the metal sink and invited Greg to look out into the lagoon at the gators while she mixed a mash. Beneath lowered lashes, she gazed at him while he peered out the tiny Plexiglas window. Seeing the muscles tense in his jaw as his strong hands gripped the window frame, she thought he seemed nervous. Had he spent all that money on alligator food to spend the morning with her? The thought made *her* nervous.

He really was good-looking, Andi decided, and polite. His shyness and sense of humor appealed to her, as well as his lopsided grin. She shook her head to clear it. Whatever his attributes, or motives for alligator adoption, they were beside the point and he could keep them to himself. All she owed him was a tour of the swamp.

So Andi began to lecture as she worked, glad to fill the quiet of the concrete room with impersonal chatter. She taught Greg to tell the difference between a crocodile and an alligator by the pointed or squared snouts. She commented on the similarities in their natural environments and how they hatched: if the average temperature was below eighty-five degrees, the hatchlings would likely be female; above ninety degrees, male. She told him how the young first fed on small creatures such as insects or frogs, then graduated to fish and, finally, to mammals and birds. She said that they could live as long as seventy-five years and, most interesting of all (she hoped), though both species

resemble giant lizards, they were actually more closely related, biologi-
cally speaking, to birds.

Greg stood on the wooden observation platform at the edge of the
swamp as Andi put out the food. He listened politely, even apprecia-
tively, nodding and asking questions to keep her talking. Feeling his
gaze upon her, she looked with increasing frequency into his face. It
was a kind face, she thought, searching and . . . sad. The word came
again to mind and she wondered for a moment what could make the
sadness disappear from those gorgeous blue eyes.

Her morning tasks completed, Andi climbed onto the deck,
pulled off her rubber waders, and joined Greg on a bench overlooking
the lagoon. Simians chattered on nearby Monkey Island and exotic
birds whistled, hooted, and squawked in conversation throughout the
zoo. Surrounded by the ancient palms and lush bamboo, ignored by
the alligators, Greg and Andi were alone.

Sitting this close to him, Andi felt suddenly shy. Confused, she
began to lecture again. Or rather, she wanted to lecture but was
amazed at how quickly she could forget facts she had known minutes
before. She no longer knew, for instance, the name of the birds that
fed upon the algae on the crocodiles' tough hide or which fish the alligators particularly favored. At last, Andi had to admit to herself that
she was having difficulty concentrating on anything aside from the
finely chiseled features of the man who shared her bench.

She drew a deep breath and wondered if she were coming down
with something. She must be. Andi Reynolds prided herself on clear
thinking and common sense. She would never be attracted to a
stranger this way. She was catching cold, she decided. There was no
other reasonable explanation for the chills she felt when he looked
into her eyes.

Greg glanced at his watch and wondered where the time had gone.
He could have listened to her lecture all day, though he would have
failed a pop quiz on the material. He still didn't know a thing about
alligators, couldn't tell them apart from crocodiles or even from the
logs they resembled. But he had memorized every inflection in Andi's
voice and knew just how she tilted her head and dimpled into a smile
at the call of a crane. He had learned to love the light in her eyes and
the serenity of her nature and wished he knew the source. All in all,

Greg couldn't say much for the swamp things, but Ariadne Reynolds was the most enchanting creature he had ever encountered. *Divine.* Yes, she was divine.

"Thanks for the tour of the swamp," he said finally. "It was really impressive."

"You won't worry about your adoptees, then?"

"No, they're obviously in good hands."

"I'm glad you approve. We want to keep our Zooper Parents happy."

They fell silent, each searching for something more to say, then began to speak at the same time and laughed.

"You first," Andi insisted.

"I asked how long you've worked at the zoo."

"I've been here about five years, counting the time I was a teenage volunteer. Now I'm a part-time keeper's assistant, three days a week. The rest of the time I attend ASU where my dad teaches."

"Are you studying alligators?"

"No," Andi laughed. "I'm an education major. I'd like a career in the public education program here at the zoo." She paused, surprised at herself. As it was, Sterling thought her job at the zoo was frivolous and only distracted from her studies. She wasn't planning to stay on at the zoo after their marriage. What was she thinking?

"That's what I studied . . . education, I mean," Greg said. "At Northwestern."

"You're a teacher?" Andi could see this quiet man working with children.

"Actually, no. I switched to math when I got too involved in sports to start student teaching, and after graduation my life went another direction. Now I travel so much that I haven't had time to think about finishing the program. But I'd like to teach someday."

"Then you're only in Phoenix for a couple of days on business?" Andi hoped the twinge of emotion she felt was curiosity. Its resemblance to disappointment was disconcerting.

"I'll be in town another week or so. I go home the first of April."

"And where is home?"

"Chicago, uh, Iowa." Greg gazed up at the trees. *Simple question.* Too bad he didn't have a simple answer. He'd meant Chicago, but the furnished apartment on the shores of Lake Michigan had never meant more than a place to kill time between games at Wrigley Field. Was home his parents' house in Peosta? He still had a room there, he supposed, though he hadn't slept in it a dozen times in six years. Surely the carbon-copy hotel rooms in cities strung across the U.S. couldn't be considered home, even if he did spend almost half his life in them. *How can anybody have all this money and still be homeless?* "Chicago, I guess."

Andi dimpled. "You don't know where you live?"

Greg smiled, but without mirth. "My parents live in Peosta, Iowa. I grew up there, but now I have an apartment in Chicago. And, like I said, I travel a lot in my job." *Okay,* he thought, lowering his eyes, *here it comes. She's going to ask me what I do.*

Instead, Andi asked, "Do you like what you do?"

Greg had given hundreds of interviews and answered thousands of questions, yet no one had ever asked him if he *liked* to throw a baseball. He glanced up in surprise. Her green eyes were searching, her lovely face earnest. "I used to," he said honestly. "I used to like it a lot. I don't know anymore."

"Then why do you do it?"

"It pays pretty well, I guess."

She affected a mock scold. "Didn't anyone ever tell you that money can't buy happiness?"

Greg nodded, studying his shoes. He had believed once that he could buy anything in the world with money and use it to solve all his problems. Now he knew that, at best, wealth might offer pleasure and comfort, but little happiness, and no security. All the money in the world couldn't have bought another day of life for Jim.

Dismayed at the slump of his shoulders, Andi asked, "What's wrong, Greg?"

He looked up, startled to hear her use his name. "Nothing," he said. "I'm fine. Small talk isn't my strong point, but everything's great."

"Is it?" Andi wanted to touch him to comfort him in some way. She folded her arms and said lightly, "I have a reputation for being a good listener. Ask any of the crocodiles. They come to me with all their problems."

He smiled thinly. "Too bad I don't have any problems you can solve." Still, he felt she was waiting for an explanation. After a few moments, he found himself trying to supply one. "It's just that work hasn't been going too well lately." *Boy, is that an understatement.* Greg thought about what he would likely face in the manager's office and sighed. "I'm just tired, I guess."

Now, Andi did touch him, her fingers gently brushing his hand. "I don't think you're tired. I think you're sad."

Greg couldn't remember the last time someone had reached out to him. He looked at the delicate hand atop his and said quietly, "My brother died not long ago."

Mourning doves gurgled softly together in their nest amid the palm fronds as Andi waited silently for Greg to continue, encouraging him with a gentle squeeze of her fingers.

Greg didn't want to talk about it, didn't know how they'd arrived here from alligators even. He tried to think of a way to change the subject and was surprised to hear his own words when he finally spoke. "His name was Jim. He was the best. It was just the two of us kids, and he was like a brother and father and best friend to me. He was the only one who listened and believed in me, and told me I could do anything."

"It sounds like he loved you."

"Jim loved everyone—kids, old people, dogs. Everyone loved him, too. My dad's auto shop was always full after Jim went to work there. People brought in cars just to be around him. He was amazing, Andi. He had a way of making you feel like you were something special, and he was always going out of his way to help somebody. It's like he didn't even stop to think of himself. He never had a bad day and was hardly ever sick." Greg paused. "Or, at least that's what I thought. He'd been talking about headaches for a couple of months. I should have wondered when they seemed to clear up so fast. I should have noticed the changes in him, too. But I was so caught up in my own life . . ." His voice trailed away as he watched a croc slip beneath the surface of the murky water.

"We're all like that."

"Believe me, I was a lot worse. Whenever I talked to Jim it was about me and what I was doing. Maybe if I'd gone back to Iowa more often, I'd have seen what was happening and could have helped him before it was too late." Greg frowned at the memory, then glanced self-consciously at Andi. *You sure can't go there, Howland. You can't talk about Jim and Zeke to anyone. Not now. Not ever.*

"How did he die?"

"Cancer. Like I said, he'd been having headaches that he just ignored." *With a little help from Zeke,* Greg added bitterly to himself. "Then, one day after Christmas, he said he thought his eyes were going bad. He finally went to a doctor for glasses—joked about getting old—but he wasn't even thirty." Greg's eyes swept Andi's face. She was listening intently, biting her lower lip. "The next day he was in the hospital for tests. They treated him for a couple of weeks—chemo and even surgery. At least I got to stay with him."

Those days had been the longest, most frightening of Greg's life as his mother, consumed with grief, rarely left her room and his father closed the shop to disappear with his private source of comfort. Jimmy's estranged wife, Bobbie Jo, had been hysterical, wailing that she was too young to be a widow, while her sons sat alone in their room with white faces and frightened eyes.

Greg had done all he could: sitting with Jim, holding the plastic bowl through long days of medically induced illness; taking the boys on outings to distract them from their misery; and, in the end, numbly arranging for a casket and grave site when no one else was around to visit the funeral home. Afterwards, he reported to spring training because he was being paid an obscene amount of money and, really, what else was there to do? Life goes on whether *you* want to or not.

Here, in the quiet of the zoo, Greg chose small, mostly bittersweet portions of the story to share with Andi. Finally, he shook his head. "The doctors said they did everything they could." It sounded like an indictment of the medical profession and, perhaps, the universe at large.

Andi's eyes were wide and moist. "I'm sorry, Greg."

He tried to shrug it off, embarrassed that he had told her in the first place. "It was eight weeks ago. I should be over it by now."

Andi bent her head, trying to meet his downcast eyes. "Why do you say that?"

"Because it's true. Jim's gone and nothing I do is ever going to bring him back."

"Where do you think he's gone?"

This girl asks the strangest questions, Greg thought. He said, "He didn't *go* anywhere. He's dead."

"His body's dead," she said gently, "for now. But his spirit, the part that made him him, the part everyone loved, is still alive. You'll see Jim again, you know."

"No, I don't know. How would you?"

Andi's eloquent eyes finally met his with confidence. "God told me."

What could you say to that? Greg wondered. God had never told him anything.

"You have to ask Him."

Greg looked up in surprise at her perception. "Well, I did ask . . . sort of. A couple of days ago." He remembered asking for . . . something. He drew a deep breath as he gazed at Andi.

"Didn't He answer you?"

"No. Maybe. I don't know." Her smile at his confusion brought a trace of the lopsided grin. He would definitely have to give this more thought. "At any rate," he said, "the crocodiles are right, Andi. You are a good listener, and I guess I needed to talk. Thank you."

"Just another of the many fine services offered here at the Phoenix Zoo." Andi dimpled again.

"Do all your lectures include theology?"

"No. I reserve that for special clients." Andi's color betrayed her as she realized how sincere she really was. Fortunately, Greg hadn't noticed. He was consulting his watch.

"I'd better get back," he told her reluctantly. "I have an appointment in another city and I need to change for it." He flinched at a twinge of conscience. He'd always been a lousy liar and felt guilty now, even when every word he said was true.

Andi jumped to her feet, certain that she had offended him. And no wonder. Who was she to claim to talk to God? "I'm really sorry," she said, starting across the bridge that led from the exhibit. "I can imagine what you must think. I shouldn't have kept you here so long, and I certainly shouldn't have pried into your private life."

"Andi," Greg called, snatching up the waders she had abandoned in her haste and hurrying to catch up. "Please wait . . . you didn't pry. You listened. I wish I could stay all day, honest I do." He reached for her elbow to slow her down. "I should have come when I had more time, but, well, I couldn't wait to meet you and this was the first chance I could get back."

Andi slowed, brushed aside a bamboo stalk and made no effort to free her elbow. Had she heard right? "Really? You wanted to see me?"

"I'm not surprised you didn't catch on since I'm such a great actor. Your boss believes I have a passion for toothy reptiles and only live to provide their room and board," Greg said ruefully.

Andi smiled. This Greg Howland was turning out to be a particularly nice sort of eccentric.

As they climbed aboard the cart and Andi steered it away from the alligators, Greg tossed her boots in back and wondered if the same quick thinking that got him to the mound in the majors could get him to first base with this girl.

Andi had some idea what he was thinking as she drove the short distance back to the office. Her heart beat faster. She wouldn't go out with him, of course. Andi had made up her mind before junior high school never to date nonmembers. She sighed. Not even handsome-funny-quiet-shy-sad ones with heart-stopping azure eyes. Besides, she reminded herself, she was practically engaged to Sterling.

She glanced at Greg. As she did, the front wheel of the cart left the pavement with a bump. Embarrassed, she overcompensated and nearly swerved into a banana tree. Andi frowned in annoyance. Thinking about Greg Howland and driving a zoo cart were apparently mutually exclusive activities, although she saw absolutely no reason she shouldn't be able to handle both.

"Are there airbags in these things?" Greg asked with the grin that had gotten Andi in trouble in the first place.

"Sorry."

As she braked gratefully to a stop at the front office, Greg took another look at her porcelain profile and wondered where he had lost all that quick thinking. "Would it be okay if I, uh, maybe call you, or something, sometime? I mean, before I leave town?" *Boy, Howland,* he thought, rubbing his forehead, *that was smooth. No wonder you have the social life of a Tibetan monk.* He tried again. "I'd like to, um, continue our conversation after I've had time to think about what you said. You're the first person I've ever known who talks to God." *A little better.*

Andi suppressed a smile. He was so sincere, and so shy, and so darn cute. She spoke without thinking. "Why don't you come to my house for dinner tonight?"

"What?"

Andi was as surprised as he was, probably more so, but couldn't turn back now. She tried to shrug casually, convinced it looked more like a nervous tic. "Dinner. I invited you to my house to eat. You could meet my family and we could talk and eat." Andi bit her thumbnail to keep her mouth busy at something besides talking. How dumb could she be? She'd invited him to dinner; of course they'd eat.

"I like to eat," Greg grinned. "What time?"

Andi could not believe she was doing this. "Six o'clock?"

"Great."

"I live in Mesa. It's east of here."

"That's where I'm working, mostly. My hotel's there."

Andi ripped a sheet of paper from a note pad in the cart and dug a pen from the pocket of her pants. "Where's your hotel? I'll give you directions to my house." When she had finished her simple map, she handed it to Greg. "It isn't hard to find, but if you do get lost, look for the stadium lights at HoHoKam Park—the monstrosities are practically in our backyard."

"I think I can find it."

"Then I'll see you tonight."

"I'll be there." Carefully pocketing the paper, he slid from the cart and smiled. "Really, Andi, thanks."

"I'll look forward to seeing you, Greg." It was true, she thought as he walked into the office. She would look forward to seeing him. But it wasn't like a date, or anything, she quickly assured herself. It was more like . . . like missionary work. Of course, that's exactly what it was. He had recently lost his brother so it was a perfect time to teach him the plan of salvation. That, of course, was the only reason she'd asked him over—to share the gospel. Sterling would be proud of her.

Before she could congratulate herself further on the purity of her motives, Carol and the girls from the ticket booths surrounded her cart. They all began to talk at once, and Andi had trouble sorting out what they were saying.

"Is he as gorgeous in person?"

"Did he make a pass at you?"

"What did he say?"

"Did you at least get his autograph?"

"Why was he here? Is he coming back?"

"I can't believe Waverly wouldn't let anyone near him!"

"What is he like?"

Andi held up her hands in surrender. "Who? Greg?"

"Listen to her!" Carol giggled. "'Who, Greg?' Like you meet the most eligible man in America every day!"

Most eligible man in America? Andi was nonplussed. "What are you talking about?"

"Greg Howland!" Carol swooned. "Who else? Won't you tell us anything?"

The other girls joined in, clamoring for details.

Andi tried to ignore them as she searched Carol's face for a clue. "The most eligible man in America?" she repeated.

Carol hushed the others and grabbed Andi's shoulders. "You really don't know who he is, do you?"

Andi shook her head. As she looked with bewilderment into Carol's excited brown eyes, she felt the beginning of a lump form somewhere near the pit of her stomach. "Who is he?"

The women stared at her in amazement, then all spoke at once. It made as much sense to Andi as monkey chatter. Carol quieted them and said grandly, "Greg Howland is the All-Star pitcher for the Chicago Cubs, that's all. Didn't you see the World Series?"

Andi shook her head.

"You don't watch Letterman?"

"No."

"Leno?"

"No."

"Oprah, Rosie, *Saturday Night Live?*"

"No, but . . ."

"His picture's on cereal boxes, for goodness' sake!"

Andi closed her eyes. "We only buy the kind with that Quaker guy on them, but I'm beginning to get the idea."

"He's in all the tabloids. He's a millionaire, of course, and he dates all these actresses and supermodels . . . "

There was definitely a lump in Andi's stomach. It was roughly the size of a rhinoceros, and she felt she might be ill. "Excuse me . . ." She climbed from the seat, then felt too dazed to continue. Besides, she couldn't think where she wanted to go. She leaned against the cart.

"Aren't you going to tell us what he's like?" Carol persisted.

Andi rolled her eyes. "He's . . . eccentric," she said quietly, "and he loves alligators." She couldn't believe she'd invited Greg Howland, sports superstar, to her house for dinner.

HAPTER 6

Greg Howland, sports superstar, had been invited to dine at the Waldorf, a trio of Planet Hollywoods, and the White House. But the best invitation in his book was the one pending to the Reynolds' home. The elevation of his mood had a corresponding effect on his statistics. Morning practice was a breeze. His sprints were sprier, his fastball really was (for a change), and his curve balls were sailing straight to the plate then arcing sharply outside—just like they used to.

"Howland, you oughta try throwing like that when there's another team on the field," Jerald Riley, the pudgy starting catcher, observed wryly as they finished the 40-odd pitches comprising an off-rotation workout. "We was all beginning to think a swelled head had replaced that swell arm."

Greg had to make an effort to widen his grin. "I was beginning to think you were right, Riley. But I've got it under control now."

"Tell that to Biderman." Riley hooked a thumb toward the lackey who had come to summon the young southpaw into the hallowed halls of the Main Man.

Well, Greg thought, feeling suddenly more like the turkey invited to Thanksgiving dinner. *I knew it was coming.*

Ushered into the general manager's inner sanctum, Greg stood, hat in hand, waiting anxiously while Evan Biderman sustained his end of a long-winded conference call.

At least they aren't talking about me, Greg noted with relief. *That was probably earlier.*

Grumbling into the receiver, Biderman continued to ignore Greg. The young ballplayer shifted his weight uncomfortably, his eyes trailing to the glints and flashes from the gold ring on the manager's index finger. Greg wondered if Biderman remembered whose pitching had led the Cubs to their first World Series win in more than nine-tenths of a century. He doubted it. All a good manager remembers is what you did for him today; all he cares about is what you're going to do for him tomorrow.

After half a lifetime by Greg's reckoning, Biderman tossed the handset on the desk and leaned back in his chair, hands laced behind his neck. Greg watched him scan the acoustic tiles as if seeking divine revelation as to why fate had cursed him with this particular lefty ball-tosser. Apparently finding no answer, the older man rolled forward with a deep sigh and trained steel-gray eyes on Greg.

"Sit down, Howland."

"Thank you, sir." Greg sank into a hard, vinyl-and-chrome chair specially designed, he suspected, to make nervous players as uncomfortable as possible.

"Do you know why I want to talk to you?"

"No, sir." Greg lowered his eyes. "Yes, sir."

The manager paused to give the perspiration on Greg's forehead ample time to bead. "Did you see a paper this morning?"

Greg shook his head.

The boss slid a *USA Today* sports section across the desk. Greg didn't need to look at it, only at Biderman's scowl, to know it was about him. And it was bad.

Mercifully, there was no column. Of course, now that he looked at it, the feature picture pretty much said it all. It showed Greg, in full color, on the mound between batters. A large, pink bubble protruded from his lips. The press, Greg knew, found his addiction to Bazooka endearing, especially when it made clever copy.

"Golden Greg Blows It Big Time!" the headline announced. Below, in smaller type, *"Padres burst Chicago southpaw's bubble in sticky pre-game action. Are the Cubs stuck with Howland?"*

Biderman waited patiently for Greg to digest the feature, then pulled it back and stuck it under a daytimer. He regarded the young man narrowly. "Do you know how many men from this training are going to make the roster, Howland?"

Greg shifted in the chair, trying to sit up straighter. *Counting myself?* He could only hope. "Twenty-five."

"How many pitchers?"

"Eight or nine pitchers, sir?"

"That's right, nine. We'd like to field ten or twelve, but we can't afford a dozen pitchers, Howland. Do you know why?"

Greg did, but didn't think it was in his best interest to own up to it.

"Because we pay one of those pitchers more than the bullpen put together." He paused for the weight of the pronouncement to sink in. "That would be you, Howland."

"Yes, sir, I know."

A vein throbbed in Biderman's neck as he shouted, "Then why don't you pitch like it?"

Greg wished he knew that.

"Exhibition games beneath you now that you're a celebrity?"

"Of course not."

"You want more money?"

"No, sir," Greg said earnestly, catching himself before he added "please."

Biderman rubbed the silver stubble on his chin and surveyed Greg calmly. "So, you're doing drugs on us?"

"No!" Greg's heart pounded in his chest then moved up his throat to settle in his temples. He wondered if Biderman could hear it, too, it was so loud. Zeke hadn't surfaced since Monday, and Greg had hoped the man had crawled back under his rock with no harm done. Now he could only wonder who had overheard them in the locker room.

"Level with me. Better men than you foul up. It seems like part of the game anymore. You kids don't stand a chance." The manager's eyes bored into Greg's. "We can get you help, Howland, private like. Have you back in form before the season gets much underway."

Greg was relieved, and grateful, that there had been no mention of Zeke. Perhaps Biderman was grasping at straws to justify his lousy performance in spring training. He pulled his chair forward, leaned his forearms on the desk, and looked the manager in the eye. "Mr. Biderman, I do not take drugs. I don't even drink. I never have. Ask anyone. Ask Jeff Jensen." As his roommate at training and buddy on the road, surely Jensen could vouch for him.

"I have asked him, and he told me the same thing. But I want to hear it, on the record, from you."

Greg's hopes lifted. "I know I'm having problems pitching right now, sir, but I give you my word, it has nothing to do with drugs."

Biderman picked up a pencil and bounced the eraser on the glass-topped desk. It was a shame about this kid, he thought. Howland was one of those rare naturals, blessed with a good head and one heck of a throwing arm. But the manager's years of experience suggested that Greg lacked the ego and aggression to make it through the long haul of major league baseball. For now, at least, he was hugely popular with the fans and selling seats like nobody else in the business. If the Cubs could squeeze a couple more seasons like the last two out of him, then the owners would be satisfied. It was Biderman's job to do it. He cleared his throat. "Jensen said you might still be brooding over your brother's death."

Greg's eyes strayed to a grass stain on his right knee. He considered it carefully, unsure where it had come from. "I guess I might be."

"That's hard to fix, you know, and it's my job to fix all the problems on this team. Any suggestions?"

The edge in Biderman's voice suddenly didn't seem quite as sharp. If Greg didn't know better, he'd think he was out from under the ax. He leaned forward hopefully. "I think I can fix it myself, sir. I had a good practice today. I'd like a chance to pitch again. Just an inning, even. Please."

"And I'd like to win a game before we head back to Chicago."

"Yes, sir. Me, too."

The manager picked up his phone and nodded toward the door, his eyes never leaving the numbers he was punching. "Shouldn't you be down with the coaches, Howland?"

Greg rose immediately. "Yes, sir. Thank you, sir." He left the room clutching his cap and grateful to still have a head on which to put it.

CHAPTER 7

It was after five by the time Greg returned to his hotel. He'd survived Biderman, the batting tunnel, an hour of pitching coaches, a hoard of autograph seekers, nine innings on the bench, and a short trip downtown. Examining his reflection in the bathroom mirror, he decided the last was a barely.

In the hour following the game, Greg had found a florist and a barber on Main Street. The flowers were okay, but the haircut was a disaster. Even in his sunglasses, everyone in the barbershop had recognized him. He'd signed autographs and talked baseball for nearly twenty minutes before politely reminding the men what he'd come in for. The sixty-something barber who finally picked up the scissors was so excited to be working on Greg Howland's head that his hands shook even more than usual and the finished style reflected it. Greg's thick blond hair was clipped so short that a white line of untanned skin ran across his forehead, down his sideburns and around the back of his neck. *I look like a Marine*, he thought. *A Marine with a bad haircut.* He slapped on his cap, scowled, and pulled it off again. He couldn't wear a hat to dinner.

By 5:15 his palms were sweating like crazy. Wiping them on a towel, he retreated into the main room, anxious to be anywhere that wasn't in front of that mirror. *It's your own fault you're so nervous to see Andi again*, he told himself, checking his duffel on the chance it contained a spare bag of resin for his clammy hands. *You should have been up front with her from the start.*

It was too late for that now, he suspected. Surely someone had told her who he was. He wondered what she was thinking.

If Greg had paid a penny for Andi's thoughts as she collapsed on her bed at five o'clock, surrounded by most of the clothes from her closet, he would have regretted it. She was furious.

Her emotions had been on a carousel since morning. They went up and down, spun around, and took her nowhere. There were times, even, when she could have sworn she heard sappy music.

When the initial shock had worn off that morning, she was back in control of her reason, if not her emotions. Who did Greg Howland think he was? Well, she knew who he thought he was, but where did he get off pretending to be some forlorn boy-next-door type? That routine must have girls falling all over him. Angry and embarrassed, she grabbed the first phone she saw, in the zoo gift shop, to inform Mister Baseball All-Star that he should plan to eat elsewhere that evening.

"Can you connect me with Greg Howland's room, please?" she asked the swamped switchboard operator.

"May I ask who's calling?"

"Ariadne Reynolds."

There was a long pause as the operator consulted a computer screen. The short list didn't include a Reynolds. In a monotone she repeated, for perhaps the twentieth time that morning, "Mr. Howland isn't taking calls or messages, but appreciates your interest."

"I'll bet he does!" Andi tossed down the receiver and stormed out of the shop without a word to the surprised volunteer behind the counter.

As the morning passed, Andi told herself that anger would get her nowhere. She would handle Mr. Big Shot Sports Celebrity in short shrift this evening. In the meantime, she had a bigger problem. Despite her best efforts to disable it, the automatic video camera in her head continued to replay archival Greg Howland footage. She saw his muscles rippling as he got on and off the safari train on Monday. She replayed him identifying the kookaburra bird, professing love for alligators, and looking pleased and boyish in Mr. Waverly's office. The stupid camera kept sticking in the scene at the swamp. Andi reviewed it dozens of times. When she analyzed what she remembered of his words (and she remembered every one), she had to admit that everything he said was probably true. When she assessed what she remembered of his face (and her memory was even better on this point), she began to believe that maybe he *was* just a sweet guy who had lost his brother and needed a sympathetic ear.

At this point, the sappy music began and she saw jumbled images of his full lips over the square jaw breaking into a shy, endearing grin, and, always, those breathtaking blue eyes. Then, the video cam switched itself off altogether, and she lapsed unconsciously into supplying dreamy, if imaginary, scenarios of her own. When she realized what she was doing, she was furious all over again.

She'd been on this ride for eight hours and was sick of it. Andi rose from the bed and glanced at her reflection in the mirror. No, she decided, she wouldn't even look. She'd wear whatever she had on. She certainly wouldn't resemble the cover girls Greg Howland was used to, no matter what she wore.

As she pulled the band from her hair and shook out the spiraled locks, Andi heard the closet door open in the hallway. Her mother must be retrieving the good linen. She had a momentary twinge of guilt, thinking that she should be downstairs helping her mother rather than up in her room, alternating between fuming and fantasizing. Still, she was irritated at her mother's insistence that she could not withdraw a dinner invitation at the door, and even more irritated at her mother's subsequent fuss despite her repeated protests.

At any rate, dinner's almost ready and Clytie will set the table, Andi rationalized.

Clytie. Andi caught her breath at the thought of her disfigured little sister. If Greg Howland so much as looked at her wrong, then she'd . . . She didn't know what she'd do, but it would be something he wouldn't soon forget. Finally, ignoring the mess on the bed, she went downstairs to the dining room and took a dinner plate from her sister's tiny hands.

"Here, let me do that," she told her sister. "After all, this is my fault."

"There isn't any fault, dear," her mother said.

"I think it's neat Greg Howland's coming!" Clytie chirped. "Wait until Dad and Brad get home. They're gonna freak."

Andi looked at her mother in surprise. "You haven't talked to Dad?"

Margaret Reynolds was folding napkins into bird-of-paradise pleats. "I called, but your father was in a department meeting. I suppose he'll have to be surprised."

"He'll freak," Clytie repeated joyfully.

Andi suspected she might be right. On the other hand, she would enjoy seeing the look on Brad's face. Brad was eighteen, the next oldest after Andi. He'd get home from his part-time job about the time Greg showed up. Brad wasn't exactly a sports fanatic, but he would certainly recognize a famous pitcher when he passed him the potatoes.

Besides Brad and Clytie, whose given name was Catherine, Andi had a twelve-year-old sister, Darlene; a nine-year-old brother, Enos; and a little, little sister, Francie, who was six and the end of the alphabet as far as the Reynolds were concerned. Andi hadn't bothered to tell the younger kids about Greg. They were no more likely to have heard of him than she was.

Now she frowned as she placed the last plate and watched Clytie stand on tiptoe to lay out the silver. "I wish you wouldn't go to so much trouble, Mom."

"It isn't much trouble," her mother assured her. "You know I like to use these things now and again."

"Well, it isn't a special occasion, and Greg Howland isn't anyone important."

"Yes he is!" Clytie protested. "Mom, you should have seen all those people on Monday at the stadium—"

"I mean, he certainly isn't to me," Andi interrupted, absentmindedly repositioning a setting Clytie had carefully arranged a moment before. "I only invited him because we'd been talking about the plan of salvation and I was trying to be a good missionary."

"But isn't he handsome?" Clytie asked eagerly.

"Yes. No. I mean, I didn't notice."

"Then why are you blushing?" Clytie asked, then her eyes widened. "Andi, did you fall in love with him?"

Her sister gasped. "Of course not! I've told you dozens of times, Clytie, reasonable people don't *fall* in love. Reasonable people—"

"I know," Clytie sighed. "Reasonable people have a checklist-for-choosing-an-eternal-companion. Like you do."

"They do if they're smart," Andi responded.

"Well, I'm going to fall in love," Clytie declared dreamily. "It'll just be a regular day and I'll look up, and there he'll be, and our eyes will meet, and we'll know we were made for each other."

Andi swung her hair over her shoulder. "You read too many silly romances, Clytie. That never happens in real life."

"It will happen to me! I'll know he's the one I want to be with forever when I can't stop thinking about him and I hear love songs playing in my head."

Andi dropped a spoon. She jumped as it clattered against the china plate.

Clytie retrieved the utensil and placed it neatly beside the knife with a satisfied smile. She believed fervently in the power of prayer, but this was almost too good to be true. She had asked for someone to teach her reasonable, know-it-all sister something about romance before boring Sterling Channing came home from his mission. But with that date only two days away, she had almost given up hope. She peeked up at Andi. The older girl was fingering a goblet, lost in thought. Clytie's smile widened. Maybe this Greg Howland was more than Andi's celebrity missionary effort, after all. Maybe he was her soulmate—and the answer to Clytie's prayer.

CHAPTER 8

In the waning minutes of Wednesday sunlight, Enos Reynolds stood in the front yard of his house, still trying to master the pitch-back contraption he had requested from Santa last Christmas. He understood the concept. You stand a few feet back, throw a baseball into the taut net, and catch it in your glove when it bounces back. Understanding the concept and implementing it, however, were two different things. Ball after ball had disappeared into the stickery bougainvillea bushes, rolled down the rain gutters or, in the worst case, disappeared into the neighbor's living room by way of his picture window. But this is what it would take to succeed in Little League, Enos believed, so he would practice until he ran out of baseballs entirely. Unfortunately, that time was now a single bad catch away.

So intent was he on his exercise that he failed to notice a compact white car roll up to the curb in front of his house. Enos threw the ball, at just the wrong angle and velocity, as usual, and turned to watch it pop over his head toward the street. His eyes widened in admiration when, even without a glove, the man in the convertible caught it easily.

Greg held up the ball as he slid across the seats and opened the door onto the sidewalk. "Is this yours?"

Pushing thick-lensed glasses up the bridge of his nose, Enos nodded wordlessly. He had seen this man somewhere before.

Greg reached into his car for flowers, then tossed the ball back, underhanded, hitting Enos squarely in the chest. "Oh, gosh, sorry about that." He moved quickly to the boy's side. "Are you okay? I thought you'd catch it."

"I can't catch," Enos informed him matter-of-factly.

"Oh." Greg scooped up the ball and put it in the outstretched glove. "Here you go, then." The child stared at it wordlessly. *This must be the right place,* Greg thought. *This redheaded kid definitely has Andi's eyes.* "Is this the Reynolds' house?"

"Uh huh."

"Do you have a sister named Andi?"

"Uh huh."

"Is she here?"

"Uh huh."

Greg was batting a thousand. He extended his hand. "I ought to introduce myself. My name's Greg Howland."

Enos plopped onto the grass, hard.

Startled, Greg knelt beside him. "Are you okay?"

Enos nodded and pushed the glasses back up his thin nose.

"You dropped your ball."

The little boy grabbed it from Greg's hand and cradled it under his chin before finally holding it up for the pitcher's inspection. "It has your name on it, see? I got it for my birthday. It's my very best one. I'm only playing with it 'cause I lost all the rest. Most of the time I keep it in a special case in my room."

Greg smiled.

"My dad says you didn't sign it," Enos continued. "He says a machine stamps your name on millions of them so they can charge kids like me more money. Is that true?"

Success in the good ol' United States of Advertising, Greg thought ruefully. *It kinda makes you proud.* He smiled sheepishly at Enos. "Well, yes."

"Oh. I thought it was real." The boy pushed at his glasses and blinked rapidly.

"Hey, I've got a pen right here," Greg said, dropping Andi's bouquet to pull a marker from inside his wool blazer. "Let me see that ball, and we'll at least make this one real."

"Cool! You really *are* Greg Howland, aren't you?"

Greg returned the now-autographed ball with a grin. "Well, the signatures match."

"And you look the same, too. Except, maybe, for your hair."

Greg rubbed a hand over his head and rolled his eyes. So much for his hope no one would notice.

"I knew who you were right off," Enos continued proudly. "I've got your picture in my room. I bought it at a school book fair. My mom wanted me to buy a book, but I bought your poster instead. I like books. I just like you more. Oh, and my name's Enos."

"Well, thanks, Enos. Do you play baseball?"

"Uh huh. I'm on a Little League team and everything. I wanted to be on the Cubs, but they put me on the Rockies."

"Good team."

"Not as good as the Cubs."

Greg's attempt to suppress another grin failed, but he said, "The name of the team doesn't matter, Enos. What counts are the players. What position do you play?"

"Second bench."

"You mean second base?"

Enos shook his head. "No, there's this other guy who sits on the bench most of the time, too. But he's better than me so Coach puts him in first. I'm second bench."

Greg kept his face serious. "I see. But when you are on the field, where are you?"

"Outfield. Way outfield."

"Outfield is great," Greg said encouragingly. "The best hitter on our team is an outfielder."

"I can't hit."

"Oh."

"And I can't catch."

"You mentioned that."

Suddenly, Enos jumped to his feet and Greg grabbed Andi's flowers to keep them from being trampled.

"Will you sign my glove?" Enos asked.

"You bet."

"And my poster?"

"Sure."

"I'll go get it!" Enos dropped his glove into Greg's hand as he made a beeline for the front door. It closed behind him with a bang.

Greg signed the glove then gazed up at the Reynolds' house. It was a Navajo-white stucco, with adobe-tiled roof and wide, wood-framed windows. Flagstones bordered by flowers carved a path across the winter rye grass and up the wide steps to the porch. When Enos didn't immediately return, Greg stepped from the lawn over the orange and gold gazanias and climbed the stairs to the beautifully carved double doors. He slipped the glove and flowers into his right hand. While his knuckles were still raised to knock, the door opened.

Andi wore a simple cotton shift and sandals. Her silky curls fell over her shoulders, and Greg thought again how well her name suited her. All that was missing from her divine face were the dimples. She wasn't smiling.

"Uh, hello," he said self-consciously, quickly lowering one arm to extend the other. "I brought you this."

"Thanks," she said dryly, taking Enos' glove. "You shouldn't have."

"Oh, gosh, no, I didn't . . . I mean, I brought you these." Greg held out the flowers and wondered where his mind went every time he needed it to talk to this girl.

"Thank you again." She accepted the bouquet of white roses, purple iris, and misty fern coolly, noticing, despite herself, that it was exquisite.

Enos charged down the stairs and skidded to a stop at the door. The corners of his prized poster had been torn in his rush to get it off the wall and out to Greg. "This is Greg Howland," he told his sister breathlessly.

"I know."

"He's a real famous baseball player."

"I know that, too," she said, casting a withering look at Greg as she handed Enos his glove. "At least I do now."

"He's gonna sign my poster!" The boy held it up for Greg. "Will you write 'To my friend' and my name? It's spelled E-N-O-S."

"Yeah." Greg took the poster with a sideways glance at Andi. It hadn't escaped his attention that she still wasn't smiling and hadn't shown any indication that she planned to invite him in. It was his own fault, he knew. He should have told her who he was this morning.

To my friend Enos, Greg wrote, *who likes baseball and books as much as I do. Best wishes, Greg Howland.* He handed it back.

Enos read it quickly and hugged it to his chest. "Thank you! Just wait until everyone sees this. Hold it for me, Andi, I've gotta call my friends and tell them who's here!" He turned to run but Andi held the back of his shirt as well.

"Oh no you don't. Greg Howland didn't come here to sign autographs all night. He came for dinner. If you want to come, too, Enos Reynolds, you'd better go upstairs and clean up."

The little boy's eyes were round as saucers behind his glasses. "Wow! Can I sit by him, Andi? I'll go wash right now!" He whirled around and disappeared as quickly as he had come.

"Stay away from the phone!" Andi called after him.

Greg's eyes followed Enos up the stairs, then turned back to his sister. "Does that mean I still get to eat?" he asked hopefully.

Andi ignored the question as she held the poster at arm's length, her green eyes flashing between it and Greg. "It's you all right," she said finally, lowering the picture. "You know, I help that kid change his sheets every week. You'd think I'd have noticed you hanging around in his room. I should have recognized you today."

Greg smiled weakly and shrugged. "I guess you don't expect to meet us poster boys down in the swamp."

"No, you don't."

In pitching, the best defense is a good offense. "You didn't ask what I do," Greg pointed out. "Just if I like to do it." He flinched as Andi tossed his poster behind the door in frustration. *At least she hasn't thrown the flowers at me,* he thought gratefully. *Yet.*

"Well, pardon me," Andi said sarcastically. "That's usually the first question I ask a man: 'Tell me, do you pitch for the Chicago Cubs? When you're not too busy hawking every product on the planet, I mean.'"

"Is what I do important?"

"Is playing baseball important? Not to Western civilization, I suppose, but I looked like the village idiot this morning. You could have at least autographed a dunce cap for me. You must have had a good laugh. Everyone else at the zoo did."

As Greg took a step toward her, she retreated. "Andi, I'm sorry. I should have told you as soon as I realized you didn't recognize me. I never meant for you to be embarrassed."

His eyes were honest, pleading, and the deepest blue Andi had ever seen. He had never actually lied to her, she had to admit. The carousel she'd been on all day began to turn, but she stubbornly refused to acknowledge it. She turned her head to avoid his eyes.

"Look, call it childish or selfish or anything you want," Greg continued quietly, "but I felt like myself for a couple of hours this morning instead of," he hesitated, "instead of whoever everyone thinks I am the rest of the time. And I enjoyed it, Andi. I never meant for it to be at your expense, though, and I'm sorry I misled you. I wouldn't have hurt you for anything." He looked down at the top of her bent head and sighed. "I better go. Tell Enos it was nice to meet him and I wish him well on second bench."

Andi looked up as Greg turned to leave and felt her carousel take a tremendous lurch. Unlike other children, she had never reached for the brass ring on the old-fashioned merry-go-round downtown. But it had never seemed as attractive as the prize before her now.

"Greg, you can stay," she said quickly, following him one step down the stairs. "Enos will be heartbroken if you leave." He paused but didn't turn. "You must be hungry . . . and you brought these beautiful flowers," she continued, searching for a reason that wouldn't involve her personally. "My mother used her best dishes." Greg turned slowly and looked into Andi's face. Meeting his gaze caused her carousel to grind to a stop once and for all, but she could still hear the music and there was one last chance for the brass ring. "I want you to stay. Please."

Greg grinned. He was a happier man there, under Andi's porch light, than he'd ever been in the spotlight receiving the highest awards baseball had to bestow.

CHAPTER 9

By the time Greg was midway through dinner at the Reynolds', he was grateful for every baseball trophy he had, since it was becoming increasingly obvious that he'd never win one for making conversation. From the moment the meal had begun with the unfamiliar custom of a blessing on the food, he had felt like an illegal alien. He couldn't help but wonder what kind of passport he would need into Andi's world.

Her home was lovely. The white Mexican tile of the floor was off-set by large area rugs woven in deep marine shades of green and blue. These hues were picked up in fabrics draped in artistic folds over brass window sconces and reflected again in Greek-reproduction vases and tapestries. The furnishings were comfortable, not new but in good taste and artfully arranged.

It had been the artwork, though, that drew Greg's attention. Over the mantel, in the central part of the living room, was a framed print of a bearded man in a white, flowing robe. He sat on a rock with one child upon his knee and others gathered at his feet. Greg marveled at how the artist had evoked such feeling from canvas and paint. Admiring it, he thought he could feel the love. "Is this a picture of Jesus?" he asked.

Clytie was his eager tour guide. Her cheeks dimpled—*like Andi's,* Greg thought—as she said, "Yes. You've never seen it?"

He shook his head slowly. He'd never seen any picture of Jesus, at least not that he could remember. But this was the third he'd noticed since entering the Reynolds' front door.

"It's my favorite," Clytie said, gazing up at it. "My mom says that girl, the one Jesus is touching, looks like me. Do you think so?" She lifted anxious aqua eyes to Greg.

He heard Andi draw a breath and hold it as he looked from the picture down to her sister. He hoped again that his first reaction to Catherine hadn't conveyed too much of the pity he felt. He'd been surprised to meet the bubbly teenager shoulder-to-shoulder with six-year-old Francie. They were the same height. But the girl's warm greeting and animated desire to make him feel welcome had assured Greg in minutes that Catherine's lack of stature apparently bothered him more than it did her.

Standing beneath the print, he looked into her bright, beautiful face, framed with golden hair, and wondered why any Creator would place a lovely face on such a small, misshapen body. Still, he smiled as he pretended to consider her question. "Well, Catherine, to tell you the truth, I think you're a lot prettier than a picture."

She blushed at the sincere compliment. "Please call me Clytie," she begged. "All my friends do."

Now she sat on a bolster across the table from him between Darlene and Francie. Her flushed face glanced up every few moments and broke into a wide smile whenever he met her eye. Enos was to his right, carefully watching every bite Greg took, trying to mimic his hero perfectly. When a forkful of the child's peas bounced across the table and into Greg's lap, the pitcher pretended not to notice.

"Enos," Trent Reynolds said with irritation. "For goodness' sakes, watch what you're doing. What's the matter with you tonight?" Clytie's prediction had hit the mark. Her father hadn't appreciated Andi's surprise in the least. He had little admiration for athletes and less for celebrities. Since being introduced to Greg, he had been stiff and disapproving, if impeccably polite.

Margaret Reynolds, on the other hand, couldn't have been more gracious. She smiled indulgently at her youngest son. "Use your right hand, dear. You're not left-handed like Greg."

Enos reluctantly passed the fork to his other hand and looked to Greg to see what he would eat next. "Please pass the funeral potatoes."

Greg glanced up, a bite of potato casserole frozen at his lips.

"Don't call them that!" twelve-year-old Darlene protested. "Mom, don't let him call them that. We have company."

Greg forced the potatoes into his mouth and chewed.

"They *are* funeral potatoes," Enos insisted. "Aren't they, Mom? You always take them to funerals and we always have them for dinner that night."

Darlene pushed hers to the far side of the plate. "Gross."

"I did take some to Brother Hamilton's funeral today, Enos," Margaret said patiently. "But I took some to Sister Crisman when she had a baby a few weeks ago, too. So let's call them scalloped potatoes, shall we?"

Enos was mollified, but Greg was confused. *Brother? Sister?* And why did Margaret Reynolds take potatoes to people in the first place? *No one brought food when Jim died. Why would they?*

Andi touched his arm. "My mother's the Relief Society president so she often takes food to families in need."

"Relief Society?" Greg asked. "I don't think we have a chapter in Iowa. Is it something like the Red Cross?"

"I'm sure you have a 'chapter,' as you put it," Mr. Reynolds replied coolly. "The Relief Society is the women's auxiliary of our church. It's worldwide. They even have it in Iowa."

Greg nodded mutely, relieved when Andi's father shifted his attention to the other side of the table. "Speaking of church, it's Wednesday night. What do you kids have going? Brad?"

Brad's eyes were glued to his plate. He had been silent throughout dinner, wondering what you said to a guy who had pitched a perfect game in the World Series.

"Brad?" Mr. Reynolds' voice was insistent.

Without looking up, Brad mumbled, "I think the priests are planning a rappelling thing this weekend. Then we might play basketball or something."

"You're Catholic?" Greg guessed aloud, hoping that he had finally caught on. One glance at Andi's father, however, was enough for him to realize that he hadn't. Greg mentally kicked himself. Now that he thought about it, rappelling and basketball *were* pretty unusual activities for priests.

"We're Latter-day Saints," Mr. Reynolds said firmly.

And modest, too, Greg thought. *Saints? Who hands out the canonization in this church?*

"Didn't Andi tell you?"

Andi leaned forward, smiling gently at Greg, then around him at her father. "There were one or two points of pertinent information Greg and I missed exchanging this morning." She touched Greg's arm, trying to put him at ease, and explained, "We're members of The Church of Jesus Christ of Latter-day Saints, Greg. Have you heard of the Mormons?"

He had, in a history class, maybe. *Weren't they the ones with eight wives?*

"Well," she continued, "that's what some people call our church, but the first name is the preferred one. Brad is a priest."

Greg raised an eyebrow and Andi shook her head. "Not like an ordained minister-type priest. In our church, boys become priests when they turn sixteen. Well, it's more than just age," she added quickly, before her father could correct her, "but that's a general idea."

Greg took a large bite from his dinner roll and chewed slowly, hoping the Reynolds would assume he was full of intelligent responses, but too polite to talk with his mouth full.

Andi knew his obvious discomfiture shouldn't strike her as funny, but she couldn't stifle a giggle as she added casually, "If you think Brad's being a priest is something, wait until I tell you that Clytie just became a Laurel and Darlene is a Beehive."

Greg knew the dictionary definitions of "laurel" and "beehive," but wouldn't even try to put them in context with Clytie and Darlene. He was considering just how much food he would need to consume to keep from responding when Darlene saved him with a shriek.

"I didn't do my project!" she cried, jumping up from the table and disappearing into the kitchen, despite a stern protest from her father. She returned seconds later with a pencil and spiral-bound pad of paper. "I'm supposed to write down everyone's favorite Book of Mormon story for a thing we're doing in Young Women tonight."

"What kind of thing?" Margaret asked.

"I don't know, Mom!" Darlene wailed. "They never tell us why we do anything. They just act all disappointed when we don't do it."

Margaret smiled. Darlene's perspective was usually skewed, but accurate from a certain point of view. "What do you need, dear?"

"I need to know everyone's favorite story from the Book of Mormon," Darlene repeated. "Mom, what's yours?"

Mrs. Reynolds didn't hesitate. "Jesus Christ's visit to America."

Darlene scribbled and Greg blinked. *Boy, I'd better pay more attention to current events,* he thought. *Either that or repeat American History.*

Darlene finished writing. "Brad?"

"I don't know."

"Just say something," she insisted.

Brad stabbed at the peas with his fork and wished he could disappear. He could feel Howland's eyes on him. "Ammon, okay?"

"What part?" Darlene wanted to know. "Where Ammon cuts off all those guys' arms and takes them in a basket to the king?"

Suddenly, Greg's chicken seemed dry. He swallowed with difficulty.

Brad's eyes never left his plate. "Sure."

Satisfied, Darlene continued around the table. "Francie?"

"Noah's Ark," the little girl proclaimed happily. "I like stories about animals."

"That's in the Bible," Darlene informed her. "I need one from the Book of Mormon. You like Nephi."

Francie's pink lips puckered into a pout. "I like animals," she repeated stubbornly.

"Francie!"

The little girl shook her strawberry blonde ringlets. "Animals!"

Darlene saw she couldn't win. "Then I'll make something up for you. Clytie?"

"I don't know that it's really a story," Clytie began eagerly, "but I like the part where the Nephites are threatened by the Lamanites and know they're going to be killed, so they send out their beautiful daughters and the Lamanites are so charmed by them that they fall in love and they don't kill them, and everyone's saved." She looked anxiously across the table for Greg's reaction. At his tentative smile, she leaned back, eyes shining.

"Is that a story?" Darlene asked her mother doubtfully.

"Of course it is," Margaret assured her. It was just the sort of story one would expect from Clytie.

Despite Darlene's objections, her father refused to name an episode, quoting instead a passage from King Benjamin's sermon to his people. It dealt with the awful situation of men fallen into transgression as opposed to the blessed state of commandment keepers. It was, Greg suspected, for his particular benefit.

Then it was Enos' turn. He turned solemnly to Greg. "What's our favorite Book of Mormon story?"

First the lousy stamped baseball, and now this. Greg could hear his pedestal crack. "I haven't read the Book of Mormon, Enos."

The little boy pushed up his glasses. "How come?"

"I guess because I've never heard of it before tonight."

Enos' eyes met Greg's. "Then will you read it now?"

All movement at the table ceased. Even Brad looked up. Greg's eyes widened, but he couldn't disappoint that earnest little face. "Well, yeah," he said finally. "I'll try to read some of it, at least. What's your favorite part, Enos? I'll read that for sure."

Conferred with the awesome responsibility of choosing a story for his hero, Enos scrunched his forehead, considering. "Well, there's a guy in there with my same name and his story's kinda cool, but I like the brother of Jared best."

Darlene jotted this down next.

"What was his name?" Greg asked. If he were lucky, this book would have a table of contents.

Enos shrugged. "Everyone called him the brother of Jared."

"Who was Jared?"

"I don't know." Enos thought for a moment. "No one important," he decided. "His brother was the important one."

Greg's forehead wrinkled as his eyebrows rose. "The important one was called the brother of Jared?" Enos nodded. *Christ in America, sword-wielding maniacs, and anonymous heroes. This must be some book.*

Andi decided Greg had heard enough for one meal. "I like Lehi's dream," she told Darlene. "So, that's all of us."

"But," Darlene said slowly, "you skipped Greg."

"He hasn't read the Book of Mormon," Andi reminded her.

"I know, but I want to tell everybody he was at our house for dinner tonight and they'll want to know his favorite story, too." Before Andi could point out the nonsense of this argument, Darlene continued, "Just tell me your favorite Bible story, Greg, and I'll work it in like Francie's and Dad's."

Bible story. Greg's thoughts raced. *Who was in the Bible?* Noah, but he couldn't copy a kindergartner. *Adam? Moses?* Did he know anything about either of those guys? *Jesus, surely. What did He do? Come on,*

Howland, think. He'd been to a day of Vacation Bible School with a boy who lived across town. He must have picked up something. He glanced nervously at Mr. Reynolds, then he had it. "That, uh, guy in the lions' den."

"Daniel?" Darlene asked, pencil poised.

"Yeah, Daniel. That's my favorite story." He took a quick bite of funeral potatoes to avoid saying more and hoped fervently that the lions hadn't devoured Daniel in the end.

CHAPTER 10

Andi smothered the giggle but couldn't disguise her dimples as she led Greg through the French doors into the backyard. His face, which she had noted betrayed every emotion, now reflected tremendous relief. The door clicked quietly closed behind them as she asked, "Glad to be out of the lions' den, Daniel?"

"Yeah. I mean, no. I mean . . . ," Greg shook his head. "Did I ever mention I'm not real good at small talk?"

"You did fine."

"Sure I did."

Despite his grimace, Andi could tell he already felt more at ease now that he was outdoors. He breathed deeply. "What smells so good?"

"It's the citrus," she replied, motioning toward white-trunked trees lining the block walls. The waxy blossoms moved gently in the breeze, perfuming the cool night air. "The subdivision was built over an old orange grove, and they saved as many trees as they could. The whole neighborhood smells this way, especially at night. It's heavenly. I think I like the fragrance even better than the fruit."

Greg gazed around the spacious, grassy yard. It was lit softly by moonlight and a few dim orbs that encircled the patio, pool, and garden areas. One side of the yard was rimmed with raised beds, profuse with vegetables and flowers; the other was dominated by a pool where a small waterfall splashed peacefully over artificial rocks. The soft light, reflected in the still water, was magical and very appealing. "Your home is beautiful, Andi."

He seemed impressed and a little awed, she thought in surprise. With all his money, Andi could only imagine the mansion he must own. She led the way to a wide, white lacquered swing and curled herself into one corner.

"Tell me about where you live," she urged, patting the seat beside her. "What's it like in the Windy City?"

Greg hesitated a moment before moving to join her in the swing. In that moment of indecision, a green and brown blur swept in from the side yard, fully and furiously occupying the seat.

"Quark!" the mallard honked as it extended strong wings, puffed itself up to the greatest possible proportion, and dared Greg to make the next move.

Startled, Greg instinctively retreated.

"Quark." Satisfied, the duck nestled next to Andi, searching her hand for a treat.

"Sorry, Icarus," she laughed. "I forgot to bring you anything this time." Andi scooped the fowl onto her lap and turned it toward Greg. "Look, fella, there's someone here you ought to meet. This is Greg Howland. He's a famous baseball player and all-around celebrity salesman. Greg, this is Icarus. He's a duck."

"I can see that he's a duck."

"Naturally, it's easy for you, but how would Icarus know you're a big-shot pitcher? He missed the World Series, you know, and they don't make Reeboks in his size. If I don't introduce you, he might not appreciate being in the presence of super stardom."

Greg rolled his eyes. "Are you ever going to drop that?"

"No," Andi replied, but her eyes were shining. "Do you want to sit down?"

"Does he want me to?"

"Sure," she said, smoothing the still-ruffled feathers. "Don't you, Icarus?"

The onyx eyes blinked. "Quark!"

"Aren't ducks supposed to quack?" Greg asked, eyeing the mallard warily as he perched cautiously on the edge of the swing. "That's the strangest sound I've ever heard."

"He won't tell you how to throw a baseball if you don't tell him how to speak duck, okay?"

The mallard hadn't moved, so Greg inched further back on the seat. Icarus stretched his beak toward him suspiciously. "Nice duck," Greg said, extending his right hand in greeting. If he lost a knuckle, it better not be one of the ones he needed for a knuckleball.

"He *is* a nice duck," Andi insisted, stroking the side of its neck and causing it to lose interest, momentarily at least, in Greg. "And he's a good watchduck."

"I can see that. Where did you get such a fine feathered fiend, er, friend?"

Andi formed a little nest for Icarus in her skirt. "Actually, he's Clytie's. He blew into the pool during one of the monsoon storms last summer. The zoo vet said his wing was broken. Clytie prayed for him and nursed him and carried him around like a baby, and he's been here ever since."

"He can fly now?"

"Oh, sure. He only hangs around because he wants to. He adores Clytie."

"He seems pretty fond of you, too."

Andi patted the duck's back. "Clytie's his favorite but he's kind of an all-around people-duck. He could probably even learn to like you," she teased, "if he knew more about you, of course. You were going to tell us about your home." When Greg didn't respond, she dimpled. "It's okay, Howland, impress me. You have forty-seven rooms and an indoor tennis court, right?"

"Not exactly." In the stillness of the evening, his sigh seemed to carry forever. "I don't really have a home, Andi. I lease an apartment in Chicago, but most of the time we're on the road and I live in hotels. When I have to go back to Iowa, I stay with my parents. So, are you impressed?"

"Tell me about where you grew up, then."

"Then you really won't be impressed."

"Tell me anyway."

Andi watched Greg's partially lowered face as he considered a dozen meaningless responses and half-truths in the silence that followed. When he finally spoke, his face told her he had decided to be candid.

"It isn't anything like this," he said, looking around the yard at everything but her eyes. "Our house is small, for one thing, only two bedrooms, and it's outside of town in a field of weeds. We haven't got a pool like yours either, but there's one heck of a mud puddle in the road when it rains."

"It must have been nice to grow up in the country."

"Not really."

"Tell me, Greg."

He looked into this remarkable girl's questioning green eyes and, as it had that morning, something in him responded. Still, Greg directed his words more to Icarus than Andi as he slowly recalled his childhood home with its peeling paint and ramshackle porch.

Andi tried not to show her surprise as he described the poverty— broken windows mended with boards and gray tape, a leaking roof, and faucets that trickled an orangish-brown water in the first few seconds of every use. Greg's account was so vivid she could almost see the rusted chassis and rebuilt engines sitting hopefully on the weed-choked acreage, waiting for his father to scrounge up the money and sobriety to reincarnate them into automobiles. Still, she struggled to understand. "Is your father an alcoholic, Greg?"

"Actually, Andi, he's a drunk." Having come this far, he continued, "He has these binges. Sometimes he drinks more than he eats."

"Doesn't that make him sick?"

"No, just everyone around him. It makes him loud. And mean."

Andi's voice was barely above a whisper. "You mean, he's . . . abusive?"

"That's a polite word for it." Greg's brows knit as he wondered what it was about this woman that had him telling her more in one day than he'd shared with anyone else in the last twenty years. He shook his head slowly. "Anyway, it was a long time ago."

"But what did your mother do about it?" She watched Greg's lips compress into a thin line as he looked away.

"Nothing." Catching the look on Andi's face from the corner of his eye, he added quickly, "I don't blame my mother. There wasn't anything she could do. She's sick a lot and never had much . . . ," he paused, trying to choose a word, "strength. The louder my dad got, the quieter she was. It's almost as if she has this ability to subconsciously disappear. It made me feel bad to talk to her, even—like it was unfair to drag her back from wherever it is she lives."

There was a foreign heaviness in Andi's chest as she blinked back her emotions. "But what did you do, Greg? Didn't you tell anyone?"

"It never occurred to me anyone would care." His voice was flat and utterly honest.

"No one?"

"Jim stood up for me when he could. The rest of the time I took the beating or tried a disappearing act of my own." When Greg's eyes met hers and saw that they were liquid, he was embarrassed and angry with himself. He didn't know what he wanted from this girl, but it wasn't pity. He forced a smile. "You know, Andi, really, I owe all this fame and fortune you're so impressed by to my dad. If I hadn't spent most of my life avoiding him, I'd have never learned to pitch."

When he was ten, Greg told her, he began throwing rocks. At first it was frustration and perhaps even a desire for revenge that prompted him to pull smooth, round stones from the sandy soil and send them crashing into the sides of his father's old cars. He would throw all day sometimes, purposefully, ferociously, until the ache in his shoulder and arm exceeded the ache in his heart. Then he would collapse on the dirt, waiting for the first star to appear in the twilight sky so he could wish himself away from Iowa forever. He had no plan, no clearly defined idea of where he wanted to go even, just a raw hope that somehow, someday, he would find a way out.

It was several miserable years until, finally, the way found him. Greg's compulsion to throw intensified as he began to set goals, meet and exceed them, then set more. In the spring, he threw every day after school and all day in the summer, stopping only to do chores he'd assign himself in an effort to help his mother. When winter came, Greg learned how quickly an arm could spasm in the cold, snowy air so he went from school to the familiar public library. There he stayed virtually every day until closing, switching his allegiance from the fictional world of Narnia to the compelling—if equally unattainable—world of professional baseball. Then he would jog the three miles home in the dark, unless Jim managed to get away to give him a lift.

By first thaw, Greg had committed the two dozen baseball books to memory and was back outside, anxious to master the techniques he learned in theory, practiced each night in his room, and lived again and again in his dreams. When April came, and baseball season finally began, he spent the hours after dark hunched in the hallway, invisible to his father, but within sight of the magical images of genuine big-leaguers flickering across the small black and white TV in the living room. He analyzed every play, trying to anticipate each pitch, swing and infield throw.

Of course there was no money for Little League, or even a real ball or glove, but Greg had a strong body, plenty of rocks, and a good imagination. He enlisted car parts, shrubbery, and the occasional stray mutt in closely contested games on his home field. His natural ability, sheer determination, and copy-cat form improved his throwing so dramatically that, by the age of thirteen, he could hurl a rock fifty feet and hit the same dent in the '58 Ford eight times out of ten. He began to experiment and found that he could also curl the tips of his fingers to make a round stone fly straight as a Frisbee and drop like a, well, rock, almost anywhere he wanted it.

It was toward the end of this summer, Greg told Andi, that Rusty Trenzle drove by in a station wagon full of kids, bound for a picnic. The fan belt snapped just across the field from where Greg was throwing. Roy Howland was home at the time, semi-sober, and had leaned under the hood while Sadie chatted self-consciously with Mrs. Trenzle, and the little Trenzles whooped and chased around the field. Greg threw rocks into an apple crate, oblivious to the commotion and to the man leaning against an ancient auto skeleton, watching his every move.

Within minutes, the picnic was forgotten (at least by Trenzle) as he trotted to Greg's side. "Hey, kid. Where'd you learn to do that?"

Greg shrugged. He was just throwing rocks.

"How old are you?"

"Thirteen." That put him one year away from the freshman class at Fairmont High in Dubuque, where Trenzle, a former minor-league pitcher, coached the second-best baseball team in the state. The coach eyed Greg's lanky build doubtfully. "Can you keep it up?"

"I throw rocks all day, mostly."

Trenzle let out a low whistle. "So, kid, you want to go on a picnic?"

That afternoon, Rusty Trenzle became his coach, his counselor, and eventually helped provide a passport away from Peosta forever. Greg, in turn, exchanged rocks for baseballs, worked harder than anyone asked, and saw to it that, for his four years at Fairmont, Trenzle coached the best high school team in five states. Meanwhile, the innate intelligence that enabled him to master trigonometry as quickly as the infield fly rule assured Greg a full ride at Northwestern University in Illinois, where he went to prepare himself to teach math and coach baseball, like his mentor.

"And that," he told Andi with a self-deprecating grin, "is, in two thousand words or more, everything you never wanted to know about where I come from."

He was wrong. Andi wanted to know everything about him. She had listened, almost without breathing, to every word he said and understood much of what he wouldn't say. She recognized now the source of those little lines around his beautiful eyes—lines she had thought him too young to have. She wanted to trace them lightly with her finger to see if, by touching them, she might make them disappear. She leaned toward Greg, disturbed the duck, and spent the next few moments soothing it back to sleep and recovering her emotional equilibrium. "But after college you didn't teach. You decided to play professional baseball instead?"

"It was so much money." The way he said it sounded like an apology. Greg told her briefly how hard those college years had been. The time spent in physical training conflicted with the hours needed to study, and both competed with sleep in the few hours left outside of class, the ball field, and a very inconvenient convenience store job. He almost failed to enroll his senior year after becoming eligible for the draft. He was sorely tempted by the legion of scouts who had flocked to his games with clipboards and radar guns, then followed him from his dorm to classes and back again, offering him everything this side of the moon. He had stuck it out in school but by the end of his senior season, with a diploma in hand and the bushes still full of talent scouts, he had gratefully signed with the Cubs. "At the time, I thought the money would make a difference," he explained.

"To your family?"

"Yeah."

"Did it?"

Greg shook his head. It was becoming increasingly obvious that he lacked the ability to change, or even understand, the cause of his anguish. "I thought if I gave my dad money he would sell the shop. Then that would take some pressure off him and maybe get Jim out of there too."

"Did he take it?"

"He took the money, all right. He moved to a new building, sank thousands into shop equipment he doesn't know how to use, and bought a fancy new truck with what was left. That's okay," Greg added quickly, "I don't care what he does. He totaled the truck, anyway, coming home from some bar."

"But what about your mother? Didn't you buy her a new house?" Andi saw the pained expression cross his face and regretted her question immediately. "I mean, not that you should have, or that she needed it, or . . . I'm so sorry, Greg."

"Of course I should have and she did need it—does need it. Andi, she'll never budge from that spot of earth. She doesn't see anything wrong with the way she lives. Her parents were poor and her father was . . ." He shrugged as his voice dropped. "It's hopeless. I've given her more than enough money to move or at least fix the place up. I don't know what's happened to it all, but the house is the same as ever. She's the same as ever. Nothing will change there, no matter what I do."

There, he thought, *I finally said it.* But could he accept it? Greg cleared the growing thickness from his throat as he glanced sheepishly at Andi. Her eyes, a deeper green than the citrus, were dewy at the corners. Mentally, Greg berated himself for sharing this sob story. He had forsaken the social practices of a monk to be with this girl, but wished now he had exchanged them for a vow of silence instead.

As he looked out over the yard, his gaze fell on the citrus trees. How long did it take for a tree to grow? At least a couple generations must have come and gone for an orchard to be planted, pruned, and finally divided into housing plots. So much had changed here, but the orange trees circling Andi's yard had remained the same. *Is that how it is?* Greg wondered. *The world goes on, but my family stays the same? My grandparents, my parents . . . me? Can't I at least change myself? No matter what I want? No matter what I do?*

HAPTER 11

Before he turned away, Andi had seen the lines deepen around Greg's eyes and wanted him to smile—wanted it as much as she had ever wanted anything. Leaning toward him, she touched his arm gently. "Tell me the most wondrous thing you can remember, Greg. Something that changed the way you look at life."

Greg's surprise at her words melted into gratitude as he settled back onto the swing, considering. "Well, when I used to walk home across the fields at night, away from everything, the stars were tremendous. It was like they came right down to the ground, and I thought if I tried I could reach up and rearrange them, they were that close. It's the one thing I miss about home."

"I love stars! And I know what you mean. When I was a teenager, I went to girls' camp every summer. I liked to pretend the stars were hung out at night just for me. They always made me feel special and close to God."

The muscles in Greg's jaw contracted. "I liked them because they were a billion reasons for God to be too busy to notice me."

Andi's eyes traveled from the shadow on Greg's cheek to his clasped hands and rested there. It wasn't the first time that evening she had wanted to cry for him. She considered her response carefully. "Can I tell you the most comforting thing I've ever heard?" When he nodded she continued, "One of our church leaders, Elder Jeffrey R. Holland, said that everyone believes, from time to time, that they live too far away from heaven for God to notice them. With all the important, intergalactic business He has to take care of, God's got to be too busy to notice one little person here on earth. Right?"

"Right."

"But that isn't true. Elder Holland said that when we die we'll be amazed to learn how well God knows us and has loved and watched over us our whole lives. And he promised each of us that there is nothing in the universe more important to Heavenly Father than our individual hopes and happiness."

"And you believe that?"

"I really do."

"What is this Elder Holland? A philosopher?"

"No, he's a General Authority."

Greg raised an eyebrow. "A general authority on what?"

Andi smiled. "Spiritual matters, I suppose. You see, Greg, I believe that Jesus Christ has organized His church today as He did when He was on earth, with prophets and apostles. Elder Holland is an apostle, which also makes him a General Authority."

"How old is he?"

"I don't know . . ."

"You call him 'Elder,'" Greg prompted, "so I assume he's ancient, or in his fifteenth life like the Dalai Lama."

"Oh, no! Elder's a priesthood office. You know, like Brad's a priest. There are several offices: deacon, teacher, bishop . . . well, several, anyway. The apostles, like Brother Holland, are prophets and also General Authorities. The Seventy are also General Authorities." Andi could see that, for Greg, this was dinner déjà vu.

"And let me guess," he said, "none of the Seventies are seventy, and there probably aren't seventy of them, either. Right?"

"Well . . ."

"Andi, does your church by any chance publish a Mormon/English dictionary?"

Her laughter woke the duck. She set it on the ground and watched it waddle off, offended, to nest beneath its favorite bush. "Maybe I can write one and get rich."

"You are rich," Greg said softly. "You have a beautiful home, a great family, and something you believe."

"What do you believe, Greg?"

His eyes trailed to the pool. After everything she had said, he might as well wrap any hope of seeing her again around a rock and chuck it in the deep end. He wondered what flaw in his character made it so difficult for him to lie, even when he really wanted to.

"You don't believe in God?" she persisted.

"I don't know," Greg said finally. "I never thought much about God, and He seemed to return the favor."

"Maybe He thought of you and you just didn't recognize it."

"Maybe." Greg shifted uncomfortably. "But if there is a God, Andi, He seems very different from the one your Elder Holland describes."

"In what way?"

Greg leaned forward to rest his elbows on his knees, his gaze shifting involuntarily back to the still water. "Well, He's cruel, or at least indifferent. Most people in the world are poor, or living in areas torn apart by crime and war. You don't see God doing anything about their hopes and happiness."

"Poverty and war aren't God's fault. Everyone has free agency and everyone's agency affects everyone else's. What you're talking about are things that men do to themselves, and to each other, when they turn away from God," Andi asserted firmly. "I believe that Heavenly Father wants what's best for all His children and blesses them accordingly."

"Like He blessed Clytie?"

Andi stiffened. How many times had she asked herself the same question? Had Clytie chosen to come to earth this way? Why would she? But if she hadn't had a choice . . . "I don't know," Andi said, "why Clytie has the body she has. But I do know that she doesn't feel sorry for herself or think that she's cursed. She's grateful for what she has and makes the most of it."

"She's remarkable," Greg said sincerely. "What's wrong with her?"

"Nothing's wrong with her!" Andi's dismay at Greg's lack of faith had caused her to speak more sharply than she intended. When she saw his startled, remorseful face, she was sorry.

"I didn't mean it that way."

"I know you didn't. I'm touchier about it than she is. Clytie's an achondroplastic dwarf. It's a genetic condition that doesn't affect her life span or intelligence or anything. It just means that although her torso and head grow normally, her arms and legs won't get any bigger. That's why she's so small and hunched looking."

"Isn't there anything they can do?"

"It isn't a disease doctors can cure; it isn't a disease at all. It's just the way some people are born. Clytie has had surgery a few times to correct bows in her legs and to straighten her spine. Still, it's hard for such little legs to support much weight."

"Is she always as happy as she seemed tonight?"

"Well," Andi smiled, "just between you and me, I think she has a major crush on this ballplayer who came to dinner." Her dimples deepened along with his coloring. "But she really does have a good attitude, even when it's hard. You wouldn't believe how people treat her sometimes. Strangers pat her on the head like a puppy and most adults talk to her like she's a child. She hates that kind of thing, but she's used to curious looks by now. Since she was little, we've told her that people only stare because she's pretty."

"She *is* pretty."

"Maybe Clytie isn't the only one who's developed a crush. Should I be jealous?"

Greg grinned. "That'd be great."

Andi hastily retreated to safer ground. "Do you know why we call her Clytie?"

"No, but I'll bet it's Greek. Even your duck's Greek. Wasn't Icarus that guy with wax wings who fell into the ocean?"

"Yes, and Clytie was a nymph who loved the sun. Every day she sat and watched it cross the sky. When she died she became a sunflower, the symbol of constancy."

"Uh huh," Greg said, circling his hand for her to go on, "and you call her Clytie because . . . ?"

"Because our Clytie is just as dedicated to the Son of God. She never takes her eye off Him and that's why she can be happy, even if she isn't perfect by society's standards. She has absolute faith that Heavenly Father wants only what's best for her."

"We've been here already," Greg observed, "with Elder Holland, last time." He leaned back, crossed his arms, and asked hopefully, "You said that Ari—your name's—Greek. Is there a story behind it, too?"

It didn't escape Andi's attention that he couldn't pronounce her name and that he was changing the subject, but she smiled anyway. "There's a story behind all our names; Dad made sure of that."

Greg was pleased. Greek mythology, without applied Christian morality, he could handle. "Tell me about the Greek Ari—Andi, then."

Andi settled into the swing and gave it a gentle push. "Have you heard of King Minos?"

"My classical education's as good as the next guy's," Greg assured her with mock indignation. "I knew Icarus, didn't I? Minos was the king of Crete, right? He had this Minotaur thing, a monster that was half man and half . . . uh . . ."

"Half bull. Minos built an elaborate maze called the Labyrinth to keep it in."

"The world's first bullpen?"

"Excuse me?"

"You know, bullpen, like in baseball." He smiled at her blank expression. "Never mind."

"Well, every nine years the people in Athens had to send Minos a tribute of seven maidens and seven young men for the Minotaur to devour. One year, at the time of the sacrifice, Theseus, the son of the king of Athens, volunteered to go himself."

"Theseus is our hero?"

"Yes. Everyone loved Theseus for his goodness and admired him for his strength. They knew he was the only one who could slay the Minotaur."

"Did he?"

"We're not to that part yet. When Theseus arrived in Crete, Minos paraded him through town and prepared to send him into the Labyrinth. Well, the king's daughter saw Theseus and fell in love with him."

"And this was . . . your namesake?" Someday, he told himself, he would have to try to say this girl's name.

"Yes."

"Did they call her Andi for short?"

"No, Greg, they were Greek. They could pronounce her name. Do you want to hear this story, or not?"

Greg laced his hands behind his neck as he leaned back. "I'm all ears, professor."

"All right, then. Ariadne told Theseus that she could get him out of the maze alive but in return he had to promise to marry her. He agreed and she slipped him a sword and a small spool of thread just as he entered the door. She held one end and he unwound it as he went along, then he eventually followed the thread back out to her."

"So, he killed the monster?"

"Of course, he was the hero."

"Did he marry Minos' daughter?"

"Yes. What kind of hero would he be if he hadn't loved the heroine?"

This was the best story Greg had ever heard. "And the moral is that two people from different worlds can fall in love at first sight and live happily ever after?"

Andi's cheeks burned despite the cool night breeze. "No. Well, yes, in a way. No. I mean, they only live happily ever after in Homer's version. In most, Theseus leaves her heartbroken and his father even kills himself."

"So, how are you going to twist this story around to show God in His heaven looking tenderly after the affairs of mortal men?"

Before Andi could frame a protest, the patio door swung open. A pajama-clad Enos appeared, his autographed ball and glove in one hand, a shiny aluminum bat in the other. "Mom says I can stay three minutes then I have to go to bed. I'm supposed to say that it was nice to meet you, Greg, and thank you for signing my poster and my glove and my ball and my baseball card and all those papers for my friends. So, thank you." Having delivered the prepared remarks, he clinked the bat up and down on the brick patio beneath his bare toes.

Greg reached inside his jacket for the pen. "It was nice to meet you, too, Enos," he said, "and I'd be honored to sign that bat of yours."

"Would you?" Enos had it, and himself, in Greg's lap almost before Andi saw him move.

"Sure." Greg paused, pen in midair. "But you know what, pal? I'm a lousy hitter, even for a pitcher. But my roommate's Jeff Jensen, and he's one of the best sluggers in the league. He's an outfielder like you, too. Do you want me to take your bat to him?"

"Would I get it back?"

Greg chuckled. He really liked this serious kid. "Yeah, Enos, Jensen has his own bats. I'd just ask him to sign it for you."

"Could he use your pen?"

Greg ruffled the little boy's hair. "If you want him to."

Enos nodded vigorously, almost losing his glasses. "Then you could bring it to my game tomorrow night! I play at eight o'clock at Whittier School."

"Eight o'clock at Whittier. Got it."

"You mean you'll come?"

Greg started to agree, then stopped himself. "I can't, Enos, I'm sorry. I've got a radio interview at 7:30 tomorrow night and the station is in downtown Phoenix. I bet your game'll be over before I get back." He lifted the little boy's chin with his thumb. "I really am sorry. But I promise to get your bat back to you with Jensen's name on it. Okay?"

"Okay," Enos said, trying to smile as he slid from Greg's lap. "Thank you again for signing all that stuff and sitting by me at dinner."

"It was my pleasure. Good luck in the game tomorrow night."

Margaret Reynolds appeared at the door and Enos reluctantly followed her inside.

"I should probably go," Greg suggested. He hoped Andi wouldn't be overly receptive to the idea, though he wouldn't blame her if she showed him out to strains of the "Hallelujah Chorus." Right now, he couldn't remember saying two dozen words he didn't regret. He must have looked like an idiot in front of her family at dinner, and then gone on afterward to describe himself to Andi as a compulsive, agnostic chump from a thoroughly dysfunctional family. If he had carefully planned it, Greg decided, he couldn't have made a worse impression in one short evening. More than likely, this evening would be the last chance he'd ever have to impress Ariadne Reynolds.

Suddenly, Greg couldn't bear to look into the shifting, emerald lights of Andi's eyes. He stopped the swing and rose from it in one fluid motion, offering her his hand. "Thanks for dinner, Andi, and thanks for listening to me again tonight. All things considered, I'll bet talking to those crocodiles is more interesting."

Not knowing what to say, Andi extended her own hand awkwardly, feeling like a self-conscious fourteen-year-old at her first stake dance. Once his hand was in hers, she didn't know what to do with it. The reasonable, well-ordered part of her, the part that carefully checked her list and charted the course of her perfect life, insisted that she give this strong hand back, show its owner to the door, and bolt that door tightly behind him. But another side of Andi had a suggestion as well. This unfamiliar part whispered that the warm tingling that she now felt in her own hand was a rare and precious thing. Certainly it was something she had never felt before and might never feel again if she let go of him now.

Andi couldn't rely on a foreign instinct, however, without first testing its worth, so she released Greg's hand and walked him through the house to the front door, relieved that he was leaving. In two days, she reminded herself, Sterling Channing would come home and this strange carousel of a day would be in her past and easily forgotten. As she closed the door behind Greg, Andi resisted the urge to peek out the curtains.

CHAPTER 12

The phone rang, fell silent, and rang again. Jeff Jensen opened one eye to the dim morning light, consulted the glowing digits on the clock, then rolled over and pulled the pillow tighter around his ears. The phone rang again. In the other bed, Greg stirred and looked bleary-eyed at the time. It was six a.m. and he'd slept less than three hours.

When Greg had flopped onto his bed before nine the night before, he'd felt anything but tired. He tried to read, but found the problems H.G. Wells' characters faced in a lost world trivial compared to his own in this one. He didn't want to talk to Jensen either, since every time he opened his mouth he said something he'd later regret. Greg only wanted to lay on top of his bed, fully clothed, and brood.

How, he asked himself, *could you have been so stupid?* Andi Reynolds was probably still wondering how he had crammed so many skeletons into one closet. He wondered what had possessed him to open the stupid closet and pull them all out for her in the first place. *Not even all,* he reminded himself. *At least you left out Zeke.*

When Greg finally did drop off, sometime after two, he had the strangest dream. He was on the mound, pitching the most important game of his career, but before he could throw the first ball, an unseen crowd booed him from the field. Trying to get away from the jeers, he stumbled into the bullpen and became lost in a maze of twilight mist, pursued by monsters with Zeke's face and the body of a duck. There was no sword with which to defend himself, no thread to follow out, no Ariadne waiting for him at the end. He woke with a start. It was a stupid dream. He didn't know why it had left him so cold and shaken, trying with little success to sleep again before dawn.

The phone rang again. Greg grabbed the receiver and mumbled a monosyllabic greeting.

"Hello? Greg?" The woman's voice was high and insistent. "Why didn't you answer the phone?"

"Bobbie Jo? Are the boys okay?"

"I guess."

"Is something wrong with my mother?"

"I don't know. I haven't seen her."

Greg rubbed his face, still groggy, as he tried to recover from too little sleep and too much nightmare. "Bobbie, it's six o'clock in the morning."

"It's eight," his sister-in-law insisted.

Greg groaned. *Maybe in Iowa.* "Well, what's up?"

"I need to talk to you, Greg. Do you want me to call you back?"

"No, I'm awake now. Shoot."

"Are you alone?"

How am I supposed to deal with this woman? Greg wondered. Everything he had tried so far—brotherly affection, cool indifference, and even hundreds of miles of distance—had failed. Greg had been in high school when she married Jim and was more than a little relieved when they separated six years (and two children) later. Bobbie Jo Howland, from the very beginning, had been a grand pain. But now she was his brother's widow—and still the reluctant mother of Jim's two sons. "Jensen's here," he said. At her giggle, Greg dropped his head back onto the soft pillow and winced at the sudden pain. "What do you need, Bobbie?"

"The kids miss you, Greg."

"I wish I could spend more time with them, but—"

"We could move in with you in Chicago."

"No."

"But—"

"Bobbie Jo," Greg said sharply, "we've been through this. I have a one-bedroom apartment . . ." He stopped, frustrated at himself now for offering excuses.

"So you move. The boys need you."

"I'm doing my best. I talked to them Tuesday. They seem okay under the circumstances."

"Well, that girl you hired isn't working out."

"What's wrong with her?"

"I don't like her. She's so . . . foreign."

The girl was from Mississippi, Greg knew, a practical young woman who had come to Iowa after high school to be close to her grandparents. She needed money for college and Jim's little boys needed stability. It seemed like the perfect arrangement. Greg paid Wanda to live with his sister-in-law so someone would be up in the mornings to get the boys dressed and off to school. Later, she met their bus, played games with them, and provided every meal that didn't come from a freezer case or drive-through window. It couldn't last forever, but their uncle would hate to see it end so soon. "Can you try a little longer? The boys like her."

"She talks funny," Bobbie Jo insisted, "and she messes with my clothes."

One woman's definition of laundry, Greg suspected. He waited for her to finish.

"And, Greg, she finally told me how much you pay her—she practically forced me to make a federal case out of it—and it's way too much."

"It's not very much," he said tiredly, "and I can afford it."

"Well, for the money, I'd rather have a maid."

"Then hire a maid, too. I don't care." He didn't, but couldn't help but wonder what Bobbie Jo did with herself as it was. How much time could one woman spend in a beauty shop or bingo hall?

"Really? I could hire a maid?"

"Hire a maid, butler and chauffeur if you think you need them. Go down to the bank and they'll arrange the money for you."

"I probably won't need the butler and chauffeur until you come home, and we get a mansion and limo—"

Greg cleared his throat. "Just hire anyone you want, okay?"

"I need you to help me. I can't do the interviews the way you did with Wanda."

"You don't like Wanda, remember?"

"But I need your help. You promised Jim you'd take care of his boys."

Greg closed his eyes, sure now he had a headache. "Bobbie, you know I can't leave training. I'm in big trouble with management the way it is."

"But this is important. I need your help."

"Someone at the bank will help you. I'll talk to them. Now, if that's all you called about—"

"I didn't call about that at all."

Greg rolled onto his stomach and buried his face in the mattress. *I can't do this.*

"Greg?"

He didn't answer.

"Greg? Zeke said—"

Now she had his attention. As he sat up, Greg knocked his pillow into the lamp and just managed to catch it before it fell. "I told you never to talk to him!"

Jensen stirred and pulled his pillow tighter. Greg lowered his voice. "Bobbie Jo, he's scum."

"He works for you."

"He's still scum."

"He called me. He's worried about you."

Greg rubbed his throbbing forehead. "The only person Zeke Martoni worries about is Zeke Martoni."

"You don't know, Greg," she persisted. "You're gone so much. He helped Jimmy with the pain."

"Helped Jim? He killed Jim, you mean."

Jensen lifted his pillow and eyed his roommate quizzically. Greg motioned for him to go back to sleep and counted silently to ten. When he spoke, his voice was lower, but as firm as he could make it. "Look, I've told you he's dangerous, okay? You've got to keep him away from the kids."

"But he's so nice to us."

"He is *not* nice. Nothing about him is nice." Greg wished, for the first time he could ever recall, to be in Peosta. Maybe then he could shake some sense into his sister-in-law. Finally, inspired, he tried a different approach. "Listen, Bobbie, just do this one thing for me, will you?"

"I'd do anything for you, Greg."

He sighed. "Then don't talk to Zeke anymore, ever. Let me handle him."

Saying he'd handle Zeke was one thing; handling him was another. Greg lay on his back, after finally hanging up the phone, and turned the problem over in his mind, examining it again from every angle. As it was, Zeke had the bases pretty well covered. He might be able to end Greg's career in baseball. He could probably kill his endorsements. He would, beyond doubt, ruin the young pitcher's reputation. Of the three, Greg most dreaded the latter. How could he look a kid in the face after *World News Tonight* led off with a story about Greg Howland's alleged point shaving to pay for his brother's drug habit?

Greg's fingers massaged slow circles around his throbbing temples as he stared up at the tiny silver flecks in the textured ceiling. In the dim, pre-dawn light they resembled faraway stars. *What did Andi say? "Nothing in the world is more important to God than your hopes and happiness."* He frowned. How had he gotten into this mess then, when his greatest hope had been to help his family, and all it would take to make him happy right now would be to get rid of Zeke?

Apparently, Howland, he thought, *you failed some heavenly aptitude test and didn't qualify for the program. Maybe gullibility is the eighth deadly sin.*

They say that hindsight is 20/20, but Greg still wondered how he could have been so myopic last summer. Jim had changed dramatically since meeting Zeke. It was so obvious in retrospect. Jim had asked Greg so many questions: *You pitching this game? How's your arm holding out? Is Wilson gonna relieve or Marley? Jensen back up to 100%?* Greg had been pleased with Jim's interest in his career and anxious to keep in touch with his brother. He had said a lot of things he should have kept in the locker room, he knew now. He used inside information to speculate on the outcome of most games, unaware that Jim was tape-recording every word to pass along to Zeke. Martoni used the information to figure point spreads, wager on the games, and win—big.

Now, Zeke had the tapes and Greg had only his word that he thought he was shooting the breeze with a brother who had nothing to gain. The tenuous agreement struck after Jim's deathbed confession was that Zeke would keep the tapes to himself in exchange for his job as Greg's publicist. If the relationship terminated, or Greg went to the authorities with what he had learned from his brother about Zeke's moonlighting in gambling and drugs, Martoni would go public, using what he had and insinuating a good deal more. Greg knew better than anyone what a master the man was at mixing lies with truth. The end result would be one Greg didn't think he could live with. Still, he asked himself, could he live with things as they were?

It wasn't that he minded the money, even. He had more of that than he could reasonably spend. What he minded was the reluctant admission that no matter how strong and successful he appeared on the ball field, there was a man who could turn him in a heartbeat back into the frightened little boy who had cowered in a field of rocks outside his home in Peosta. Physically, he'd come a long way from Iowa. Emotionally, he knew he still had a ways to go. Mostly, he feared abusing the trust that his team and thousands of strangers had placed in him. Even without evidence to legally indict him, Zeke had more than enough scandal to headline every paper in the country. What would the kids think then? The kids who collected his cards, treasured his baseballs, and bought his posters at book fairs. Kids like the wheelchair-bound batboy and Enos Reynolds.

Greg shook his head and winced again at the pain in his skull. No matter how much light he tried to cast on the matter, it remained stubbornly gray. It hadn't been hard to forgive Jim under the circumstances. All his life, his brother had given him so much and asked so little in return. Besides, Greg had soon learned firsthand how easy it was to be entrapped by Zeke. Even though he would never again speak an unguarded word about the team, he couldn't get rid of Zeke. At least, he couldn't today. Feeling vaguely unclean, Greg rolled off the bed to head for the shower.

CHAPTER 13

Lupe Rodriguez put on another pot of decaf and took a cursory swipe at the counter top with a soapy cloth. She glanced up at the sound of the door chime and smiled. In her three-decade tenure as morning waitress at the Eat Inn, she had served hundreds of hungry Chicago Cubs. Her favorite had just walked in the door.

She poured a tall glass of orange juice and strolled to the booth in the rear where Greg usually sat with his back to the other customers in the hope of making it through breakfast undisturbed by autograph seekers.

As Lupe handed him the glass, her gaze lingered on the bruised half-moons beneath his eyes. Her tongue made a little *tsk* sound in the back of her throat. "You no feel so good, *mi jo?*"

"Just a headache, Lupe," Greg replied, laying aside his newspaper to sip the juice.

"You don't look so good. You cut your hair." He grimaced and she placed a warm brown hand on his forehead. "That flu, it has been going around. Did I tell you my Guillermo had it last week?"

Greg tried to nod under her hand. She had not only told him about her husband's illness; she'd brought in a bottle of cayenne. The hot pepper she'd stirred into his tomato juice had burned his throat and opened his sinuses for a week. "No more chili, Lu, please."

"*Gringo.*" But she patted his cheek fondly. "No fever, I think."

He smiled into her dark eyes, grateful for her concern. "I don't have the flu, just a headache. I didn't get enough sleep last night, I guess."

Her hand shot from his head to her ample hip as she glowered. "You tell me, Greg Howland, that you were not out with those party boys all hours. They are nothing but trouble. They—"

Greg laughed in spite of the pain in his head. "You know I'm a regular saint, Lupe. I just couldn't sleep." He nodded reassuringly at this middle-aged Hispanic woman who had mothered him since he first stepped off the bus and into the big leagues three years ago. In February and March, she did it in person, supervising his breakfasts and often inviting him to her home to share homemade tamales with her extended brood. The other ten months she accomplished it by mail, sending long letters, newspaper clippings, and care packages of her famous marzipan. Greg appreciated Lupe's cozy kitchen, and in many ways, the Rodriguez family had come to seem more real to him than his own. Now he squeezed Lupe's hand. "Honest."

"*Bueno.* I'll bring you some pancakes," she decided. "They're blueberry today, your favorite."

"Thanks, but could I just get toast? I'm not hungry."

"I knew it. You are sick."

"No, really."

"Your throwing, it cannot be good if your eating is not good."

"You're going to bed before the sportscast again, Lu. I've eaten in here every morning this season and I still can't pitch to the wide side of a barn."

She ignored him. He was the best pitcher in the world and she knew it. "I did not see you here yesterday."

"No." Greg's gaze shifted to a small placard advertising breakfast specials. "I wasn't here." *I was at the zoo. But I don't want to think about Andi. Or Enos. Or Bobbie Jo. Or Zeke. Especially, Zeke. What does that leave?* "Lupe," he asked impulsively, "do you know anything about a Church of Christ of Saints—something like that?"

"You mean Mormons?"

"Yeah."

The waitress shrugged. "My neighbor's a Mormon. They are nice people, mostly. Why is it you ask, Greg?"

"I'm curious. I, uh, had dinner with a Mormon family last night." He avoided her eyes. "It was no big deal."

"You met a little Mormon girl, you mean."

"What?"

"*Mi jo*, this is Lupe. I've raised three *niños* of my own, *no*?" She wiped her hands on her apron. "Lupe knows the kind of sick you are." A nearby table of businessmen was waving her over so she patted Greg on the shoulder. "Drink your juice. The pancakes will come, *pronto*."

Greg rubbed his temple as he glanced at the paper, turning pages abstractedly. It was the same old everyday stuff: crimes, corruption, war . . . life. Oh, and the Cubs hadn't won a game in two weeks.

As she balanced the overflowing plate of hot cakes, Lupe was deliberately slow to return to Greg's table. She needed time to think. Over her dead body would she let this young man get hurt. Most of the men she served were all ego, or all insecurity in a *mucho-macho* package. Greg, she believed, was all heart.

Lupe had noticed him the first morning of training, three years before. It was Valentine's Day and he was alone, just out of school, and more than two thousand miles from home. Over the first week, she noticed that he was painfully shy and a natural loner, so she befriended the rookie pitcher as she did the homeless *gatos* that skulked warily around the kitchen door for scraps. It wasn't the first time she'd done such a thing. In thirty years she thought she'd met every kind of stray there was. But Greg had surprised her.

The surprise came the first week of March that year, a few days after the tiny *Iglesia de Paz*, a clapboard building where her father had preached, burned to the ground. It was the church in which Lupe had been baptized, married, and intended to be eulogized. But, with no insurance, and most of the small Hispanic congregation living hand-to-mouth like she and her grown children, the hope of worshipping again on that site had dissipated with the smoke. She stayed home from work three days, mourning.

She had forgotten Greg. Nor did she give him a thought when the restaurant manager called to verify her return to work and mentioned that the young pitcher had asked about her. Late that night, the preacher made his rounds. He had received an anonymous donation, through a local bank. The account contained funds enough to rebuild the chapel and add the additional meeting rooms for which they'd petitioned the Lord. Lupe had thought of Greg then. Although the newspapers had told her that an eight-figure salary and hefty signing bonus had made the newest Cub an overnight multimillion-aire, he'd never acted like he knew it. Nor, in the weeks to come, did he mention Lupe's church or comment on her absence. Lupe didn't bring it up. She didn't need to. The Lord had told her where the church money came from.

Now, she set the plate in front of Greg and determined to protect him as best she could. "About those Mormons . . ."

He looked up into her dusky, serious face.

"They are nice people, *mi jo, es verdad.*" Lupe was a Christian woman and not one to speak unkindly of anyone, so she chose her words carefully. "But they're . . . close, Greg." She laced plump fingers together to illustrate. "*Comprende?*"

"No."

The waitress ignored management rules to slip onto the bench across from him. "Mormons, they like only to be with Mormons. They are friendly to you at the start, while they see if you want to join their church, but if you don't, they drop you like a hot *tortilla*."

Was it her imagination or were the circles beneath his eyes deepening? Still, she believed, it was better for him to hear the truth from her than to find out on his own by having his heart broken by some thoughtless girl. She continued, "I talked to their missionaries once. They were fine young men, *muy intelligente*—but they thought they owned the Lord Jesus."

"What do you mean?"

"God talks only to them." Lupe leaned across the table. "They think they know it all."

"General Authorities," Greg mused aloud.

"*¿Perdón?*"

"Nothing." He pushed away the plate and rubbed a hand across his face.

Lupe knew when she had made a point. She pushed the plate back in front of him. "Now you eat those pancakes, Greg Howland, *no?* Then you go out and find yourself a good Christian girl."

Greg mustered a half smile. "They haven't made any more as good as you, Lu. I wouldn't even know where to look."

CHAPTER 14

The door chime played "Onward, Christian Soldiers" as Greg stepped into the brightly lighted store and paused to survey unfamiliar territory. Remembering Lupe's admonition, he smiled. A Christian bookstore might be a logical place to shop for a good Christian girl. Actually, though, he planned to purchase a book to keep a promise to a little Mormon boy.

For a bookstore, it seemed to feature everything but. To Greg's right was a display of T-shirts, posters, and CDs—teenage stuff with a Christian theme. Along the back, spilling into the center of the room, were paintings, prints, and statuary. To his left was a children's play area flanked by rows of videos, toys, and even storybooks.

A picture book caught his eye. *Noah's Ark Full of Animals* was brightly illustrated, written in rhyme, and featured animals galore as well as a holographic rainbow on the last page. Francie Reynolds would love it. Greg planned to send Enos a bucket of balls when he returned his bat and thought now he should send little Francie something as well. He stuck the book under his arm.

There was a display of gift volumes just before the novelty section. One title was familiar: Henry Van Dyke's *The Fourth Wiseman*. Lupe had sent him a copy one year for Christmas. It was the best story he had ever read. He picked one up for Darlene, who seemed to collect people's favorite stories, and after some thought, added an illustrated Charles Dickens' *The Life of Christ* for Andi's parents. That left Clytie and Brad. He'd send Brad tickets to Saturday's game and a duffel, or something, from the team shop. Now Clytie.

A pretty, perky brunette approached and flashed him a radiant, flirtatious smile. "Good morning! Can I help you find something?"

As she looked at him more closely, Greg averted his face. "Uh, no thanks. I'm just looking."

"I could take those things to the counter for you," she offered slowly. She appeared perplexed, as if trying to decide why his face looked familiar.

Greg gave up the books with a mumbled thank you. Receiving no encouragement from him, the clerk said, "Well, I'll be up front if you need anything."

As he passed through the novelty section, Greg slipped his sunglasses on under the gaze of a nondescript man shopping nearby, then paused to return the stare. Hadn't he seen the same man outside the restaurant this morning and . . . where else? He shook his head at his own paranoia. It was probably a coincidence, or perhaps the man was a shy fan.

Greg lingered at a pasteboard box to let the man pass behind him. The carton was filled with soft foam sports balls, each small enough to fit in the palm of his hand. He picked up a football. "God is the Safety" was imprinted in bright, white letters. A soccer ball proclaimed, "Set a Goal for Heaven," and the basketball suggested, "Shoot for Eternity." Greg rummaged in the box until he found a baseball. "Run Home to God." *Corny.* Still, the ball was irresistibly squishy, and Greg found himself kneading it reflexively between his thumb and middle finger as he moved on.

There were no pictures of Christ like the one he'd admired at the Reynolds', though there were dozens of variations on the theme. Very few featured children however and, of them, none looked like Clytie. Greg turned to another shelf. There he picked up a wooden curio box painted with sunflowers. *Perfect.*

As he considered looking for something for Andi, his head throbbed. *She'd probably like nothing better than to forget she ever met me.* Greg walked quickly to the few rows of books to locate what he'd come for.

He found four shelves of Bibles, but no Book of Mormon. Just as he was about to take his chances with the flirtatious salesclerk, he spotted a book that at least had Mormon in the title: *The Mormon Mission.*

This must be the place. But there was no Book of Mormon among the dozen or so titles. Greg glanced at the placard above the shelf: *Apologetics/Cults.* An apologetic, he knew, is a defense of Christianity.

Confused, he pulled out a thick volume and felt his heart sink as he read the flyleaf. He put it back and chose another, eventually reading the summaries of several books as he worked his way along the row. Each book asserted that the Mormon Church was non-Christian. Yet Greg was sure Andi's church at least had Christ in the title, and Lu had said they thought they owned Jesus.

That's the thing about religion, Greg thought. *Everyone who says he believes in God wants to define Him in his or her terms and send to hell whatever portion of humanity happens to disagree.*

Scanning the titles, Greg noticed that the Mormon Church wasn't the only "cult" targeted by so-called mainstream Christianity. *What makes people write this stuff?* he wondered. *Do you really have to tear down someone else's belief to feel good about your own?* Still, Greg was anxious to learn *something* about the Mormon Church, so he picked up the first volume and took it to the front with Clytie's box.

"This is a really good book," the brunette said approvingly as Greg lay it on the counter.

He lowered his eyes.

"I have some pamphlets here about the Mormons," she continued, selecting two from a rack at the side of the register.

"No, thanks." Greg pulled a bill from his wallet. "Just this stuff."

"They're free."

"Thanks anyway."

"You're not a Mormon, are you?"

"No," Greg said quickly. *Too quickly,* he thought.

She smiled again. "I'm sorry. It's just your short hair, I guess. You look kinda like one of their missionaries."

Greg made a mental note: *Mormon missionaries have bad haircuts.* He was filing away information at a steady clip.

"Do you want that, too?" the girl asked, nodding toward the foam baseball in his hand.

Greg had forgotten he had it. "Uh, sure." He lay it on the counter and watched her enter the price in her computer.

"Well, come back soon," she said, after she had carefully bagged his purchases and made change. As he passed through the electronic theft-prevention checkpoint on the way out of the store, she called after him, "Jesus loves us!"

Really? Greg thought. You'd *think some of it would rub off and we'd love each other.*

Outside, Greg consulted his watch and regretted leaving his car in the lot at the hotel. Now it was four blocks away, he felt increasingly unwell, and he didn't have much time to make it to the field before batting practice.

Despite the dull ache in his head, he started back to the hotel at a jog. He surprised himself by stopping short at the entrance to a used bookstore. On impulse, he pushed open the door and blinked in the dim interior.

"Morning," an ancient man grunted from behind the counter, his squinted eyes never rising from the pulp fiction propped open in front of them. "Help you with something?"

"Well, maybe," Greg said, removing his glasses as he stepped further into the store. He was the only customer and it was a good thing. With so much merchandise spilling from the shelves, there was barely room enough for one person to pass down the narrow aisles. Cases, eight feet high, overflowed with books while boxes, bins, and even paper sacks held the multitude for which there was no other berth. Greg considered the thousands, possibly hundreds of thousands, of volumes in that room alone and wondered what would prompt anyone to write another book about anything.

"Do you have a section on religion?" he asked doubtfully.

"Nope."

"Okay, well, thanks." *Good. Maybe I'll make the game on time, after all.* He turned to leave.

"What religion?"

Greg paused. "I'm looking for a Book of Mormon. I don't guess you'd know if you've ever gotten one in."

The old man's hearty laugh turned into a hacking cough. He rapped his chest with a gnarled fist. "One? One! The Mormons give those things away by the truckload. Seems like most of them end up here—or would if I'd take them."

This was more interesting information for Greg's growing file on Mormonism. "But you don't take them?"

"I sell books, son. You can't sell what some folks give away, now can you?"

"I guess not. Thanks, anyway."

"You know," the man said slowly, as Greg put his hand on the doorknob, "I just might have one in that box of Bibles and stuff back there . . . if you want to look."

The crate the man indicated was large and stuffed to overflowing. Greg shook his head and turned the knob to leave.

Just a quick look.

He found it midway through the carton. It was softbound and well worn, with a corner of the sky-blue cover torn away. The part that remained featured a picture of a golden figure holding a trump. Greg flipped through the pages on his way back to the front of the store, feeling some dismay at the twin columns of small type. *Thank goodness I didn't promise Enos I'd read it all.* But it was indexed, thankfully, and even illustrated.

The book must have belonged to a child, he thought. The inside covers were plastered with stickers and several passages were marked with uneven boxes drawn in red and yellow crayon. He lay the book on the desk and reached for his wallet.

"That'll be a quarter," the old man said, never raising his eyes from the space epic he was reading. "I don't know if it's worth it, though."

"It's worth it, if only to keep a promise." Greg dropped the change on the table and slipped the book into the bag with his other purchases. It lay beneath the "Run Home to God" ball, atop *The Mormon Mission.*

I'll sort that out later, Greg thought, *when I figure out who Enos and the brother of Jared are and what the Enos I know likes about them.* Right now, he'd better worry less about running home to God than making a quick dash for the ball field.

CHAPTER 15

The rock in Andi's hand was a light, chalky color, not very heavy, and harder than her fingernail. She raised it to her tongue. It was tasteless, so she could eliminate halite. It didn't seem hard enough to be chert. Most likely, she decided, it was dolomite or microcline. With a sigh, she reached for a knife blade and eyedropper bottle. This lab seemed to be taking her and Justine forever. It was curious, because Andi liked geology. It wasn't a life science where she might distastefully dissect the smelly remains of a former creature; or a social science where she would sit, skeptical and bored, barely listening to contradictory theories on human behavior. Earth science was solid and reliable. She could hold a rock in her hand, classify it easily, and move on. At least she always could before today.

Why can't I think? Andi wondered. *What's wrong with me?* The defect, if there was one, was probably in that tiresome mental video cam of hers. Still stuck on the Greg Howland footage, it apparently lacked an eject button. *This is so unreasonable,* she told herself. *I've spent fewer than four hours with that man and I've known Sterling all my life . . .*

Justine Fletcher, Andi's lab partner this semester and best friend since grade school, was perched on the next stool, pencil poised. "What is it, Andi?"

"I don't know what you mean," Andi responded defensively. "There's nothing wrong with me."

"Huh?"

"What *do* you mean?"

Justine tapped the rock with the tip of a long, manicured nail. "Specimen six. We're classifying minerals, remember?"

"Oh, of course." Andi turned her attention back to the task at hand and scraped the stone with the edge of the knife. "It's probably dolomite," she said when it scratched easily. "Try the acid."

Her friend dropped a single bead of liquid from the eyedropper along the abrasion and smiled at the obliging fizz. "Yep, dolomite."

As Justine noted the results in their lab book, Andi watched the little bubbles with fascination. Reason told her that it was a chemical reaction caused by hydrochloric acid dissolving the carbonates in the rock, yet she marveled at the magic nonetheless. Then her eyes trailed to her hand and she examined her fingers carefully. Last night when Greg held them, a warm, fizzing sensation had spread up her arm and into her heart. Was such an unreasonable reaction to his touch chemical or psychological? And why had it never happened with Sterling, the man whom she loved? She jumped when her partner pressed another rock from the specimen tray into her palm.

"Wake up, Sleeping Beauty," Justine teased. "Daydreaming isn't going to get your prince here any sooner." She tilted her head at Andi's startled expression and examined her friend's face carefully. "This *is* about Sterling, isn't it?"

"What is?"

"The feeling I have that we're going to blow this lab, for one thing," Justine said. "And all that sighing, for another. "

"I haven't sighed once."

"No, you've sighed dozens of times." Her best friend smiled knowingly. "And the way you were looking at your fingers just now, it's pretty obvious the only rock you're interested in will be on a diamond engagement ring." She took back the specimen. "I might as well do this. You'll be useless until tomorrow afternoon."

"Tomorrow afternoon?" Andi repeated. She'd been so busy watching her mental videos, she'd failed to consult the calendar. As realization of her mistake dawned, she drew in her breath sharply. "Sterling's plane comes in tomorrow afternoon!"

"I know. Pick me up at two. No, never mind. I'll pick you up, then you can ride home with him and his parents."

Andi was still so shocked at her lapse of memory she could barely speak. Finally she managed to whisper, "I can't go."

Justine dropped the rock. "What?"

"I can't go, Justine," Andi repeated, her eyes wide with alarm. "I told Les I'd work for him at the zoo tomorrow. His brother has a bar mitzvah and—"

"Why did you say you'd work when you've been planning for months to meet Sterling?" Justine interrupted, astonished.

"I don't know." Unfortunately, Andi admitted to herself as her discomfort grew, that wasn't entirely accurate. Somehow, with Greg beside her in the zoo cart yesterday morning, she had forgotten Sterling. *No, I didn't forget Sterling*, she corrected herself quickly. *I simply forgot when his plane was coming in.*

"Can't you get out of it?"

"I don't think so," Andi replied slowly. "I don't want to let Les down. It's too late for him to get anyone else." She reached for the specimen on the bench and pretended to study it closely to give herself time to sort out her confused feelings. As the shock of her forgetfulness faded, Andi wondered why she didn't feel worse about having to miss her missionary's airport reception. It was her reasonable nature finally reasserting itself, she decided with relief. "After all," she told Justine, "a bar mitzvah lasts a few hours of one day once in a young man's lifetime. Sterling will appreciate my willingness to sacrifice. We *will* have eternity to be together, you know."

Justine shrugged her slender shoulders. "I guess so . . . "

Andi raised the rock and examined it for cleavage. "It's quartz." While she waited for Justine to write it down, Andi's reasonable nature retired and her thoughts drifted back to the night before. Why *had* her flesh responded so oddly to Greg's touch? She sighed. Whether her body's baffling reaction had been biological or psychological, she was stuck in geology—definitely the wrong branch of science to help her figure it out. But it didn't matter. With Sterling on his way home, the Greg Howland video would surely be on its way to the previously viewed bargain bin. And that, Andi reflected as she reached for the next rock, was precisely where it belonged.

CHAPTER 10

Less than an hour after his bookstore excursion, Greg was in the clinic at the team office complex, perched shirtless on a cold metal table as a team physician began his examination. He'd arrived late for practice, been fined $100 for it and, worse, drawn the attention of a trainer who didn't like the way he looked. Though Greg insisted that his only ailment was a headache, he'd been promptly dispatched to the medical center.

"Does this hurt?" the doctor asked, his skillful fingers probing the braided muscles in the top of Greg's left shoulder.

"No, sir," Greg replied. "I didn't get much sleep last night. I just have a headache."

"Hmmm." The physician's fingers moved down the star player's arm. "Any tenderness?"

"No."

He grasped Greg's elbow and flexed it, then rotated the limb at the shoulder. "You seem to have full range of movement."

Greg held his tongue. He couldn't fault the doctor for examining the primary piece of anatomy that cost the team big bucks, even if it did have the effect of reducing the rest of the man to the status of an inoperative pitching machine.

"Your wrist feeling okay?"

"Yeah."

"Any stiffness in your back or neck?"

"No, sir."

"Roll your head for me."

Greg winced but did as instructed.

"You seem okay, but we better X-ray that rotator cuff to be on the safe side."

Greg sighed. "I have a headache, doctor. It's no big deal."

"A headache?" The physician stuck a thermometer in Greg's mouth and a specula in his ear. "Everything looks good," he said, after examining Greg's ears and throat and listening to his chest. "No fever."

"Great." Greg was half off the table, ready to suit up for the game.

"You don't pitch today?"

"No, but . . ."

The doctor consulted his chart. "To be on the safe side, I'm going to send you back to your room for the day. I want you to go to bed. I'll check in later to make sure you're not coming down with something."

The last thing Greg felt he could face was more time on that bed. "Doc—"

But the medical man was on his way out the door. "Get dressed and wait here a minute. I'll bring you an antibiotic and something for the headache."

Back in his street clothes, with medication in his pocket, Greg headed through the team office building on his way to the parking lot. He turned when someone called his name.

The community relations specialist hurried to catch up, her high-heeled shoes tapping on the tile floor. "Greg! You're not leaving are you?"

"Just for the day, Sharon, unless you know something I don't. The doctor thinks I'm sick."

"You don't look so good," she agreed. "Will you still be able to handle the interview tonight? They asked for you specifically."

"Sure."

"Tell you what, I'll get it changed to a phone thing, okay? Then you won't have to leave your room. I'll still need to get with you about some Chicago promos, but it can wait."

"We're in Tucson tomorrow. Can it wait until Monday?"

"Sure, I'll expect you in my office before warm-ups. By the way, we'll forward your local mail to your agency."

Greg hesitated. He'd hired a professional answering service last year at Sharon's suggestion. It was probably the best he could do, but he couldn't shake the picture of a boy like Enos examining the stamped signature at the end of a form letter and asking, "Is this real?"

"You know," Greg said, "I think I'll take it with me this time. I'd like to answer it myself."

"Okay, Greg," she said dubiously. "It's your call. I'll get Sam and a couple of his men to carry it out to your car."

Three men? "Uh, Sharon, how much is there?"

She smiled. "Well, if you start writing today and give up eating, sleeping and baseball, you might finish before the end of the season—with this month's, that is."

"Oh. How about you give me a stack and send the rest on?"

"Good choice. Hold on a sec and I'll grab a few we've already looked at."

"You open my mail?"

"Some of it," she called over her shoulder. "Enough to see if people think you're worth the money we pay you."

"Do they?"

Greg didn't think she'd heard him as she turned the corner into her office. She reappeared a few minutes later with a modest stack of envelopes and a large, red cellophane-wrapped package of candy kisses.

"To answer your question," she said, "most people seem to think you're pretty hot stuff. Although maybe not quite as hot as the lady who brought you this." Sharon balanced the heavy gift in one arm and pulled a heart-shaped card from the elaborate silver bow. "How many Melissas do you know?"

"Uh, none."

She flipped over the card to show him a key taped under an address. "The key to her heart, I presume?"

Even blushing hurt his head. "You keep it. You can have the candy, too."

Sharon pressed the package to his chest with a smile. "I only read your mail, Howland. I don't eat it. Now, why don't you get out of here? You look awful."

HAPTER 17

Greg pulled the door closed behind him, tossed the candy and shopping bag on the dresser, and dropped himself, with the mail, onto his bed. *Maybe I am coming down with something*, he thought. The walk upstairs had seemed to take a tremendous effort.

He swallowed two of the doctor's tablets with a gulp of tepid water and unfolded the first letter. It was from a grandmother seeking advice to pass along to a grandson in Florida who dreamed of a career pitching in the majors. Greg drafted a response in his head: *Tell him to give up baseball for alligator wrestling. Like Rube Waddel said when he did it, "It's bound to be more fun."* He rolled onto his side with a groan and wondered why he had to think of alligators.

Greg was in the middle of the sixth or seventh letter, this one from a star-struck teenager, when he finally fell asleep.

He dreamed he was in Iowa. The fields were green in early spring, an ideal pocket of nature after the last late snow and before the inevitable browning by summer sun. It was a mild, breezy day—perfect weather to fly a kite.

His kite was a red dragon, the kind he'd seen in pictures, but never owned. Greg ran with it, faster and faster, sailing across the fields, nothing before him but blue sky. The kite was soaring higher than he would have believed possible, sailing up, up into the sun.

As Greg watched the kite rise, he was filled with wonder and a sense of accomplishment. Never would he have believed a kite could fly so high. Then he felt the tug and a sudden lightness in his hand as the string reached the end of the spool. It wasn't tied, he saw in dismay. He grasped for the twine and felt the burn as it slipped between his fingers. The kite was gone.

"Clumsy," his father's voice said. "Stupid. Couldn't even hold on to a string."

Greg hung his head in shame and started slowly back toward the house. As the warm sun bathed his neck and head, he couldn't resist one last glance upward. The kite had risen so high that it had become a comma against the cottony clouds.

"Let it go, Greg," Jim's soft voice whispered. "Just let it go."

Greg woke slowly and rolled toward the window, the dream fading in the afternoon sun. He felt better. The dull ache in his head had disappeared. It stayed away, even when he swung his legs over the side of the bed to sit up.

As he stretched and stood, he had to struggle to resist the impulse to get outside. When the doctor called to check on him, he'd better be where he was told. Greg settled for opening the window as wide as it would go. Then he pulled a chair into the square of sunlight and slid the books from the shopping bag. When the foam ball rolled out with them, he scooped it up and stuck it in his pocket.

Greg skimmed *The Mormon Mission* first, reading a line, paragraph, or chapter here and there, enough to catch that this writer considered Mormons anti-Christian, amoral and most likely damned for eternity. Greg didn't like the self-righteous tone of the book, though he was curious about some of the precepts.

Finally, he dropped the apologetic to the side and opened the Book of Mormon. The frontispiece was in small italic:

> *Behold, I would exhort you that when ye shall read these things, if it be wisdom in God that ye should read them . . . that ye shall receive these things, and ponder it in your hearts.*
>
> *And when ye shall receive these things, I would exhort you that ye would ask God, the Eternal Father, in the name of Christ, if these things are not true; and if ye shall ask with a sincere heart, with real intent, having faith in*

Christ, he will manifest the truth of it unto you, by the power of the Holy Ghost.

And by the power of the Holy Ghost, ye may know the truth of all things.

And by the power of the Holy Ghost, ye may know the truth of all things. Greg wondered how that worked. He didn't know what was true anymore. Could it be, like Andi had said, simply a matter of asking God? His mind wandered back to her again, a place he had studiously avoided all day. Was the divine Ariadne an answer to his prayer? He shook his head. He was no answer to hers, and she was the one who had the cozy chats with deity.

Greg turned the page. The introduction to the book was written by the hand of a guy named Mormon—hence, he guessed, the name—and was translated by some other guy named Joseph Smith, Jun. The second paragraph, however, was the one that caught his attention. It alluded to Jared—hopefully the guy with the brother—in a Book of Ether. Greg flipped pages until he found it, near the end, and began reading. After thirty-two verses of background he didn't understand and genealogy he didn't care about, he picked up a story line: *Which Jared came forth with his brother . . .*

It took him about half an hour to read the chapters dealing with the brother of Jared. He turned back to the picture of the glowing stones and the finger of the Lord and considered what he had read. Then he propped his feet up on the window sill, relaxed deeper into the chair, and resumed reading where he had left off. When he finished the Book of Moroni, Greg turned to 1 Nephi and started at the beginning.

A little after six, he felt a stirring in his stomach, but ignored it and continued to read. Finally, at seven o'clock, he marked the place and lay down the book. He had an interview to do.

Sharon had been as good as her word in calling to give him the number of the radio station. Greg looked at the cell phone that lay beside the notepad where he had scribbled the station's phone number. As his eyes took in Enos' newly signed bat and bucket of balls, he smiled. He had planned to call a delivery service to take it, and the other things, over to the Reynolds' house. But maybe he'd show up at Enos' game, after all. If he dressed carefully and kept a low profile, no one would have to know he was there. He could slip the stuff to Enos after the game. Hopefully, he'd be lucky enough to see Mrs. Reynolds there, rather than her husband.

Greg pulled a phone book from a drawer in the nightstand. What was the name of that school? It started with a W and was named after whom? *A writer,* he thought. There were three possibilities: Webster, Whitman and Whittier. Greg thought it was Whittier, but jotted down the addresses for the others for good measure. Then he changed quickly and dialed the radio station on his way out the door. His steps descending the stairs were much lighter than the ones he had taken coming up hours earlier. It was hard to believe that a couple of aspirin and a short nap could have changed his outlook on life, but he couldn't think of another reason to account for his mood. He was actually grinning when the eager talk show host came on the line.

Five minutes and four questions later, however, the grin had faded and Greg wished he had a couple more aspirin and a bad phone connection. Some twenty minutes seem longer than others, and Greg knew that these were shaping up to be some of the longest of his life.

HAPTER 18

Andi shifted uncomfortably on the hard, metal bleacher and tried to concentrate on her geology text. With her father in class and her mother at a stake leadership meeting, it was her night to bring Enos to his game. She wished she'd thought to bring a lawn chair as well.

It was eight o'clock and increasingly cool on the open dirt field. Most of the other spectators, she noted enviously, had not only remembered to bring chairs but had blankets as well. She pulled her soft, moss-colored sweater a little tighter and felt grateful she had at least had the foresight to slip from a cotton skirt into blue jeans.

Paleocene, Eocene, Oligocene, Miocene, Pliocene . . . She inserted the tip of her finger in the book to mark her place and glanced toward the Rockies' dugout while trying to engrave the epochs of the Tertiary period into her brain. Enos was still on the bench. Well, if he ever played, she would watch the game. Until then, she had a lot of studying to do. Within minutes, she was so engrossed in geologic time that she merely moved aside instinctively when someone from the present joined her on the empty bleachers.

"What's the score?"

The rich-timbred voice she had spent most of the day trying to forget so startled her now that she let go of her book. Greg caught it as it slid from her knees and handed it back with a lopsided grin. "So, are we winning?"

"We?"

"You know, our side. Enos' team."

"Oh. Uh, well, really I have no idea."

"You couldn't exactly be accused of being a sports fanatic, could you?"

Andi's cheeks turned pink. She had never watched an entire athletic event in her life. How, then, could she account for finding herself outside at dawn this morning, flipping through the paper for the sports page? She had realized with a start what she was looking for. A certain athlete was the reason she hadn't slept well all night and was out on the lawn before the robins in the first place. She had a lot to do, as well, with a two-hour geology lab taking three. In fact, Andi decided with a twinge of annoyance, it could be considered *his* fault that she would miss Sterling's arrival tomorrow. She scooted away a little and looked fixedly at the field.

Despite her best efforts to concentrate on the game and ignore Greg, Andi couldn't resist a single sideways glance. She frowned as her eyes swept his sweat pants, ASU sweatshirt, and the purple Phoenix Suns cap pulled low over his forehead. She noted the way he had flipped up the lenses on his sunglasses, rather than removing them, to be able to see in the deepening twilight. This must be some kind of disguise. She scooted a little further away as she spoke. "I thought you had an interview tonight?"

"I just wrapped it up in the parking lot. Cell phones are one of the perks of modern society, you know."

"How did it go?" she asked politely.

"Sharon blew it this time. She said it was a call-in sports talk thing, but it turned out to be some guy with an ax to grind. Apparently, he and his listeners didn't like paying taxes for your fancy new ballpark."

"What does that have to do with you? You don't play for the Diamondbacks."

Now his eyes were the ones fixed on the game. "Apparently they don't much like overpaid ballplayers, either, even if they're from Chicago."

Andi tried to ignore the involuntary pang in her heart that accompanied the formation of the little lines around his eyes. "What do you mean?"

"You know, Andi. The questions were all pretty much the same: 'Just what have you done, Howland, to merit the income of a small foreign dictator?'" He attempted a grin, but it was more like a grimace. "Outside of hawking every product on the planet, I guess."

"I'm sorry I said that," Andi said quickly, "but it wasn't meant to be critical. The companies you represent only hire you because people admire what you do."

"If tonight was a measure of my popularity, I ought to represent the IRS."

Andi looked at him helplessly. Beneath his broad shoulders and muscular chest, his heart seemed awfully soft. She started to move nearer, then caught herself. He ranked so low on her eternal companion checklist that he was practically in the negative numbers. Why then, she asked herself, did she so want to comfort him now?

Andi decided she was merely compassionate by nature and inched a little closer. She said, "Those people on the radio—theirs was only one point of view."

Greg sighed. "I know, but the ironic thing is that I agree with them. I'm *not* out on Wrigley Field to research a cure for cancer or negotiate world peace. Why don't we pay those people what they pay me? I'm just a grown man playing a kid's game, for gosh sakes."

"Well, I know one kid who loves to see you play and will be thrilled that you came to see him tonight—even if you didn't bring along a Nobel Prize." Andi felt her traitorous heart expand when his lips parted into a grateful smile.

"I brought back his bat and a bucket of old baseballs. Will that do?"

"He'll love it."

"Has the coach put him in yet?" When Andi shook her head, Greg reached over to tap her textbook. "You sure?"

"I'll have you know I look up every quarter, or set, or . . . "

"Inning."

" . . . inning. The only time he's been off that bench is to go to the water cooler."

They looked together at Enos in the dugout. He was off the bench now, his fingers curled around the chain-link fence. As he stared at the bleachers, his mouth formed a perfect O beneath the thick lenses of his glasses.

Before Greg could react, Enos whirled toward his coach and grabbed the back of the man's jacket, his excited voice rising clearly over the noise of the game. "Coach! Coach! You've got to put me in! Greg Howland came to see me play!"

More than sixty pairs of eyes followed Enos' index finger toward the spot where Greg and Andi sat. This time, when Andi let go of her book, Greg didn't even try to catch it. The thud it made as it hit the ground was the only sound on the field for several seconds. Then there was bedlam.

Greg pulled off his glasses, tossed them into his cap, and handed both to Andi. "Hold these for me, will you?" Then he dropped agilely from the bleachers and strode to meet Enos and his ecstatic peers. The game suspended by unspoken agreement as kids, parents, coaches, and umps crowded around Greg.

Andi watched as the famous Cubs pitcher smiled and shook hands, going out of his way to respond to each person in the mob. With Enos leaning into his leg possessively, Greg amiably signed every bat, ball, glove, cast, and scrap of paper thrust toward him. Andi had never seen anything like it, except, perhaps, for Moses gathering the Israelites for the exodus scene in *The Ten Commandments*.

Finally having scribbled his name on everything in sight, Greg tried to excuse himself to return to his former status as an innocent bystander. But Enos' coach had hold of his elbow.

"Howland, how about pitching one to me?" The man was a power hitter in the city's Co-Rec Triple A League and had always fancied himself major league material. "You know," he persisted, "give the kids a thrill."

A chorus of voices echoed the plea. Everyone wanted to see the celebrity southpaw in action.

Greg eyed the eager, middle-aged man thoughtfully. Under the terms of his contract, he wasn't supposed to freelance throw anywhere, ever, but a couple of careful pitches surely wouldn't hurt his baseball career and might significantly advance Enos'. Still, there were a couple obstacles. "It's a Little League field . . . ," he pointed out.

"You can stand way back," the coach suggested, "second base, even. I want you to hit me with your best shot."

Greg raised an eyebrow. "Uh huh. Do you have a catcher?"

"My son Junior here's an all-star."

Greg smiled at the pudgy ten-year-old the coach pulled forward and wondered what the man was thinking. Greg's "best shot" was a 100 mph-plus fastball. Few men in the minor leagues could catch it. It would kill this kid.

"Besides," the coach continued, "who says they'll be anything left of it to catch?"

This guy is nothing if not confident. Greg looked from one hopeful face to the next, finally concentrating on Enos'. "Come on," he told the coach with a nod toward the field, "let's see your stuff."

As the kids went wild and scuttled over one another in their eagerness to line the fences, Greg took the miniature mound. He made an elaborate deal of warming up his arm and scuffing the well-used baseball. He winked at Andi but wasn't sure she saw it, though her book, he was grateful to note, was closed. The kids cheered as he held up the ball. Then he pulled back in a showy windup and threw a slider. At least, it was sort of a slider, soft and very low, aimed to land in the catcher's glove. It curved below the coach's knees, almost to his ankles even, but still the man tried to murder it.

Hold on, mister. I'll throw you one.

Greg's next ball was a fastball, or as fast as he dared with a kid behind the plate. The coach swung and missed. *Nerves'll get you every time*, Greg thought. The man's face was flushed and beads of perspiration shimmered on his forehead and upper lip. He'd been bragging for years, Greg guessed, and now it was time to put up or shut up. Greg gave him a reassuring nod to try to put him at ease. *Just relax, guy. It's coming straight across the plate.*

It was a candy pitch and, fortunately, the coach recognized it. Greg watched with satisfaction as the ball sailed over his head and cleared the fence to drop harmlessly onto the empty basketball courts. It was a clean homer, on a Little League field, at least. The coach could die happy and Greg could go back to sit with Andi—a thoroughly satisfactory arrangement for them both.

Greg briefly joined the circle of adults congratulating the coach, then returned gratefully to the bleachers as the gang of kids retrieved the coach's coveted ball and reluctantly filed back into the dugouts to resume their game.

Andi handed Greg his cap and glasses. "I can see now why you wear these. You certainly know how to draw a crowd."

He rolled his eyes. "I wish I knew how not to."

"Well, we've established that I'm no expert, but keep pitching the way you just did and people might stop watching." She smiled. "That was nice."

"I'm a nice guy."

Yes, Greg Howland, you are, Andi thought as she watched him try determinedly to ignore all the folks who still couldn't tear their eyes away from him. He was a people magnet. There were children on the bleachers now, sitting as close as they dared, and the lawn chairs seemed to have drawn nearer as well. Greg was probably the only one in the audience trying to concentrate on the newly resumed game, absentmindedly massaging the sore middle finger of his left hand. The side of that finger, Andi noticed, was callused and even somewhat mis-shapen—probably from never refusing an autograph to anyone.

Andi suddenly realized what Greg's life must be like and what it had meant for him to come tonight for Enos. Surely he knew he'd be recognized here, even if he wore plastic glasses and a rubber nose. Yet he had come, just the same. Grateful, she moved nearer and slipped her arm through his impulsively.

Greg gazed down at her, a slow smile spreading across his face. Andi shivered at the current that passed from his electric blue eyes through her body.

"Are you cold?" he asked.

She shook her head wordlessly. She had never felt so warm.

Greg motioned toward the field with his chin. "Look who's going in."

Andi's eyes lingered for the briefest moment on the little cleft in that chin, then followed where it pointed. Enos was going to play. She frowned in concern when he stopped and turned before the edge of the grassy outfield. He didn't stand near one of the bases like the other boys. He seemed suspended and off center. "He doesn't know where he's supposed to be," Andi worried aloud.

Greg grinned. "He's playing shortstop."

"Oh."

Enos waved his glove enthusiastically and Greg gave him a hearty thumbs-up. The new centerpiece of an unofficial honor guard of base-men and fielders, Enos Reynolds still couldn't catch, and he'd proba-bly never hit anything either, but he was destined to become a legend nonetheless: the most envied and admired second benchman in the history of Mesa Western Little League.

Greg was happy for him and suddenly famished. He dug in his pocket. "Do you want a kiss?"

Andi froze, her newly moist palms gripping the bleacher to halt a forward tumble. Her body, for some reason, felt like ice; but her face was impossibly warm.

"Andi?"

She forced her eyes to open and stared in confusion at the foil-wrapped candy in Greg's palm. Her eyes traveled, with a mind of their own, to his face. It was questioning and, thankfully, unsuspecting.

"You don't like chocolate?"

"I do!" she exclaimed, snatching it from his hand. She frowned at her fingers, which had suddenly turned to rubber and wood. She couldn't unwrap the stupid thing; she couldn't even hold onto it. In dismay, she watched the candy bounce between her feet and fall into the dirt below.

"That's okay," Greg said, producing more. "I have a pocketful. Somebody left ten pounds of them at the clubhouse for me."

Some female somebody, Andi thought but said only, "That was nice. Thanks for sharing."

He popped two in his mouth. "I haven't eaten since morning. These are better than nothing, I guess."

Andi's mind was obsessed with who had left Greg a ton of candy kisses and what it might have signified, so she hardly noticed when her mouth said, "The game must be almost over. I promised Enos I'd take him out for a pizza afterwards. Would you like to come with us?" Immediately, she clapped her hand to her mouth, mortified that she'd just invited the most eligible man in America to dinner for the second time in two days. She felt only marginally better when, for the second time, he eagerly accepted.

CHAPTER 19

A knot of indolent young men loitered outside the dimly lit front of the pizza parlor. Andi barely gave them a second glance as she pulled into the empty parking lot at the strip mall and swung open her car door. She had had considerably less trouble leaving the Little League field than Greg, who had to stop and re-shake dozens of hands. After waiting several minutes, she had driven to the restaurant slowly, expecting Greg and Enos to catch up in Greg's car by the time she placed the order.

She got out of the car and walked most of the way to the entrance before realizing her mistake. She could hear the low hum of male voices verbally assess her, and frowned when one of them whistled at her approach. Andi stopped suddenly, removed the keys from her pocket, and whirled around to return to her car. She didn't have to look over her shoulder to know that at least one of the gang was following her.

Before she could decide what to do, Greg's small German import swung into the lot. He was barely parked when Andi met him and reached for the door handle.

"I missed you, too," he said, stretching out his long legs to stand beside her. His gaze moved from her anxious face to the group huddled in the entryway. "Friends of yours?" He turned to Enos. "Hey, pal, want to put the top up for me? It looks like rain." He handed the boy his keychain and indicated which button to push.

"Cool!" Enos said, climbing out of the car. "Can I do it again?"

"Maybe later, Enos."

"I think we should leave," Andi suggested.

"Before we eat? No way." Greg took Andi's hand and guided Enos toward the door. "Good evening, gentlemen," he greeted the young men casually as he pulled open the door and shepherded Enos and Andi inside. The glass door swung closed behind them. "Nice neighborhood. Kind of reminds me of Chicago."

"I would never have chosen this place," Andi apologized, "but I thought it was out of the way enough that people wouldn't bother you here."

"Good thinking. Not one of those guys asked for an autograph."

"No, but they might take your hubcaps."

"The car can take care of itself." An alarm shrieked and the headlights blinked on and off before they reached the order counter. "See?" Through the storefront window they watched the gang depart for quieter environs.

Andi had been right about the restaurant. Besides two young employees too interested in one another to notice anyone else, they were alone. Greg barely managed to draw enough attention to order a pizza and pitcher of root beer. From a nearby machine he procured a handful of tokens for Enos to use in the game area. "Go win something," he told the little boy. "We'll call you when the pizza's ready."

Enos accepted the coins dubiously. "I can't play games."

"Of course you can, Enos," Andi assured him. "You just have to try."

He shook his head, his glasses sliding precariously down his nose. "I can't do anything."

Before Andi could respond, Greg took Enos by the shoulders, turned him toward the games, and spoke into his ear. "The brother of Jared would have had one dark boat with an attitude like that. Now go try." He gave the boy a gentle push.

Enos responded, despite himself, to the authority in Greg's voice and wandered across the room to drop a token into the skeeball machine. Greg watched for a few minutes then, satisfied that Enos was actually playing, slid onto the picnic-style bench across the table from Andi. His eyebrows rose innocently. "What?"

"What do you know about the brother of Jared's boat?"

Greg scratched his head and pretended to consider. "Well, let's see. There were eight of them; I know that. And I know that they were water tight, like a dish, and lightweight—like your duck. And I seem to recall that they had some sort of cork in the top and in the bottom for air and, oh, did I mention that I know they were lighted by sixteen little rocks that had been touched by the finger of the Lord?" Immensely enjoying Andi's astonishment, he added casually, "The only thing I don't know is what those folks did about seasickness, bobbing across the ocean like fish. It sounds pretty rough."

Andi was having trouble closing her mouth, let alone using it to form words. Finally she managed, "Where did you learn all that?"

"How many places *are* there to pick it up?"

"You read the Book of Mormon?"

"Well, not all of it," Greg admitted. "I only had part of an afternoon. I read Ether and Moroni and most of the first two books of Nephi. I skipped the Isaiah parts, though. That Nephi guy admires his work a lot more than I do." He waved his hand in front of her face with a grin. "Let me guess, you never dreamed we jocks could read."

Andi recovered enough to return a weak smile. "Where did you get the book?"

"At a used bookstore. It only cost me a hundred bucks and a quarter."

"How much?"

"I was late for batting practice. The hundred was more of a surcharge tacked on by the Cubs."

"But you read it?"

"Haven't you?" As he saw how important this was to her, Greg grew serious. "I told Enos I would."

Andi carefully considered her next question. After everything he had said last night, and especially after everything she had felt tonight, she wondered if she could bear to know the answer. "You read Moroni. Do you . . . ," she swallowed, " . . . do you believe it's true?"

"I don't know, Andi. There are parts I want to believe. I wish I had the faith and hope that Moroni wrote about. But it's a lot to digest at one sitting." He didn't mention the contradictions he had found between the scripture and the other book he had read, or Lupe's caution regarding the Mormons. He shrugged. "Anyway, aren't I supposed to ponder it first?"

Andi nodded. Greg was reading the Book of Mormon. He had bought it himself and read it and hadn't rejected it entirely. A warm glow filled her heart and spilled out her luminous eyes.

Greg looked into her face and felt the same stirrings he had the first day he had seen her. He remembered his prayer and the testimonies he had read of God answering prayer. He wondered. Before he could put the thoughts into words, however, Enos and the pizza were done and at the table. The trio talked and laughed and finished the pizza in record time.

When Enos went to the counter to redeem his tickets, Greg mentally crossed his fingers for luck and turned to Andi. "I know you already have a date tomorrow night, but . . . "

Andi looked up in surprise and confusion. Who had told him about Sterling?

"At the zoo Wednesday," Greg prompted, "you told that guy with the monkeys that Friday would be fine."

"Monkeys? Oh! You mean Les. And those were lemurs, Greg." She couldn't suppress a smile. "Actually, he's one of the reasons I *don't* have a date tomorrow night. Les asked me to work for him tomorrow afternoon—driving the zoo train." Her eyes sparkled. "I assume I'll see you there?"

"I wouldn't miss it if I didn't have an early game in Tucson. Baseball's not brain surgery, but they do expect me to show up." He crossed all his fingers. "Afterwards, though, I'd like to take you to dinner."

Andi bit her lips to keep them from accepting his offer. She tried to look busy clearing the napkins and cups. Finally she realized that she would have to respond eventually. "You bought the pizza tonight."

"Believe it or not, they pay me to play baseball. But if your tastes are as expensive as those alligators of yours, maybe I could get a side job to finance the deal. Do you think this place needs a celebrity spokesman?"

"No," Andi said, turning away to dispose of the paper goods and, hopefully, her embarrassment. "I think they already have a man in a pizza suit."

"I look good in pepperoni."

"I can't go to dinner with you. I'm busy."

"But I thought you just said . . . "

"Well, I did. But that's not what I meant." What did she mean? Andi wondered. And why couldn't she think around this man? She pushed the plates into the receptacle with more force than was necessary. Perhaps it engaged her brain because she suddenly remembered the ward party. "I meant that I don't have a date, but I do have an obligation. My mom's in charge of the ward's spring social tomorrow night."

"Is that Mormonese for 'I don't want to go out with you'?"

"It means that my church congregation is having a dinner party. I need to be there." Andi wiped a trace of pizza sauce from her fingers, satisfied. She absolutely, positively could not date this man. As she glanced up at him through lowered lashes, her satisfaction evaporated. She wondered how far she could stretch the fellowshipping thing in good conscience. "Have you ever been to the Superstition Mountains?"

"Is this where you tell me to take a hike?"

"This is where I ask if you'd like to meet me at the social after your game." When the words were actually spoken, Andi wanted to cover her face and slink away. She hadn't asked a man out since she took Sterling to the Sadie Hawkins dance in high school. Now her big mouth was three for three with Greg Howland—twice now in one day. Would she ever stop offering to feed this man?

"As a matter of fact," he responded quickly, "I've always meant to visit the Superstitions, wherever the heck they are." Greg pulled out his pen and grabbed a fresh napkin to take down directions.

By the time he had finished outlining a simple map, Andi felt better. Inviting Greg had been inspired. Sterling and his parents would surely come to the social. Greg would meet Mr. Perfect and get the dual message that here was what God expected in a man and that Andi would settle for nothing less. She smiled confidently as her little brother approached.

Enos had redeemed his tickets for a black plastic eye patch and glow-in-the-dark skull ring. He balanced the patch over one lens of his glasses and held up his fingers for admiration. Andi knew this had been the best night of the little boy's life. She glanced at Greg as he gave Enos a high five. It was the one pointer he might be able to give Mr. Perfect, she thought. An only child himself, Sterling was, at best, indifferent around children.

Out in the parking lot, Greg gave Enos the keychain to pop the trunk of his convertible. Enos opened it reverently and peered inside. To Andi, he looked like a pirate with a treasure chest. The contents were apparently better than gold doubloons. Here were the baseballs Greg had brought him, more than a dozen of them.

The unpatched eye he turned to Greg was wide. "Wow! Do you take baseballs with you wherever you go?"

"No, Enos," Greg laughed. "They're for you. I figured you could use them with that bat Jensen signed."

"Wow!"

"They're not new, though. We've used them in practice. Most of them show it."

"Wow," Enos repeated, "real major league baseballs. Have you pitched them yourself, Greg?"

"I don't know. Probably some of them."

"But you've touched them all?"

"I put them in the bucket."

"Wow!"

Andi saw the glimmer in Enos' eye and said quickly, "Don't get any ideas about Greg signing these. He's written his name on enough things tonight. Just pull them out. We need to go. It's late."

Greg helped the child carry the heavy bucket to his sister's car, then reached back inside his trunk for the shopping bag. As he handed it to Andi, he said, "Since I had the balls for Enos, I thought I should send something to Francie and then I saw a book for Darlene and . . . anyway, these are for your family to say thanks for putting up with me last night."

"That was very nice," Andi said, impressed again by his thoughtfulness. "Thank you."

"I want to give you something, Greg!" Enos declared impulsively, his booty safely stowed away in his lap and at his feet.

Greg walked over to where Enos leaned out the window. "You don't have to give me anything, buddy. I had a great time at your game tonight."

"But I want to!" Enos insisted. "I really do." His glasses slid down his nose as he pulled at a finger on his right hand. Greg thought he was about to receive the plastic skull, but the ring Enos dropped into his palm was smaller and silver.

Greg held it up to the light to examine the inscription on the blue shield. "What's this, Enos?"

"It's my CTR ring. I got it last year when I was baptized."

Sensing its significance, Greg tried to hand it back. "I can't take this, pal, but thanks."

The little boy sat on his hand. "It's mine," he insisted. "I can do what I want with it. And I want to give it to you."

Greg looked to Andi and she nodded. Greg felt something he couldn't explain, something strangely close to tears, even. He slipped the ring securely past the first knuckle on his little finger and tousled the boy's rusty hair. "Thank you, Enos. Thanks a lot. I'll take good care of it."

"You'll wear it?"

"Yeah. I'll wear it all the time."

If Andi hadn't been so touched by Enos' gift, and Greg's grateful acceptance, she might have thought to point out the man leaning casually against one of the few cars in the dim lot. She wasn't certain, but she thought she had seen him at the Little League field and then again, standing in that same spot when they went in the restaurant door. As it was, she forgot him as she wished Greg good night and pulled away from the mall. So none of them noticed the man climb into his car when Greg did and follow, at a discreet distance, as he left the lot.

CHAPTER 20

No one, he was certain, had seen him slip up the seldom-used back stairs to this hotel suite. That there was no one who cared to look for him, or wonder at his after-midnight visit, was beside the point. Being invisible was Simpson's business and he took that business seriously.

The private detective's shoes sank inches into the carpet as his keen eyes darted from the chandelier, down and across a pair of brocade chairs, to rest with interest on the mirror-backed bar. "Not a bad place you've got yourself, Mr. Martoni."

"It'll do." Zeke motioned Simpson into one of the plush chairs and lowered himself into the other. His gaze slid languidly over his newest employee. The man was milquetoast, he thought, with fair skin, brown hair, and just a bit of paunch beginning to show on his slight frame. He could be an accountant or a meter reader; the sort of man you might see every day without noticing or remembering. It was this quality of genuine ordinariness that made the detective so good at what he did. Coupled, of course, with an admirable lack of scruples. Zeke could almost like him. "What've you got for me?"

Simpson opened the manila envelope and extracted two sheets of neat, even type. "Not much, Mr. Martoni. Your guy's a regular altar boy."

"You didn't miss anything?"

"Not a chance. I'm on him from the time he leaves his room 'til he checks back in, and that's always early. You oughta thank Howland for what he's saving you on overtime."

"What have you got?"

The detective consulted his paper. "After he left you Monday at the stadium, he drove around awhile and finally ended up at the Phoenix Zoo."

"What's at a zoo?"

"Nothing but animals," Simpson shrugged, "as far as I can tell. Howland stood around on the bridge for a while, then went in. We rode the train most of the afternoon. That's where he met the redhead. Then he went in the zoo office and left. He went to supper at—"

"A redhead?" Zeke interrupted.

Simpson pulled out another sheet. This report was shorter, perhaps five paragraphs. "A girl. Her name's Ari—I don't know how you say it—Andrea Reynolds, something like that. Howland met her Monday, like I said, then saw her Wednesday morning back at the zoo. Wednesday night he had supper at her house, then hooked up with her again tonight at a Little League game."

Zeke's eyebrows rose slightly with his interest. "So who is she?"

The detective passed him the report. "Nobody. Here's everything I've got. She works at the zoo, goes to the university, and lives with her folks . . . "

"Got a picture?"

"Fresh out of the darkroom."

Zeke took the packet and pulled out the top photo. It was an 8x10 glossy of Greg and Andi leaving the pizza parlor. His eyes narrowed as he studied Andi's face and form. "She's nothing to write home about. Who's the kid?"

"Her little brother. He's got a weird name, too. Enos. Six kids in the family, if you can believe it. The girl's the oldest."

Zeke nodded, considering. "She and Howland do anything interesting?"

"I tell ya, all Howland does with this girl is talk. He's in his room by ten every night—alone."

Zeke frowned as he flipped through the set of pictures. They were useless. "What else?"

"Nothing else." Simpson looked back at his notes. "Monday, zoo. Tuesday, game and back to his room. Wednesday he was at the zoo early. I couldn't get in, but I found out he met the girl there. Then he went to the field, bought some flowers, got a haircut and, like I said, went to her house for supper. He was home early." His finger moved down the page. "Yesterday he dropped in at a couple of bookstores, then went up to the stadium where—"

"All that kid does is read," Zeke interrupted. "What's he into now?"

The detective looked up from the paper. "Well, the first store was a Christian place. He bought a little box and a couple three books—I couldn't read the names. The second place sold used books. I didn't risk following him in again, but the guy there said he sold him a Mormon Bible."

"A what?"

"A Mormon Bible," Simpson shrugged. "That's what the old man called it."

Zeke didn't like the sound of this one. Greg Howland's ethical proclivities were already a healthy pain in the posterior. He wasn't going to stand around and let the kid go religious on him to boot.

"Howland showed up late for practice," the detective continued, "but left in less than an hour. Went back to his room until—"

"That's enough." Zeke was thinking through this Bible thing, and the man's droning got on his nerves. He needed to make a decision. The boys in Chicago weren't especially renowned for their patience, and he didn't have much time to deliver—not nearly as long as he'd thought. He leaned forward. "That thing we talked about before— you can still do it?"

"Yeah, but it won't be easy."

"It's about time you earned your money. When can you get in?"

"The guy I know on the crew is off weekends, so Monday's the earliest."

"Do it Monday, then."

"You still want a tail on Howland?"

Zeke considered. There had never been a time when he wasn't as concerned about a buck as he was unconcerned about an ethic. He'd drop in on the kid himself. Still, you never knew. "Yeah, and don't miss anything."

"I never do."

Martoni stood, indicating an end to the meeting, and Simpson scrambled to his feet. He collected his fee in cash, slipped out the door, and smoothed himself into the night. His gift of practical invisibility had netted him a couple grand and was good for at least five more.

CHAPTER 21

A startled jackrabbit scooted for the shelter of a creosote bush as the convertible swung into a dirt parking area in the foothills of the Superstition Mountains. The young man at the wheel hoisted himself up on the side door to watch the desert creature pause, sure now of safety, and energetically scratch the base of its ample ear with an elongated gray leg. It looked stronger and much leaner than the cottontails in the flat fields back home.

Greg's gaze swept from the hare up the impressive breadth of the famed Superstitions. His hotel concierge had provided a booklet on the history of the area, and during the bus trip back from today's game, Greg had read the fable of the Lost Dutchman, a legendary prospector who found the richest lode in the West, then mysteriously disappeared, leaving a mule as the only living creature to know the location of the mine.

I'd have made a good prospector, he thought. *You live outside and go months without talking to anyone but a jackass.* His eyes shifted toward the group gathered in a clearing just off the road. *As it is, I'm more likely to talk like one.*

He considered for a moment hiking up into the canyons. Maybe he'd get lucky and fall headfirst into the lost gold mine. *Yeah, right,* Greg smiled to himself. *That's just what you need.* Besides, he suspected that he'd already fallen headlong into more than he could handle. He knew for sure that the only gold he'd come looking for tonight was in the highlights of a certain young woman's hair. He walked quickly to meet her approaching parents.

"Greg, we're so pleased you could come," Margaret said, lightly squeezing his upper arm in greeting. "Thank you for the thoughtful gifts."

"Thank you. I mean, you're welcome. I mean, I'm glad I could come tonight, and I appreciated the dinner Wednesday." Greg wished he had gone prospecting after all as he turned to Mr. Reynolds. "It's nice to see you again, sir."

Trent extended his hand slowly. "Andi thought maybe you weren't coming."

"I'm sorry I'm late."

"You're just in time," Margaret assured him. "We're only starting dinner. I'll let Andi introduce you around. She's right over there."

"Thank you." Greg purposefully skirted the group on his way to Andi's side. He caught up with her as she delivered pie tins of food to an elderly couple whom she introduced as the Lesters. "Hi. Sorry I'm late."

"You were probably late on purpose," Andi said with a smile, surprised at how pleased she was to see him, despite the absence of her planned object lesson. Sterling had been anxious to report to the stake president so neither he nor his parents had come to the activity. "Admit it," she teased Greg. "You wanted to miss the introductions."

"Oh! You shouldn't have!" Twila Lester exclaimed. "It was such a fun little game. I don't know how the girls think of such creative things, do you, Lucas?" She beamed at her husband of sixty years, then back at Greg. "Can you imagine? I was Catfish Sue!"

"And I was Doc Holliday," the old man added. "Doc and Twila are kissing cousins, don't you know? Sealed for all eternity." He covered his wife's soft, wrinkled hand with his own.

"Oh?" Greg wished Andi would hurry with that Mormon dictionary. A little white-haired woman "sealed" to a gunslinger would mean what? Deciding that he would never master Mormon-speak, Greg froze his face into what he hoped was a look of interest and intelligence. Apparently, it was close enough.

"Oh, yes," Brother Lester continued, "Ol' Doc was baptized in Provo, just a few years ago. His mother is Twila's grandmother's second cousin, once removed. Isn't she, dear?"

"She certainly is!"

Lucas Lester tapped Greg's arm. "So you can see why we're tickled."

Greg couldn't see it at all. In fact, he wasn't looking. Now he was trying to figure out how you'd baptize a guy that must have been dead for at least a hundred years.

"Tell him who you were, Andi," Twila urged, pulling Greg back to the present.

"I was Calamity Jane."

"And you're sealed to her?" Greg guessed.

"What a kidder!" Brother Lester chuckled. "You'd have liked the game, young man."

"It sounds like a lot of fun," Greg agreed doubtfully.

"They pinned the name of someone out of the Old West on your back and you had to guess who you were by asking people 'yes' or 'no' questions," Andi explained briefly. "The game's been around longer than we have, Greg. Now aren't you sorry you were late?"

"Oh, sure."

"Let me tell you another thing about Doc," Lucas interjected.

Andi reached for Greg's arm, hoping to get him safely away before she'd have any more to explain. Temple sealings and baptism for the dead seemed like topics enough for one evening.

Unfortunately, Sister Lester already had hold of Greg's other wrist. Fortunately, she changed the subject. "Were you working late, dear?"

"Well, yes."

Twila nodded at her husband, then Andi. "He looks like a fine, industrious young man, doesn't he, Lucas? Now, let me guess. Are you a doctor?"

"No, I—"

"An engineer?"

"No, ma'am, I—"

"He's a lawyer," Brother Lester decided. "Lawyers wear sunglasses, Twila."

Greg pulled off the glasses and stuck them in his shirt pocket. "I'm not a lawyer, sir . . . "

"Such nice eyes," Sister Lester told Andi. "Now what would someone with such nice eyes do, Lucas?"

"I play baseball."

Twila smiled tolerantly. "We were guessing what you do for a living, dear."

"I, uh, play baseball."

Sister Lester dropped his wrist as though it were suddenly warm. "Oh, my!" She looked doubtfully at Andi, who nodded.

"Greg's a pitcher for the Chicago Cubs."

The elderly couple looked from Andi to Greg to one another. Greg thought he could read their thoughts: *Sweet little Andi Reynolds taking up with some ballplayer. What is the world coming to?*

"We don't watch much baseball," Brother Lester said finally, in an effort, Greg thought, to be kind. "Sometimes we'll watch the Angels, though. Maybe we'll see you pitch to them on TV."

"Well, no," Greg said. "We're in different leagues. The Angels are American." Lucas Lester averted his eyes and nodded sadly at Greg's public confession of communist leanings.

"I mean—"

"Excuse us, please," Andi interrupted, taking Greg's arm more firmly. "Your food is getting cold."

"I take it the Lesters won't want an autographed ball for their den?" Greg asked as he and Andi approached the now-deserted buffet table.

"Probably not, but a lot of others here would," Andi replied with a glance over her shoulder. "They're just afraid to come over and ask."

Greg turned to look at the eyes following them. As he did, the faces turned quickly away. "They look to me more like a jury than a fan club."

"It's your imagination. Are you hungry?"

"Always." He watched her ladle beans onto pie tins and add barbecued meat and corn bread. "Nice plates you've got there."

"We're being authentic tonight. Well, I don't know how many cowboys had Marie Callender's name stamped on the bottom of their tin plates, but for a dime apiece at D.I., they're not bad." She passed him the food. "Everyone was supposed to bring their own pie plate, but I covered for you."

"Thanks. I don't know what a D.I. is, let alone where to find one."

"D.I. stands for Deseret Industries."

"And a deseret is . . . ?"

Andi shook her head. If he'd missed the honeybee definition in Ether, that was probably the only thing he'd missed. "The D.I. is a thrift shop run by the Church."

"Meaning your church?"

"Yes." That was easy, Andi thought, but wondered what she should say when he asked about the Doc Holliday/Sister Lester affair. While considering, she led the way through the wild lupines to a rocky outcropping a short distance from where the others were seated. "I hope this is okay, Greg. I seem to have a problem remembering to bring a lawn chair. Last night my forgetfulness put me on the bleachers, and tonight I've downgraded us to boulders."

Greg brushed loose pebbles from the rock before she sat down. "Hey, it's authentic. I've never seen John Wayne with a lawn chair strapped to his horse."

"The best part is that we don't have to sit with the others." Unsure how Greg would interpret her last remark, or even how she had meant it, Andi busied herself at balancing the tin of food on her knees while carefully separating the beans and beef. Finally, she trusted herself enough to turn to Greg. He held his own plate at an angle that threatened to spill the contents onto his lap. His eyes were fixed on the horizon. Andi reached for his tin and righted it. "You don't like cowboy food?"

"I've never seen anything like that," he said slowly, his eyes flicking to hers then returning to the scene before them. A molten, copper-penny sun was just beginning to deposit itself into the bank of the western horizon, turning the sky a smoldering carmine gold, brushed with thin wisps of salmon and coral.

"Arizona's famous for sunsets," Andi said, with a sigh over the rare beauty of this particular one. "You can see why people come from all over the world to photograph them." She turned back to Greg, but his eyes never left the sky. To Andi, they looked as though they had absorbed all the blue from the day. When she looked closer, she realized they had captured a few of the clouds, as well. "Sunsets come around pretty regularly, you know," she teased gently. "You couldn't have missed every one but this."

"I'm beginning to think there may be a lot of things I've missed."

"Such as?"

"I don't know. What did Hamlet say? 'There are more things in heaven and earth, Horatio, than are dreamt of in your philosophy.' Maybe I don't know as much about heaven and earth as I think I do."

Andi's heart skipped a beat. "Shakespeare also said, 'We know what we are, but know not what we may be.'"

Greg turned to look into her face. The golden glow of the sky must be reflected in her features, he thought. *Either that or she's an angel.* He felt he could accept either explanation with equal ease. God, he felt sure, did talk to Andi. He looked into her eyes.

"How does God answer your prayers?"

"The scriptures say—"

He interrupted with a shake of his head. "I've read your scriptures. Enough at least to know about dreams and visions and voices from heaven. I want to know about you, Andi. Have you really talked to God?"

"Only in prayer."

"And you heard His voice?"

"No."

"Then how do you know He heard you? How did He answer?"

"In different ways, I think," she said slowly. "Usually, it's an idea I didn't have before or a feeling that I can't deny or explain."

"Could it ever be another way?"

He was fishing for something, she suspected, but couldn't imagine what. "Well, yes, of course. He knows us each so well that He can answer our prayers in just the way that we will understand."

Greg's thoughts returned to the bridge at the zoo. Was it conceivable that God had heard him? And if He had, had He answered? Could He have sent an auburn-haired Mormon girl to turn his life upside down? Dared he ask her? He looked into her face earnestly, "Andi—"

"Ariadne!"

Her head turned instinctively toward her father's voice. When she looked back, her face was apologetic. "My dad . . . "

"That's okay," Greg said, taking the tin from her lap. "Go. I'll hold your plate."

"He can wait a minute," Andi said, thinking that her father must have the worst timing in this world and the next. "What were you going to ask?"

"It's not important."

"Please tell me."

Looking over her shoulder, Greg could see the impatience on her father's face. "I don't think your dad wants to wait, Andi. I'll tell you later."

Exasperated at both men, Andi left the boulder to meet her dad. Greg watched as she searched the pockets of her denim skirt, then hurried to the buffet table to rummage through the boxes that had been pushed underneath. He set her dinner aside and watched the sun set as he began to eat his own. From the corner of his eye, Greg caught Brother Lester's shuffling approach. Even with his cane, the old man was unsteady on the gravel path, so Greg set aside his meal and hurried to meet him.

The older man took a firm grasp of Greg's proffered arm and looked up at him appraisingly. "Andi's mother tells me you're not of our faith."

Greg eyed the cane and wondered if this elderly gentleman had come to defend Andi's honor. "No, sir," he said. "I'm not."

"Let me give you something, son." Lucas hung his cane from his wrist as he reached beneath his coat to pull a bundle of folded papers from his shirt pocket. The homemade pamphlet he offered Greg was about six inches long, typed on an old machine, and badly Xeroxed. Its hand-printed cover read *My Philosophy of Life by Lucas P. Lester*. "I wrote that after my mission—in 1938. I've spent the rest of my life trying to live by it. Maybe it can help you some, I don't know. But you read it, will you?"

"Yes, sir," Greg said, his steady fingers accepting the gift from the gently trembling ones.

The old man's eyes twinkled as he looked at Greg's hand. "That's some ring you have there. Do you mind it?"

"Mind it?" Greg rotated the wrist below Brother Lester's grasp to look at his gold World Series signet.

"Not that one, the other."

As Greg held up the pamphlet, Enos' small ring glinted in the dimming light. "Oh," he said. "Enos Reynolds gave it to me. I appreciate it very much."

"But do you mind it?"

"I don't understand."

"Do you do what it says? Do you choose the right?"

Greg's brows knit as he examined the ring on his little finger. He had assumed that the letters were Enos' initials, though now that he looked closely, the first letter was clearly a C. *C-T-R. Choose The Right.* Greg's eyes met the older man's in surprise.

"You haven't answered me. Do you mind it?"

"I, uh, try to, sir."

Brother Lester clasped Greg warmly on the arm. "That's all the Lord asks, son. That's all He asks." Refusing assistance, Brother Lester made his way carefully back to his companion and Greg returned to his rock. The meal forgotten, he leafed thoughtfully through the thirty-two pages of humble testimony of Jesus Christ and His restored gospel. Greg didn't know what to make of the doctrine, but deeply appreciated the dedication it had taken to write and distribute it. He searched the crowd for Brother Lester's silver head and thought, when he found it, that he might truly be looking at a latter-day saint.

Was Lucas Lester raised to be that kind of man? Greg wondered as he pulled the sunglasses from his pocket to make room for the booklet. *Is it too late for me already?* As the bronze sun disappeared, Greg reflected on what it must take to commit to a lifetime of devotion. *Faith? Courage?* He thought suddenly of Zeke and shook his head. *It takes more than you've got, Howland.*

By the time Andi returned, the corals and golds in the clouds had dulled to slate and gray, almost as though someone had turned a knob to decolorize the sky. She offered Greg a slice of pie with an apology. "I had to find the keys to the van and get the pies out. I'm sorry to have missed the sunset."

Greg seemed solemn now, Andi thought, though he said, "They come around pretty regularly, I hear."

"Not like that one." Andi touched his arm. "What were you saying before my dad called?" Greg shrugged so she prompted, "We were talking about prayer."

"Were we?"

Andi didn't know what she had lost, but knew that it was precious. Still, she wouldn't press. She tried, instead, to tease. "I saw you talking with Brother Lester. More Doc Holliday stories or a lecture on patriotism?"

"Neither. He gave me a copy of a little book he'd written."

"His *Philosophy of Life*, no doubt," Andi said slowly, suspecting that Greg's sudden aloofness was because he had taken offense. She was a little piqued herself. Brother Lester should have known better. "He passes those out to everybody, Greg. Most people just ignore him."

"Do they? I can't help but think it's a pretty great thing for the man to do."

Andi smiled, her relief so great that she wanted to hug him. She nudged him instead. "I thought you were hungry? You'd better at least eat your pie. The entertainment committee's planned another game and a sing-along around the campfire. We can't sit here forever, you know."

Greg was gazing past her now at a car that had just pulled into the parking area. He squinted in the dim light, then was sure. Not only could he not sit here with Andi forever, he didn't have five more minutes. "Andi, I've got to go. I'll call you, okay?"

"What?"

Greg was on his feet and moving around the outcropping that lay between them and the parking lot. "The car that just pulled in—he's a tabloid photographer and I don't think he's out looking for a sunset. He came into town with some movie star and showed up at my hotel late this afternoon. I thought I lost him coming up here, but he must have driven around until he found a crowd."

"He won't even see you," Andi objected. "It's almost dark."

"When he sees my car he won't leave until he sees me. I need to meet him in the lot before he talks to anyone. You stay here—keep talking."

Andi followed him stubbornly. "I may talk to crocodiles, Greg, but I don't talk to rocks. If you think you have to leave, fine. But I'll at least walk you to your car."

"No, Andi. I don't want to be seen with you." When he saw the shocked, hurt look fall over her face, Greg rushed back and took her shoulders gently. "Andi, I mean—"

"You don't have to explain. I understand. You're the most eligible man in America, after all. You have an image to maintain." His face was so close that when he sighed, Andi could feel his breath on her cheek. She was furious with her eyes for filling with tears.

"Most eligible . . . ? You *don't* understand, Andi. I should have said I don't want you to be seen with me. One picture of us eating dinner would be enough to make your life miserable."

Andi blinked back the tears and tried to smile. "Your table manners aren't that bad."

Greg frowned impatiently, but his voice was unbearably tender. "Look, Andi, those tabloids manage to make everything seem . . .

dirty. I have to go, right now, because I couldn't stand for you to get hurt because of me. But, please, can I call you?"

She nodded.

"Okay, good. Thanks for inviting me tonight." Greg cupped her face in his palm and, for one dizzying moment, Andi thought he might kiss her. Instead, his fingers trailed slowly from her cheek to the back of her neck and away. "I'm sorry about this."

Andi raised her hand to her tingling chin as she watched Greg jog toward the parking lot. *Reasonable people don't fall in love*, she reminded herself firmly, *and you're a reasonable person.* She turned to retrieve the pie tins and tried to ignore the question being raised by the traitorous little voice within: *Why, then, is there so little reason in your reaction to a simple touch of this man's hand?*

Greg saw the photographer standing on tiptoe, trying to locate his white convertible, when he arrived in the parking area. He tapped the man on the shoulder from behind. "Looking for anyone in particular?" then raised a hand in front of his face as the camera swung up. "Wait! This isn't my best side."

The man lowered his camera suspiciously. "Where's Jacy?"

"Who?"

"Jacy Grayson, the movie star."

"Beats me. Have you looked around Hollywood?"

"Very funny, Howland. I know you snuck up here tonight to meet her."

"Sorry, mister, you've got the wrong sneak. I was out for a drive when I happened to run into this church group. I'm leaving now, but feel free to hang around for an exclusive with the Lost Dutchman." Greg grinned as he started toward his car. He had gotten away with that one.

"Mr. Howland!"

He spun at the sound of the familiar voice, his jaw dropping as Andi hurried toward him. He recovered quickly enough, however, to plant himself solidly between her and the now-alert reporter.

Andi looked up at Greg and couldn't help thinking how handsome he was when he was mad. "You left your glasses," she said innocently. "I thought you might need them."

The photographer leaned around Greg for a shot then paused, unsure. This girl didn't look like Howland's type.

Greg moved Andi another step away. "Thank you, Miss," he said tersely. "Sorry—I've forgotten your name."

"Jones," she replied sweetly. "Gertrude Jones. We had dinner together tonight." His eyes, she saw, had turned almost indigo. That alone was worth making him angry.

"I don't remember you."

The photographer stepped around Greg. "Do you know who this man is?" he asked hopefully.

Andi's eyes grew wide. "No, who?"

"Greg Howland, the pitcher."

"Pitcher?" Andi repeated with obvious disappointment. "Darn. I thought maybe he was related to that cute guy who sells rice cakes on TV." She stifled a giggle as Greg rubbed a hand across his face.

The photographer snapped the lens cap on his camera and turned back to Greg. "Come on, Howland. Gimme a break here. You know as well as I do that Jacy Grayson's in town to shoot a movie. When are you two getting together?"

"I don't think the lady's interested."

"The lady said, and I quote, 'Greg Howland's the hottest thing in the Valley of the Sun,' unquote."

Greg cleared his throat and ignored Andi. "Look, I've never even met the woman."

"One picture, Howland, that's all I ask. In Jacy's room or her hot tub, maybe. Just one. I could put my kid through college."

"Or," Andi suggested, "you could get a real job and do it the hard way like everyone else."

Greg couldn't believe this. He spoke quickly. "Thank you for the glasses Miss . . . Jones, but don't let me keep you from your friends. I was just leaving. Good night." He turned and walked purposefully toward his car, hoping the photographer would follow and Andi wouldn't. He stole a backward glance as he lowered himself into the leather seat, pleased to note that he was okay on both counts. If he had been more accustomed to the practice, he might even have offered a prayer of gratitude.

CHAPTER 22

The sight of a pale, yellow light spilling through the curtains from the window beside his door caused Greg to pause on the cement stairs outside his hotel room. He was sure he'd left the curtains open and the lamp off. Jensen's wife had come in yesterday to spend the last week of spring training with her husband, so Jeff had moved his stuff to the room he would share with his wife. Greg now had the room to himself. At least, he thought he did.

He looked over his shoulder toward the parking lot, relieved to see that the photographer had apparently gone after bigger prey. Taking the last couple of stairs in a single bound, Greg knocked once on the door, just in case, then inserted his key.

Zeke looked up from the chair. "How's it goin', kid?"

Greg's volume on Mormonism lay open on Martoni's lap while the Book of Mormon lay at his feet, alongside the small foam baseball. Recovering from his surprise, Greg scooped them both up on his way into the room, then backed away until he was against the dresser.

The publicist nodded at the ball. "Run home to God, Grego? Why not just run home to Daddy?" His lips slid over his pearly teeth in a self-satisfied smile. "Oh, never mind. I remember now. Your own father never wanted you. What makes you think God does?"

"How did you get in here?"

Zeke dangled a silver key. "I turned on the ol' charm and told the girl at the desk I forgot the one you gave me. You can't be too careful, kid. People are gullible. They'll believe anything." He winked. "Won't they?"

"What do you want, Zeke?"

"Business, as usual. The contract's on the dresser."

Greg lay down the Book of Mormon to pick up the contract and frowned at the multiple pages of small type. "What is it this time?"

"Does it matter, Grego? I arrange it, you sign it. That's our deal."

Greg scanned the legalese uneasily, looking for the name of a product, a company, anything. Lawyers, he decided, were the only people on earth harder to understand than Mormons.

"Wieners."

"What?"

"Hot dogs. The contract's to sell hot dogs, Grego."

"You're gonna kill the market, Zeke. People are getting sick of me." Greg tossed the contract on the bed.

"I'll worry about that. You worry about charming the nylons off Jacy Grayson. You're having dinner with her tomorrow night in her hotel room—and breakfast Sunday morning." He raised a dark eyebrow as Greg leaned back against the dresser. "What's the matter, kid? You like girls, don't you? She's all girl."

Greg's fingers kneaded the foam ball, belying the intended offhandedness of his reply. "You don't need me for your fairytales, Zeke. You haven't had any trouble selling bad fiction before."

"Pictures, Grego. Grayson's people want publicity for her new movie. I told 'em you'd be in her room by—"

"No."

"I didn't hear that."

"Sure you did." But the words sounded strange even to him and Greg swallowed hard. He was surprised he could manage it, given the dryness of his mouth. Still, he continued, "I'm not spending the night with Jacy Grayson or anyone else just so you can make a buck."

Zeke closed the book slowly. Despite his claim, and the contract he'd brought to back it up, his real business had been complete before Greg even set foot in the door. His dark eyes narrowed as he glanced toward the bathroom, then back to the book on his lap. Finding out what the kid was up to with this religion stuff, then jumping him through a few hoops, was just icing on the cake. He rubbed his chin, considering the Grayson thing. If he spooked Howland now, he might never get the final hold he needed. Already the young ballplayer's arms were crossed resolutely and his eyes were glacial ice. Zeke extended a conciliatory hand. "Hey, Greg, kid, no need to get worked up about this. How about you do breakfast with Grayson? Leave the rest to the imagination."

Greg considered the offer. The end result in the media would probably be the same, but that wasn't necessarily his concern, was it? He ignored the small voice that claimed it was. "Make it someplace public, then."

"Whatever you say, Grego." Zeke leaned forward to retrieve the contract from the bed and held it out to him. "I gotta make a profit somewhere, kid."

"What do they want?"

"Just a picture and your name. Simple."

As Greg extended his hand to accept the contract, Zeke slowly opened his fingers. Greg watched the papers flutter to the carpet, then looked into Martoni's expressionless face. Their eyes locked in the brittle silence. Finally, Greg looked away. *You don't always strike 'em out*, he thought. *No matter how good you are or how hard you try.*

He bent to snatch up the contract and flinched at the reflection he caught of himself in Zeke's well-polished shoes. Still, he pulled out a pen, scribbled away another part of himself, and thrust the papers at Zeke. "Now get out of my room."

Zeke rose slowly and strolled out the door, *The Mormon Mission* still in his hand. As Greg stepped onto the walkway behind him, the publicist turned. He leaned very close, pressed the book to Greg's chest, and whispered, "You don't need these Mormons, Grego. I'm the one who can make you a god."

The first lung full of air Greg drew as Zeke descended the stairs hurt his chest. He clutched the book and remembered its scorn-filled description of Mormons as god-makers. As he thought of Lucas Lester's philosophy of life as a God-seeker, his fingers tightened on the book's spine.

Twin lights glowed red as Zeke began to back his car from its space. It was a good distance to the lot, and the book in Greg's hand was much heavier than a baseball, but he threw it for all he was worth. One rear light blinked out as the book smashed against it and bounced away, landing a few feet from the garbage dumpster. Greg watched the pages rifle in the breeze. Then, compressing the foam ball in his right hand, he went in to his room and locked the door. The yellow light continued to spill from the window as Greg picked up the Book of Mormon and began to read.

CHAPTER 23

"Okay, Andi, I'll use small words and short sentences this time," Justine teased. "You try to keep up. Today is Saturday. Sterling is home. Are you with me so far?"

"Yes, of course," Andi said, trying to mask her reluctance to take an active role in the conversation. Justine was easy to ignore when she entered her chat mode. Andi had had no difficulty keeping half her mind on her friend and the other half on the sunset she had watched with Greg in the Superstitions. But now Justine apparently required intelligent responses instead of murmured agreement. Andi sighed and pushed her mental pause button. "You were saying?"

"I was saying, what's with you? This is the happiest day of your life and you're acting like you're not even here."

"The happiest day of my life?"

"Of course, silly. Sterling's obviously ready to pick up where you two left off. Andi, you can be a June bride!"

Andi's eyes swept the crowded room and rested on the striking guest of honor. Off the plane scarcely more than twenty-four hours, Sterling Channing stood in his parents' spacious home, surrounded by well wishers whom he regaled with stories of his Peruvian mission. When he met her eyes with a smile, Andi looked quickly away. To Justine she said, "Well, it's not like that, exactly."

"Oh, Andi, everyone knows that you and Sterling were made for each other. You're soulmates."

"I don't believe people have soulmates, Justine."

"Did you see that darling picture Sister Channing has on the table with the rest of Sterling's stuff? If that isn't proof that you were destined to be together, I don't know what is."

"I didn't see it."

Taking Andi by the arm, Justine led the way into the foyer and pointed out the focal point with a dramatic flourish. Andi wondered how she had missed the veritable shrine in the first place. An antique cherry wood table boasted an impressive paper trail of the young missionary's life. It seemed to Andi that every straight-A report card, good citizenship certificate, and Duty to God award ever bestowed on mankind was here on display with Sterling A. Channing's name on it.

There were pictures, too: Sterling the student body president, Sterling the Eagle Scout, Sterling the valedictorian. Picking up a silver-framed snapshot, Andi rolled her eyes. It was of Sterling and her boarding a long yellow school bus for the first day of kindergarten. He wore a starched shirt and pants and a confident smile. It was obvious, even at the age of five, that this boy knew where he was going. Andi thought she looked like Pippi Longstocking with her red braids flying at odd angles as she followed him up the steps. She put the picture back on the table, tucking it behind a larger photo.

Justine returned it to its original position with a smile. "See? You were meant to be together." She turned to admire the room full of flowers, people, and food. "Andi, you're so blessed. Isn't all this beautiful?"

"Sister Channing certainly went to a lot of effort," Andi acknowledged, ignoring the "blessed" remark as she ran her finger over the table before turning away. "Of course, no one could deny that Sterling deserves it."

Justine cast her a sideways glance. "Have you two already quarreled about something?"

"Of course not. I only spoke with him for a few minutes last night on the phone and today, with all the fan club gathered, I'd have to take a number to even get close to him."

"You are definitely acting strange."

"It's your imagination."

"I don't think so." Justine tried another tack. "Everyone was surprised you didn't come to the airport yesterday."

"I told you," Andi said, lowering her eyes. "I had to work."

"I know. And then you had to help at the ward social. And when I called to see why you were late today, Darlene said you were waiting for a phone call that never came." Justine's blue eyes narrowed. "Andi, why do I think there's something you're forgetting to tell me?"

Why *hadn't* she told her best friend about Greg? Andi wondered guiltily. Over the years they'd shared everything from chicken pox to high school graduation jitters. But what could she say? she wondered. *"I met this man who makes my fingers tingle and my legs turn to putty? He's kind and funny and sweet . . . and everything I never thought I wanted."* Andi couldn't explain something she couldn't understand. She avoided Justine's eyes. "I don't know."

As another group arrived and joined the fringe around Sterling, Andi glanced at her watch. Brad had left for the Cubs' game at noon and it was almost three now. How long did those things last, anyway? Maybe, to be on the safe side of not missing Greg's call, she'd leave now. Sterling would never miss her. As she tried to think of an excuse to give Justine, a remarkable new thought occurred. If there *were* a place to take a number to be close to Sterling, would she take it?

Chicago's starting pitcher picked up his phone in the locker room before most of the fans had picked up their stadium cushions. He'd thrown some of his best stuff today and hoped immodestly that Brad would tell his sister about him. It had proved too much to wish for Andi to come to the game he'd sent tickets for, but having her brother and his friends there was the next best thing. Greg had promised them a tour of the locker room after the team cleared out, but he ought to have time to call Andi first.

Darlene answered the phone at the Reynolds' house. "Thanks for the book," she said when Greg had identified himself. "I haven't read it yet because I think it's a Christmas story and it isn't even Easter yet, but Francie loves her book and Enos still has most of the balls you gave him. My mom says it was nice of you to think of us, and Clytie says—"

"Uh, Darlene," Greg interrupted, sure this could take a while. "You're welcome. Is Andi home?"

"No. She's at a party for her missionary."

"Her what?"

"Her missionary."

Greg had heard that part; he just hadn't understood it. "Who is her missionary?"

"She didn't tell you?" Darlene asked, pleased to be the source of information. "Well, maybe she forgot. She forgot she was supposed to go to the airport, too. Clytie says it's because—"

"You were telling me who this missionary is."

"His name is Sterling Channing. He just got home from—I don't know. Somewhere a long ways from here."

"What makes him Andi's missionary?"

"You know, the regular stuff. She dated him before his mission, wrote to him while he was gone, and waited for him to come back. That makes him her missionary. See?"

"No."

"Well, that's how it works. So now they're going to the temple. Only members can, you know." Darlene paused to be sure she got it right. "Well, Clytie doesn't think they will," she conceded, "and Andi says she might go on a mission first, but Justine says that Sterling will have Andi to the altar by June." She paused for a breath.

"What does that mean?" Greg asked, wondering if Justine were another kind of general authority.

"It means married, of course. You have to get married in the temple," Darlene told him, "and you have to marry a returned missionary."

"Why?"

"Because you have to."

At least now, Greg thought, someone had told him the rules. Andi ought to include them in the appendix to her dictionary. He said, "Well, uh, thanks Darlene."

"You're welcome. Do you want me to tell Andi to call you?"

"No. That's okay. I can call back later." *To find out where to send the wedding gift.* Leaning back against the cold steel of his locker, Greg wondered idly if it was too late to take Lupe's advice and find another nice Christian girl. The weight in his chest, right about where his heart used to be, warned him that it probably was.

CHAPTER 24

Trent Reynolds returned home from an early high council meeting, set his scriptures and planner on an end table in the family room, and noted with pleasure that he still had thirty minutes to glance at the Sunday morning paper before taking his family to church.

A methodical, well-ordered man, it was important to him that his paper was similarly appointed. He didn't mind Brad or Darlene taking the comics, and he appreciated his wife for removing the bulky ads, but the remaining sections he liked undisturbed. Today they were a mess. At first, as he arranged them into the proper order, Trent couldn't determine what news was in Section D, the part that was obviously missing. A quick scan of the index, however, revealed that it was the sports section. He scowled.

Margaret happened into the room at that moment, in search of Francie's shoes. The little girl had been wearing them a few minutes earlier.

"The sports pages are missing."

"I imagine so," his wife replied, unaware of the gravity of the situation.

"Do you know who has them?"

Margaret moved aside a cushion on the couch. Francie's shoes could have been anywhere. "No. All the children were anxious to see Greg's picture and read about the game."

Trent dropped the paper into his lap. "I don't believe it!"

"What?" Margaret asked, brushing back the drapery at the window. "You don't ordinarily read that section."

"That isn't the point. Aren't you concerned about the influence this Howland person is having on our children?"

She checked under his recliner, then abandoned the shoe search for a moment to perch on the chair arm. "What influence would that be, Trent?"

"Well, Enos hasn't stopped talking about Greg Howland since Wednesday night. It's Greg this and Greg that . . . "

"Greg made quite an impression at his Little League game. Enos is a celebrity at school now. It's understandable that he'd be excited."

"How do you account for Clytie? She's almost as bad."

Margaret held her tongue, knowing her husband wouldn't appreciate the answer. For the last three days, Clytie had floated through the house whispering to herself, "Greg Howland thinks I'm pretty."

"Brad took off work yesterday to use those baseball tickets. Did you know that?" Trent demanded.

"Yes. He and his friends had a wonderful time. Greg even took them into the clubhouse."

"That's the last place I'd want them!" He tapped his paper sharply. "Do you know how many times Francie has asked me to read that ark book to her?"

"Oh, Trent, does that worry you, too?"

"Well, no, but . . . Andi hasn't seen Howland again, has she?"

"Not since Friday night. Greg hasn't called." Margaret didn't tell him what effect this was having on their eldest daughter.

"Good. I know she was trying to be a good missionary and all, but she's better off staying away from that young man. He's nothing but trouble."

"He seems very nice to me."

"Nice?" Trent asked incredulously. "Nice? Do you know what the papers say about him?"

"No."

"He's a womanizer, Margaret."

"Greg?" she laughed. "You met him, Trent. He's so shy he can barely talk to Clytie." Margaret stroked her husband's cheek affectionately. "These papers wouldn't by chance be the same ones you call trash sheets, would they?"

"As long as Andi doesn't have any more to do with the man," Trent grumbled. "She never should have invited him here in the first place."

"Because?"

"If for no other good reason, Margaret, because he isn't a member of the Church. We raised our children better than that."

"Your mother was a convert," his wife pointed out quietly.

"That was different."

"Because she's your mother?"

"Because she was different. We don't know anything about this . . . this pitcher. Who knows what kind of background he comes from?"

Margaret knew. She and Andi had talked late into the night, and the mother's heart, like her daughter's, had gone out to Greg. Now she said, "If he were a fine, decent man who learned where he was going, and if Andi truly loved him, would it matter to us where he came from?"

Trent paused to straighten his paper. "Margaret, let's not be ridiculous. Andi could never love this ballplayer; she's too sensible. Sterling is home now and Andi will marry him unless she chooses to go on a mission herself. I don't know why you're getting all worked up about this. Greg Howland is a moot point."

His wife sighed as she patted his shoulder. "I suppose you're right, dear."

Trent picked up the paper as she resumed her search for the missing shoe. "Of course I'm right. I'm always right. And, Margaret, please let me know if you find the sports section."

By late Sunday afternoon, the butterflies of anticipation in Andi's stomach had expired and were apparently now being mounted to better preserve her lesson. There was no other way to account for the sharp pinpricks of disappointment she felt at every thought of Greg. He wasn't going to call. She sat in the family room, inches from the phone, and leafed idly through the pages of an *Ensign.*

"Haven't you already read that?" Clytie asked, coming in from the kitchen with a bowl of freshly popped popcorn and an LDS romance.

Andi looked at the magazine cover. It was the December issue. She tossed it beside her on the couch.

"Greg hasn't called?"

"No, but I'm not expecting him to." She wasn't, at this point, and Andi knew why. He'd read more of the Book of Mormon and decided righteousness wasn't for him. Or, more likely, he'd been out with the chocolate kisses lady last night and forgotten all about the Book of Mormon—and Andi as well. That was okay, she told herself. No, it was good. Great, even. Sterling was home, more perfect than ever, and had already asked her to dinner at his house Tuesday night. Why had she said she'd have to check her calendar? She'd call him right now and accept the date. Justine was right. She'd always loved Sterling. Andi reached for the phone then pulled her fingers back into her lap. She didn't want the line to be busy if . . . She sighed. She was so relieved to see her mother come in from ward visits a few minutes later that she jumped up to hug her.

"Well, thank you," Margaret said, brushing a curl from her daughter's cheek. "Since when have you started missing me?"

"I always do," Andi said sincerely. "It's just that today I . . . Oh, Mother, what's wrong with me?"

Margaret smiled sympathetically and pulled Andi down beside her on the sofa. "Nothing's wrong with you, dear." She glanced at Clytie and the younger girl squirmed around in her father's chair so that her back was to them. She appeared deeply engrossed in her book. "The stake is hosting an open house tonight. Why don't you call Greg and invite him?" Margaret suggested.

"That's a great idea!" Clytie declared, flinging aside the novel and all pretense of disinterest. "I know he'd come. I just know he would!"

Andi shook her head. "I've invited him out three times already. He said he'd call me."

Margaret patted her hand. "He's very busy, dear. He probably just got back to his hotel."

"The game was yesterday."

"Yes, but he was at the hospital much of today." Clytie's sharp gasp carried across the room. "The Children's Hospital, Clytie. I just came from Sister Walther's house. You remember that her grandson's been hospitalized several days now? When she visited late this morning, Greg was there. One of the nurses said that he was stopping in each child's room."

"He wasn't at the hospital yesterday afternoon," Andi pointed out. "Or last night."

"Who wasn't at the hospital?" Darlene asked from the doorway. Her violin was in one hand, her music in the other.

"Greg *was* at the hospital," Clytie told her. "That's why he hasn't called Andi."

"Yes he has," Darlene said airily, "but he didn't sound sick, so I don't know why he's in the hospital. Do you mind if I practice in here?"

"Greg called?" the three Reynolds women asked at once.

Darlene opened her violin case as she shot them her best "what's with the Greek chorus?" look. "He called yesterday. I thanked him politely for the book and he asked if Andi was home and I said that she'd gone to a party for her missionary." She reached for her bow.

Andi was at her side before she could tighten it. "Is that all you said, Darlene?"

The freckles on the girl's nose shifted as she tried to remember. "Well, I might have told him about you and Sterling getting married. But I'm not sure," she added defensively as the horrified look on her sister's face began to register. "Anyway, he didn't leave a message. He said he'd call back."

"Call him," Margaret and Clytie said, almost in unison.

Andi turned to face them, the color drained from her face. "I can't. I'd be too embarrassed. What would I say? Besides, when I tried to call him last Wednesday the operator wouldn't connect me or take a message."

"I'll call him," Clytie offered, seeing that Andi never would.

"Clytie, you can't," her older sister argued. "They'll never put you through and besides, what would you say?"

"First I'd tell him my sister Darlene is ditzy," Clytie said with a meaningful glance at the younger girl.

"Mom!" When Margaret did not immediately come to her defense, Darlene flipped back her hair, put her violin under her arm, and flounced from the room.

"Then I'd say that you want him to come to the missionary fireside tonight."

"No, Clytie, I don't," Andi said quickly. "I don't want to take him. I . . . "

"Then I'll ask if he wants to come with me."

"You'll never get through," Andi repeated. "He gets dozens of calls from women every day, so they screen them all. Your name probably has to be on some kind of list and—"

"I could try," Clytie insisted.

"But . . . "

"She's the one who wants to invite Greg," her mother pointed out. "It wouldn't hurt to let her try."

Andi tossed her hair with a shrug. "Well, I don't care what she does." It was a good imitation of Darlene but, Margaret noted with a smile, Andi stayed close by.

After her mother helped her find the number, Clytie punched the buttons on the phone and held her breath until the switchboard operator answered.

"May I please speak to Mr. Greg Howland?" She paused, listening. "Yes, you may tell him it is Miss Catherine Reynolds." There was another pause, then Clytie began bouncing up and down. "It's ringing, Mom! . . . Oh, hello? Greg?" She covered the mouthpiece. "It's him!" Into the phone she said, "Greg? Hi, um, how are you? . . . This is, um, Clytie. Clytie Reynolds . . . Fine, thanks. I called because we're, I mean there's a missionary fireside at my church tonight and we can invite our nonmember friends and I hoped that you, um, that you might be able to come with me. If you want to."

Looking at Clytie's anxious face, Margaret regretted encouraging her. If Andi was right and the Church had offended Greg, she hoped he wouldn't say anything now that would hurt Clytie.

"It's okay if you don't want to," the girl added hurriedly. "What? . . . Really? . . . Oh, wow! . . . Seven o'clock. You could just come here first if you want to and . . . Well, church clothes or, I don't care, just wear anything . . . Thanks, Greg. I'll see you in a little while . . . Bye."

Clytie lay the receiver reverently in the cradle and stared at it for a moment as though more magic might pour forth unbidden. "He's going to come," she whispered. "I invited Greg and he's really, truly going to come." She whirled to face her mother, her bright eyes shining. "What will I wear?"

CHAPTER 25

Greg drove slowly through the Reynolds' neighborhood. Green lawns surrounded a few of the softly lighted homes, while others were landscaped with gravel and rock; borders of cacti and desert flowers completed the picture. Almost all the houses had bicycles, basketball hoops, or chalk drawings evident from the street. Each could have been a set from any Nick at Night sitcom—with saguaros standing in for elm trees and Pathfinders subbing for station wagons. Suburbia, Arizona-style.

Trying to picture himself in one of these homes with a family of his own, Greg shook his head at the fuzziness of the reception. This was Andi's destination, if Justine could be believed. He was on his way to Chicago, or Pittsburgh, or L.A. In other words, nowhere.

Greg wondered what he was doing here in the first place. Why had he ever accepted Clytie's invitation? Actually, when he considered, there were a couple of reasons. Foremost was that an hour and a half with the synthetic Ms. Grayson, followed by a day of pale, drawn faces at the Children's Hospital, had left him more than a little disillusioned and depressed. The prospect of an evening with Clytie, whose genuineness and joy had deeply impressed him Wednesday night, had seemed irresistible.

Too, he admitted to himself, he wanted to know more about the LDS Church. He had read the Book of Mormon late into the night both Friday and Saturday, and felt things he had never experienced before. Still, the scripture made no mention of the strange practices cited in the other volume. Maybe a night observing Mormons in their native habitat would help him clarify things. At any rate, he thought as he pulled into the Reynolds' driveway, Clytie hadn't said a word about Andi being there. For that, at least, he was grateful.

Greg tightened the knot in his tie and shrugged into his suit coat as he got out of the car, hoping that he was dressed appropriately. He had worn this suit to the last Cy Young Award ceremony. If it was good enough for the cover of *Sports Illustrated*, hopefully it was good enough for Clytie's fireside.

The front door flew open before Greg reached the first step, and Clytie appeared on the porch in a long, blue dress, anxiously fingering a strand of her mother's pearls.

He paused at the foot of the stairs so they were almost eye to eye. "Hi, Clytie." Greg looked down at himself as she stared at his navy suit and ran his fingers self-consciously over the tiny embroidered baseballs on his tie. "Am I okay here?"

Clytie clasped her hands. "Greg, you're absolutely gorgeous!"

"Uh, well, thanks Clytie. You, too. I mean, you really do look nice. That's a pretty dress and your hair is, well, nice." Greg knew that he was stammering and that his face had colored, perhaps even to crimson, but no one had said anything like that to him before and obviously meant it. He looked into her rapt face. She was, what? Sixteen. He hoped her parents knew about this. He said, "Are your folks home? I ought to say hello before we leave."

She shook her head. "My dad's at a meeting and Mom went down to the church early to set up for refreshments. Brad's staying with the kids, so we can just go."

"Does your mother, uh, know you've invited me?" He didn't want to hurt her feelings, but . . .

"Of course. She told me to call you. Andi knows you're coming, too. She wore her best dress."

Before Greg could decide what, if anything, that could mean, Clytie started down the stairs, tripped, and fell into his arms. Righting her carefully, he noticed her shiny, heeled shoes and smiled. Then he extended his arm gallantly. "Miss Catherine, ma'am, your carriage awaits."

She reached up to take his arm breathlessly, her joy bubbling in her laugh and shining from her eyes. "I've never ridden in a convertible before."

Greg opened her door, then went around to the other side. "I'll put up the top so the wind doesn't mess up your hair."

"No!" she protested. "I don't care. I love wind." Clytie giggled as they pulled away from the house and the breeze lifted her hair, trailing it in gleaming streamers of gold.

"I like wind, too," Greg said, pleased at her excitement. "Now, where are we going?"

"Oh!" Clytie squirmed in the seat, trying to make herself tall enough to see over the low dashboard. "Go out to the main street and turn left. I'll tell you from there. Thank you for coming, Greg."

"Thank you for asking me. I can't remember the last time I took a beautiful blonde to church. Come to think of it, I never have." He smiled at her fondly. "May I ask just what's in store once we get there?"

"Well, it's a missionary fireside. We have them once or twice a year to invite friends to learn more about the gospel. We'll see a video broadcast, probably, and there might be some displays."

"Why is it called a fireside?"

"I don't know. We have meetings every month called firesides. I've never thought about it. Why do you think they call them that?"

"Clytie, I have no idea why you Mormons—excuse me, Latter-day Saints—call *anything* what you do."

"Inspiration, I guess," she said brightly. "Turn left at the next street."

CHAPTER 20

The stake center was unassuming, and even attractive, in the soft Sabbath twilight. Its tall spire reached from adobe brick walls into an earth-toned sky. Walkways leading to the mirrored double doors were wide, tree-lined, and inviting. Still, Greg eyed the building uncomfortably as he circled the car to open Clytie's door. He could count on one hand the number of times he'd been inside a church and have three fingers and his thumb left over.

As he followed Clytie up the walk, Greg was sorry to have left his sunglasses on the dash. It made no difference that it was almost dark, that no one was paying attention to him in the first place, or that he didn't know from what he wished to hide. He entered the foyer with an enthusiasm generally reserved for trips to Biderman's office.

Andi looked up and smiled tentatively in greeting. Her best dress was soft lace, in the hazy coral of an Arizona sunset. A few disheveled ringlets escaped her upswept hairdo, forming a coppery-gold setting for her cameo complexion. Greg gazed at her and knew his first impression at the zoo had been mistaken. She was, beyond doubt, the most beautiful girl he had ever seen.

When Andi's companions, a young man and woman, turned toward him, Greg knew with certainty why he had wanted the anonymity of his shades. He wanted it even more when Clytie led him over to where they stood.

"Greg, I'd like you to meet Justine Fletcher and Sterling Channing."

Greg evaluated the handsome young man honestly. *Not all Mormon missionaries*, he noted, *have bad haircuts. This guy's hair is perfect.* He accepted the extended hand and said insincerely, "Nice to meet you."

"This is Greg Howland," Clytie continued. "He's the absolute best pitcher in the world and our very good friend." She looked pointedly at Andi.

The blonde took Greg's hand next as she, too, looked at Andi. "A pitcher?"

"You know, Justine," Andi said, "like in baseball. Greg plays for the Chicago Cubs."

The girl still held his hand and Greg worried it was becoming decidedly damp. Justine smiled. "I know who he is, Andi. The whole country knows who he is. I only wonder what he's doing here."

Greg extracted his hand carefully to run it down a pants leg. "I'm here for the, uh, fireside."

"Clytie invited him," Andi pointed out.

"So he's Clytie's very good friend." Justine looked Greg over and turned back to Andi suspiciously. "Well, he'd certainly give me amnesia."

"So, Howland," Sterling said amiably, "how long have you played baseball?"

"A couple of years professionally."

The young man nodded. "That explains why I haven't heard of you. I've spent the last two years of my life in an undeveloped nation, representing our Savior."

Greg smiled thinly. "That kinda puts tossing baseballs in perspective, doesn't it?" He wished they would start this fireside thing. No matter what it was, it had to beat this conversation. But Elder Channing, Greg soon had to admit, was not only tall, dark, and handsome, he was also confident, polite, and accomplished at small talk. In ten minutes of mostly one-sided remarks on Sterling's part, Greg could find nothing to dislike about the man, but managed it nonetheless.

An organist played quietly as Greg and Clytie finally entered the chapel. Although most people filled the back benches first, Clytie, to Greg's dismay, chose a seat at the front. When Andi and her friends slipped into the padded pew behind them, he felt a warm flush creep up the back of his neck. *Cool it, Howland*, he told himself. *You can handle this.*

As the meeting began, Clytie passed him a hymnal, which he opened cautiously. To date, his public singing experience had consisted of a line or two of the national anthem on the field before a game. He had caught himself singing along several times, his hat over his heart, wrapped up in the wonder of being in the major leagues and feeling—what? Curiously, Greg now experienced the same prickly sensations as at the ballparks. He still didn't know what caused them, but felt pretty sure at this point he could rule out patriotism. He tried to ignore the goosebumps to concentrate on the words of the hymn.

"Where can I turn for peace?" Greg's voice dropped as he glanced apprehensively at Clytie. There was no way they could have chosen this song for him. Could they? He fell silent as he listened to her soprano *". . . when other sources cease to make me whole . . . "* and Andi's clear alto, *". . . Where, in my need to know, where can I run? . . ."* The voices in the congregation rose, intertwined and reverberated as one, and Greg felt pulled into a prayer that was at once unanimous and intensely personal. *"He answers privately, reaches my reaching . . ."* By the time the hymn ended and the broadcast began in the now-darkened room, Greg felt at ease enough to peer intently into the projected face of an apostle of Jesus Christ. He couldn't help but admire what he saw.

The painted bricks left a pebbly pattern on the young pitcher's shoulder blade as he leaned against the wall in the hallway, awaiting Clytie's promised return with refreshments. Although Greg thought he craved anonymity, it was strangely uncomfortable now. If anyone recognized him they were too shy, or perhaps too polite, to acknowledge it. More likely, they were oblivious to his presence as they talked in twos and threes, reminding Greg of the companionable turtles at the zoo.

After counting the ceiling tiles and studying the stitches in his shoes, Greg looked with relief upon the approach of a man balancing a brownie in one hand and a plastic cup of punch in the other.

"You don't belong here, either," the man observed with a sympathetic nod.

"Is it obvious?"

"Yeah. So who dragged you here? Your wife?"

"No, I was invited by a friend."

"But a female friend?" The emphasis was on female.

"Well, yeah, but . . . "

"That's the way it goes," the man declared, pulverizing a large bite of brownie between his strong, yellow teeth yet still managing, to Greg's fascination, to talk around it. "My wife carried on like nobody's business to get me here. She said if I loved her I'd want to find out what she believes."

The words touched a chord in Greg's heart and realization began to vibrate through him. *I love Andi*, he thought, with some surprise. *I have from the first day I saw her. Is that why I'm here?* Greg blew out his breath between pursed lips as he recalled the recent hours he'd spent reading the scriptures and on his knees. Had he fooled himself into thinking he felt drawn to God, when, in reality, he was infatuated with a woman?

As he considered, he missed much of what the man said and tried to force himself to pay attention.

"She found this church, or they found her, more like," the man continued. "It was about a year ago. A couple of missionaries came by our house one night while I was bowling. That's the way they work, you know. She was ripe, I told her, ripe for the picking. She joined right up. You know why?"

"Because she believed in it?"

He hesitated. "Well, yeah, that's what she said. She read some book, prayed about it, then she gave up wine, smokes, everything— just like that. Now all of a sudden she wants to kick in ten percent of her paycheck to this cockamamie outfit so she can get ready to go to some temple they won't let sinners in. She says she'd be 'tithing the Lord's money,'" he added sarcastically. "Ten percent of a paycheck. Would you pay it? Would you? Just because she asked you to?"

Greg considered both sides of the question. If Andi asked him to contribute money, how much would he give? He thought he could give it all and not miss a cent. *And if all they say is true, then it isn't my money in the first place.* Both concepts were too new to be decided now in the hallway. He said honestly, "I don't know."

The man had apparently finished his tirade, along with his brownie, and regarded Greg more closely. "Hey, did anybody ever tell you that you look like that Cubs pitcher—whatshisname?"

"Wilson?"

"No, the white guy."

"Howland?"

"Yeah, him. Not a lot maybe . . . "

Greg raised an eyebrow. *Not the hair again.* He extended his hand. "I am Greg Howland."

The man dropped his cup and napkin to grasp Greg's hand and elbow as he gaped around the hallway, anxious to see if anyone noticed whose ear he'd been bending. "Well, I, uh . . . "

Greg smiled as he withdrew his arm. "Good luck to you and your wife. Now, if you'll excuse me, I see the girl I came with." He walked down the hall toward little Clytie, leaving the man to close his mouth in his own good time.

CHAPTER 27

"So, what did you think of the fireside?" Clytie asked anxiously as they settled onto the stairs leading down from the stage. It was one of a few places to sit for private conversation.

Greg could hear Andi's voice from the kitchen across the hall and wondered what made her laugh.

"Greg?"

"Uh, yeah?"

"I asked what you thought of the broadcast."

Greg chewed a bite of brownie to give himself time to think, but all he could think about, besides Andi, was the treat. Oreo cookies and cherry Kool-Aid were what he remembered best about his brief tenure in Vacation Bible School. *Apparently,* he reflected, *it's doctrinally sound tradition to serve up manna with commandments.* Finally, he swallowed. "Clytie, are you ever so confused that you don't know what to think? Not about religion, maybe, but about anything?"

"You mean, like algebra? I hate it. The book says 'evaluate the equation,' and I don't know how they want me to do it. Some kids make it look easy, but when I try I always miss a part somewhere and it doesn't come out right. It's so frustrating. Sometimes it makes me want to cry."

"That's it exactly," he said. "Religion, to me, seems like some kind of advanced math problem. I think now I might be missing something, but I don't know what it is, or how to find it."

"Does it make you want to cry?"

What a question. She was so much like Andi. "I felt kinda like I wanted to cry tonight," he admitted. "But it was different, I think. I wasn't sad or even confused. I was . . . Clytie, I just don't know."

Her refreshments forgotten on the stair, she lay her stubby fingers on his arm and looked into his face. "That was the Spirit, Greg."

"The spirit of what?"

"The Holy Ghost."

And by the power of the Holy Ghost ye may know the truth of all things.

"Yes!" Clytie cried joyfully. "That's right."

Greg wasn't aware he had spoken aloud; he doubted, in fact, that he had. Elbow on knee, he cupped his chin in his hand and asked, "But if the Holy Ghost can tell you everything, why do you need all those General Authorities?" Immediately, he regretted the question. No fair. She was just a kid.

Before he could take it back, however, she responded. "Pretend you're leaving for a trip across the ocean, okay?"

Greg wasn't surprised that this would be the analogy. Someone was always crossing the ocean in the Book of Mormon.

"What's the first thing you need?"

"A boat?"

"Uh huh. And Heavenly Father gave you your body for a boat. What else do you need?"

"A sail, maybe?"

"Your boat comes with a sail."

"Well then, some kind of map so I know I'm going the right direction?"

"Yes! The scriptures are your map."

"Okay."

"And you need a compass to tell you if you're following the map right, and that's the Light of Christ, or your conscience."

That, Greg knew, he had on board. Every time he thought of Zeke, it hurt.

"So, you're ready to go, right?"

"I guess so."

"And most of the time it's clear sailing. But what happens to you when the first big wave comes, and the next, and you take on water and think you're going to sink? What then?"

Greg leaned forward, his face earnest. "I don't know."

"That's when God sends the Holy Ghost. He's the Comforter. He's the one who says, 'Hang on—everything's going to be okay if you trust God and ride it out.'"

Peace, be still. Where had he heard that? *At Jim's grave,* he thought, *and again on the bridge at the zoo. In my head. Peace, be still.* He nodded slowly.

"And everything *is* okay," Clytie continued. "At least you don't sink. But you've been blown off course by the storm and you don't know where you are anymore. Then you hear the waves crash against the sharp rocks at the shoreline. That's when you wish there was . . . "

"A lighthouse."

"Yes!" Clytie beamed. "The prophet and General Authorities are our lighthouses, and we can trust them because they're built on the rock of Jesus Christ."

Greg watched with admiration as she unzipped a paisley case and pulled out her leather-bound Book of Mormon. The place she wanted, Helaman 5:12, was already marked when she handed it to him.

> . . . Remember that it is upon the rock of our Redeemer, who is Christ, the Son of God, that ye must build your foundation; that when the devil shall send forth his mighty winds, yea, his shafts in the whirlwind, yea, when all his hail and his mighty storm shall beat upon you, it shall have no power over you to drag you down to the gulf of misery and endless woe, because of the rock upon which ye are built, which is a sure foundation, a foundation whereon if men build they cannot fall.

Greg read it carefully, then smiled. "And how, Clytie Reynolds, did you get to be so wise?"

She blushed to the roots of her golden hair. "I listen in church. A man from the high council told it in our session of stake conference."

Greg only understood the first four words of Clytie's statement although, when he thought about it, they were probably the only important ones. As he handed back her book, he covered her small hand with his. "Thanks, Clytie." Then, stretching his cramped legs, he glanced at his watch. It was just after nine and the hallway was nearly empty. As they watched, Elder Channing entered the kitchen.

Greg's wince was almost imperceptible, but Clytie noticed. She said, "Andi isn't going to marry Sterling Channing." His head snapped toward her as she continued, "Some people think she will because Andi is . . . well, Andi, and Sterling is Mr. Super-Spiritual, but she doesn't love him and she wasn't waiting for him at all."

"Waiting for him to what?"

"I mean, she wasn't waiting until he came home from his mission to marry him. And you know what?"

"No."

"When she was driving you around the zoo last week, she forgot that she was supposed to meet Sterling's plane so she told Les she'd work Friday." Clytie knew she was gossiping, probably even meddling, but for the first time in her almost perfect life, she didn't care. Turning Greg's eyes such a bright, electric blue was more than worth it. "Greg, I love Darlene, but she never knows what she's talking about. Ignore everything she tells you, okay?"

Greg grinned. "With pleasure."

"Let's go out through the kitchen," Clytie suggested. "It's the shortest way."

Sterling was leaning against the fridge as they entered, finishing off the leftover brownies. Margaret Reynolds scrubbed the last of a red stain from the counter top as Andi tied a garbage bag closed and struggled to remove it from the deep container it lined.

"Let me do that," Greg said, quickly rounding the counter. He lifted the bag easily and deposited it beside another. "Where do these go?"

"To the dumpster out back," Andi said, motioning through the open door to a bin across the parking lot. "But you certainly don't have to take out the trash."

"I don't mind." Greg picked up the bag, but by this time Sterling had finished eating and his hands were free.

"No, I'll do it," he said as he reached for the other bag.

Better yet, Greg thought as he surrendered the trash. He wondered if he could get away with "accidentally" kicking the door closed behind the guy.

"Did you enjoy the fireside?" Margaret asked. She was gracious and pretty, the prophecy of her eldest daughter, and Greg admired what he saw.

"I did," he replied, "and I learned a lot this evening. Especially from Clytie."

The teenager clasped her hands. "Can I take Greg someplace else, Mom? It's almost on the way and we'll be home before ten. Please?"

Margaret glanced at Greg and saw that this was news to him. "I think Greg needs to get back to his hotel, Clytie. Why don't you ride home with me?"

"But I want to drive by the temple," the girl explained, "to show Greg."

Her voice was pleading and the marine-colored eyes she turned on him irresistible. The Mormon temple wasn't far, he knew. He had driven by it several times. They wouldn't even have to get out of the car. "If it's okay with you, Mrs. Reynolds, I'd like to see it."

Margaret hesitated. Trent didn't know about this yet and was bound to have a fit. She looked from Greg to Clytie. She trusted this young man and appreciated his kindness, and she loved her daughter. Trent would get over it. "Well, all right then, but be back before ten and don't talk Greg's ear off."

"Come with us, Andi," Clytie suggested eagerly. "I'm really small. We can all fit in Greg's car."

Greg was too hopeful to even look Andi's way. He couldn't believe his ears when she responded, "I'd love to." Then she remembered Sterling. "Oh! I, um, I can't. I promised—"

"That's okay," Greg said quickly. He knew who she'd promised and didn't want to know what. "Come on, Clytie. We won't be long, Mrs. Reynolds."

Clytie cast Andi a withering look but allowed Greg to lead her from the kitchen through the back door. As they passed Sterling on his way in, she scowled at him as well. She couldn't think of a better place than the Andes for Elder Channing right now. Just this once she doubted the Lord's timing.

"What's with Clytie?" Sterling asked Andi as he escorted her to his parents' car a few minutes later.

"What do you mean?"

"She's been treating me like I came home with leprosy."

"It's your imagination."

"I can't believe your mother let her ride home with that man." He opened the car door.

"Greg?" Andi asked, surprised. "Why not?"

"Because, Andi, he's a, a . . . "

"He's a friend," she supplied firmly, "of the family." Andi scrutinized his face under the light from the overhead bulb. Had she really once thought dark eyes attractive? "Greg's been very thoughtful," she continued. "Clytie and Enos think he's wonderful."

"They're children. They don't know any better. I don't trust him."

As Sterling closed her door, Andi thought how sure of himself he was, how sure of everything. Then realization struck: hadn't she been that way herself, just a few days ago? What was she sure of now? Sterling opened his door and slid in beside her. Subconsciously, she pulled out her eternal-companion-checklist.

> 1. Member of the Church. (Sterling had been baptized at the hour of his birth on the morning of his eighth birthday.) *Check.*
> 2. Strong LDS Family. (His father had been a bishop, his grandfather a patriarch, and his pioneer ancestors had probably preceded Brigham Young to the Salt Lake Valley.) *Check.*
> 3. Returned Missionary. (To hear him tell it, he had converted half the South American continent, in between establishing stakes and advising the mission president.) *Check.*
> 4. Committed to the Gospel. (The Apostle Paul should have been so committed.) *Check.*

Andi bit her lip. According to her list of qualifications, Sterling Channing was everything she had ever wanted in a man. And here he was. All she had to do was move a little closer.

Instead, she leaned away, pressing her cheek against the cool window. Her breath, as she sighed, formed a foggy pattern on the glass to match the one in her mind. She'd had that checklist as long as she could remember. It was reasonable. It was inspired. It was, for some unfathomable reason, rewriting itself before her eyes.

CHAPTER 28

The temple was beautiful. *It must be the lighting,* Greg thought, but the white granite walls seemed to glow of themselves. Velvety green lawns stretched protectively around the majestic building like a setting for a precious stone: a pearl of great price. Greg parked without thinking and stepped out of the car for a clearer view. *Why didn't I ever notice it before?*

In a few minutes, Clytie's door opened and she came up beside him, the top of her head reaching barely to his waist. Greg felt bad for forgetting her. He put his hand on her hair, smoothed it to her shoulder, and let it rest. It was a brotherly gesture, loving, as he realized how much he would like to have a little sister of his own.

"This is the most beautiful place on earth," Clytie said softly. "Do you want to walk around?"

Greg looked down at her impossibly small feet. Already she was unsteady in the heels and tired from a long day. "Just over to the bench, okay? I'd like to look from here."

"I like to touch it."

Could he touch it? It seemed impossible, though there were no fences or guards to prevent it. *The House of the Lord, Holiness to the Lord* proclaimed the boldly etched letters. Somehow, Greg believed them. He stuffed his hands in his pockets. "Let's just walk over to the bench."

When they were seated, gazing into a rippled image of the temple in the reflective pool, Clytie said, "Andi told me your brother died."

Greg nodded and waited for the weight to descend on his chest and the pain to knot in his throat. His eyes, fixed on a fresco along the top of the temple, widened in surprise when neither of the familiar sensations came. "Yes," he said, his voice full of wonder at the calmness he felt, "he did. A few months ago. His name was Jim."

"That's why God gave us temples," Clytie said, "because everybody has to die."

Greg listened, without moving. The negative things he had read about Mormon temples flitted through his mind and he shivered. And yet, as he looked from Clytie's serene face to the majesty of the House of the Lord, he felt suddenly warm. "Have you ever been inside the temple, Clytie?"

"In the baptistery. I'm too short for the font, but I watch the others. It's so beautiful, Greg. Someday, I'll get my endowments here and be married for eternity."

Greg's heart constricted, but for her or himself he couldn't say. "Is that very important?"

"It's the most important thing in the world. What do you want more than to go home to Heavenly Father and spend eternity with Jim and the other people who love you?"

"Nothing, I guess."

"The temples are the only places on earth where families can be sealed together. Then, even when someone you love dies, you know that you'll be with them again forever."

A couplet by Henry Kemp came to mind. Greg had memorized it to engrave on a frame for Lupe's birthday. "The countless generations, like autumn leaves, go by. Love only is eternal. Love only does not die."

Clytie gasped. "You read poetry?"

"What's with you Reynolds girls?" Greg asked with a grin. "Everyone's amazed that I can read anything but a scoreboard."

"Have you read Emily Dickinson? She's my favorite poet in the whole world. We're so much alike."

"Really?" Greg couldn't help but wonder what this tiny, outgoing teenager had in common with the willowy recluse. He tried to recall a Dickinson poem from Lit class. There was something about swamps and seas. Then he remembered: "'Hope is the thing with feathers that perches in the soul, and sings the tune without the words, and never stops at all.'" That could be Clytie.

"You have read her! Oh, Greg, what's your favorite poem?"

He hated to tell her that he had just exhausted his almost nonexistent repertoire. "What's yours?"

She didn't hesitate. "'We never know how high we are till we are called to rise,'" she recited. "'And then, if we are true to plan, our statures touch the skies.'"

The gentle, prickly feeling began in Greg's head and flowed down into his neck and arms. He repeated the verse silently as he looked back to the temple. A young couple strolled past, arm in arm, involved in no world but their own. *Why do I feel this way?* Greg asked the bright stars in the dark, but perhaps not so empty sky behind the temple. *Am I in love? Am I being called to rise? Could it possibly be both?*

Sterling shifted his weight from one foot to the other as he stood with Andi on the front porch of the Reynolds home. He had walked her to the door thirty minutes earlier, expecting to be invited in. Like Justine, he prophesied that they would marry in June; this didn't leave a long period for courtship. Not, of course, that they would need it. Sterling knew that he was everything Andi admired; he had known it for years. The only thing that puzzled him now was why they still stood outside. Perhaps she had been too enraptured by his missionary experiences to think to invite him in. He had noticed that she hadn't taken her hand off the doorknob the entire time he was talking.

Now Andi's hand slipped to her side as she looked around Sterling to the white convertible that pulled into the driveway. He followed her gaze. "Thank goodness Clytie got home all right. Howland probably drives that thing like a maniac."

The spring breeze carried his words clearly, and Greg's hands tightened on the wheel.

"Thank you for taking me, Greg," Clytie said in his other ear. "I had a wonderful time . . . Greg?"

He dragged his eyes from the porch to smile down at her. Lowering his voice, he said, "I'm the one who needs to thank you, Clytie. Honest, you are the sweetest, most remarkable person I've ever met."

"Aren't you going to walk me to the door?"

Greg looked from her to Andi and back. "I, uh . . . " Seeing the expression on Clytie's face, he sighed. "Sure."

Clytie held his hand tightly as they went up the stairs to the porch.

Once there she guided him squarely between Sterling and her sister. "Excuse us for interrupting."

"You're not interrupting," Andi said. "In fact, Sterling was just saying good night. I have to be at work early tomorrow."

Greg knew he should leave it alone but couldn't resist. "She has to feed my alligators," he told Sterling.

"Feed what?"

"Alligators," Andi said. "I work at the zoo. Remember?"

"Oh, that." He turned to Greg. "What makes them your alligators?"

"That's how we met. I adopted the exhibit lock, stock, and lunch pails."

"Why?"

"I love alligators," Greg replied. "Alligators and zoo trains. It's a tough call which I like best."

Sterling watched Andi suppress a smile. Howland might be some kind of worldly big shot, but he was crazy. It was gratifying to see that Andi knew that as well. He took her hand. "Well, I'll see you at home evening tomorrow. Good night, Clytie." He motioned toward the stairs. "After you, Howland."

"Just a minute, Greg," Clytie said quickly. "I need to get that book you want to borrow."

"Book?"

"You know, Emily Dickinson." She had already gossiped; surely she could also repent of one small fib for such a good cause. "It might take me a minute to find it." She turned to Sterling. "You don't need to wait, though. Good night, Sterling." She waited patiently for him to walk to his car, climb reluctantly behind the wheel, and pull away. Then she crooked a finger at Greg. When he leaned down, Clytie pecked his cheek. "I love you, Greg. I'll call you tomorrow about the lesson." She disappeared into the house before Greg regained enough wits to respond.

At the sound of a sharp click, Andi reached behind her to grasp the knob, then turned to Greg. "She locked the door."

Greg grinned. "She's a great girl."

"She seems to think you're pretty great, too," Andi observed, easing herself against the porch rail. "Are you giving her pitching lessons next?"

"Actually, she offered to arrange a lesson for me tomorrow—with the missionaries." He looked down the street in the direction Sterling had taken. "No one we know, I hope."

"Sterling's all right."

"All right? I got the impression he walks on water."

"Well, there isn't much call for that here in the desert." Andi smiled shyly at Greg's grin and brushed back a tendril of hair that had been freed by the breeze. "I hope Clytie didn't badger you until you agreed to meet with the missionaries."

"No, it was more my idea. I have some questions Clytie thought they could answer."

Andi nodded slowly. She couldn't believe it. Here she was the one who had set out to fellowship Greg Howland, but Enos had challenged him to read the Book of Mormon and Clytie had taken him to a fireside and invited him to meet with the missionaries. What had she done? Andi sighed. She knew what she had done. She had fallen in love with him. "That's just great," she told herself. Then, "I mean, I'm glad you want to meet the missionaries."

Andi's words, Greg noticed, didn't match her tone of voice. Apparently Clytie was mistaken, and the man her sister wanted to be with had just left. "Well," he said politely, "I know those crocodiles get hungry pretty early. I'd better let you go."

"What about your book?"

"I think Clytie, uh, forgot about the book."

"Let me walk you to your car, then."

A gentle wind brushed the clouds from the moon as they walked together in silence. Greg breathed in the sweet scent of citrus from the trees along the drive and gazed up at the stars. He would forever associate both with Andi and, perhaps, her Elder Holland. He chose the brightest star in the sky and wished for words, and courage, to tell her how he felt.

When they reached his car, Greg turned to look down at Andi. The breeze caught a stray tendril of her hair, trailing it across her face as a dusting of orange blossoms swirled slowly around them, suspended as though caught within a water globe. Greg's hand moved in slow motion as he captured the curl and moved it back with one finger, barely brushing her lips. The blossoms settled into fragrant drifts around their feet and the night became suddenly still.

Andi's eyes, as they looked searchingly into his, were liquid as well. "What questions do you have, Greg?"

His hand lingered at her cheek until he slowly raised it to pluck a blossom from her coppery hair. "Do you want an honest answer?"

She nodded wordlessly, thinking how easy it would be to lose her balance in his eyes.

When Greg spoke, his voice was rich and low. "My biggest question, Andi, is whether I'm even asking questions for the right reasons."

The wayward curl escaped as Andi lowered her face. "You want to know the truth. What other reason could there be?"

Greg tucked the curl into her hair as his strong fingers cupped and lifted her face to his. "There could be this one."

His kiss was everything she'd dreamed it would be, Andi thought as she melted against his muscular chest. It was as shy as it was tender, but his lips held an underlying strength that left her breathless and dizzy. She sighed when, finally, he moved her gently away.

Greg looked into the starlight of her emerald eyes and thought of the temple grounds. Darlene, he realized now, knew more than Clytie gave her credit for, at least about temple marriage. Forever with Ariadne would seem much too short a time.

Greg searched again for the right words—any words—to tell her how he felt. *I want to say I'm beginning to understand,* he thought. *I want to ask her to wait for me. I want to . . . I only want to kiss her.*

With effort, and a tender smile, he handed her the blossom he had taken from her hair, opened his car door, and said quietly, "Good night, Andi. Give my best to those swamp things tomorrow."

Andi stood under the stars after Greg drove away, lightly fingering the small, waxy flower and breathing in its sweet scent. When she finally returned to the porch, she was so engrossed in replaying Greg's kiss that she failed to notice that, at some point, Clytie had unlocked the front door.

CHAPTER 20

Every creator produces a masterpiece and this Monday, in Andi's mind, must be God's. It was exquisite. The sky was perfectly clear, a glowing azure blue—her favorite color—and the sunlight was melted honey. Dripping from heaven, it coated everything it touched with warmth and made the world incredibly sweet. Even the animals noticed. At the zoo, the turtles had climbed onto their log a little earlier than usual, drawn by the rays of this peculiar new sun. On her way across the bridge, Andi paused to watch them blink and stretch their necks to admire her perfect day. She loved turtles.

The alligators and crocs—his, of course—were wonderfully designed and indescribably dear. She would have hugged them, if she could, and kissed each on its scaly snout, just for being its own sweet self. Instead, she greeted them warmly and doled out extra portions of food. The crocodilians noticed and were pleased. Their smiles were almost as wide as Andi's.

Because it was such a masterpiece, however, God must have deliberately slowed the minutes to give the world time to admire and exclaim. Andi tapped her watch, then held it to her ear, but had to admit that it was probably right. It was still eight hours until Greg would come to her home for a missionary discussion. Afterwards, he'd invited her to dinner and agreed to go to her Young Adult home evening. Somehow, she would have to wait.

Elder Vernon Pratt had known since embarking on this call that he was special. But today, one year, ten months and twenty-four days into his term as emissary of the Lord, he would prove it. He, Elder Vernon Pratt, would put the Arizona Tempe Mission on the map. He would convert Greg Howland.

Of course, he'd be humble when the *Church News* put his picture on the cover, and he'd modestly consent to an interview with the *New Era*. Or the *Ensign*? Well, both, and *The Friend* besides. He wondered for a moment if someone in Salt Lake would want to give him a plaque or something. After all, Howland was not only mega-famous, he was making, what, $15 million a year playing baseball? Who knew how much he got for all the commercials? Why, in tithing alone, that was . . . golly. Forget the plaque. They'd probably erect a statue of him outside the MTC.

Elder Pratt glanced at his companion. The greenie was still on his knees. Well, in about eight hours he'd show Elder Owens how a real missionary operates. After all, this was the day of his dreams; he'd been born for it.

Andi, who had never in her life had an unkind notion toward a servant of the Lord, thought now she might strangle this one with her bare hands, preferably before he could utter another ridiculous word. Elder Pratt had sermonized, expounded, preached, and postulated for the last thirty minutes, making it impossible for his companion (or anyone else) to squeeze in a single sane comment. If she were Greg, she would have left after the opening prayer. The senior companion had offered it (of course), thanking God for, among other things, the sword of truth to smite wayward sinners. With a rameumptom, the tableau would have been complete.

But Greg was pressed into the chintz-covered chair Clytie had offered him, still listening, apparently, as he idly fingered an old, well-worn copy of the Book of Mormon. He looked down at it from time to time and pressed his lips together firmly. But if he caught Andi's eyes on him, or Clytie's, he smiled and refocused his attention on the missionary.

"' . . . and if they will not repent and believe in his name, and be baptized in his name, and endure to the end, they must be damned.'" Elder Pratt paused, for air most likely, but before Andi could speak Elder Owens cleared his throat.

"My daddy says," the missionary began tentatively, "that damning isn't so much what God does to us as what we do to ourselves. And we mostly do it without the N, if you know what I mean."

Elder Pratt had regained his wind and started to interrupt when Greg held up his hand. "I've listened to you. I want to hear what your partner has to say. Please, Elder, go on."

The Idaho-farm-boy-turned-Lord's-representative gulped audibly. "Well, Daddy says that we start life like a stream high up in the mountains and the natural course is to run back to the sea. 'Course, we can pick up a lot of things we don't need along the way, things like sticks and stones and even big ol' logs. Leastwise, that's what rivers do. Daddy says people pick up things like doubt and fear and hate 'til, after a while, they're so dammed up they don't rightly know where they were headin' in the first place and end up going no place at all." He cast an uneasy glance at his senior companion. "Leastwise, that's what my daddy says about damning."

"Your dad seems like a very wise man," Greg said quietly. As he leaned back in the chair, Andi worried at the deepening of the fine lines around his eyes. Was he thinking of his own father? She shuddered to think what he had picked up there.

Greg was ten years old. The tip of his tongue touched his upper lip hesitantly and hastily retreated at the salty taste of blood and sharp-sour sensation of swollen tissue. He hugged his knees and leaned far forward, watching as the blood from his nose dripped a pattern of small, scarlet bursts into the dirt. *I hate him*, he thought. *I hate him. I hate him. I hate him.* Greg closed his eyes and curled himself smaller, pulling the raw part of the little boy that felt pain and humiliation deeper into the silent shell that would refuse to feel at all.

The back door opened and soft steps hurried down the stairs. Sadie's hand touched the top of his head, her fingers barely lingering, like a breeze that ruffles and passes on. "He didn't mean it."

Greg's quivering chin followed as his eyes rose in disbelief.

His mother looked down at his bruised face and quickly away. "He didn't mean it," she repeated softly to herself.

"I hate him!"

"No, Greg. Hate what drinking does to him. Hating him will only hurt you worse."

"Sadie!" The way Roy said her name was a command and a curse. Greg grasped the hem of his mother's dress. "Mama?"

She hesitated, looking down at her young son, then toward the screen door. Greg felt the thin fabric slip from his fingers. "When you're older," she said, "you'll understand."

Greg wiped the blood into a narrow streak along the back of his hand and arm. *How old?* he wondered. His hand fell to his side, bruising the knuckles on a smooth, round stone about the size and weight of a baseball. He picked it up and gazed across the field at a rusty chassis.

How old? Greg wondered, his left hand gripping the arm of the chair. *How old?*

Elder Pratt had been silent as long as he could bear. He held aloft a missionary copy of the scriptures and intoned, "I exhort you to read the Book of Mormon!"

Greg looked up. Exhort? Someone ought to tell this guy that he and Moroni play in different leagues. He said, "I have read it."

"Which part?" the missionary asked suspiciously.

"All of it." Greg looked from one stunned face to the next. "What? Would you be surprised if I said I'd read a long novel over the weekend?" He ran his thumb over an ancient crease in the cover of his book as he grinned. "I mean, Mormon's scope is a little epic, and his plot wanders off in places, but the overall theme pretty much makes up for it, don't you think?" Greg extended his free hand. "But I would like another copy, if you were going to offer me that one, for a friend." Lupe had asked what he saw in all this Mormonism as he read the scriptures over breakfast, and he couldn't think of a better way to explain than to let her see for herself.

Elder Pratt handed him the volume doubtfully, at a loss, for once, for words.

Greg took advantage of the silence. "May I ask a question?" He tucked the second volume next to him as he leaned forward in his chair. When he looked up, his clear eyes mirrored the cover of the book he still held. "How do you know when you know?" He opened to the frontispiece. "I mean, Moroni said to ask God and by the power of the Holy Ghost you will know the truth of all things." He flipped a few pages. "Nephi said that Christ is the same yesterday, today, and forever, and the way is prepared for any man to find him."

Greg turned a few more pages, frowned, then closed the book. "All through the scripture, men testify, angels appear, and prophets prophesy—all by the power of the Holy Ghost. But I just don't know how it works for me."

When no one responded, he concluded, "The apostle last night called the Holy Ghost a still, small voice and Clytie said that he's the Comforter, and I think I may have experienced both of those things. But, let's say you're a fairly regular kind of guy who hasn't seen an angel, heard a voice, or been carried away by a vision. You've just felt . . . happier and more . . . hopeful all of a sudden than you ever have. How do you know if it's the Holy Ghost, or spring fever, or epinephrine, or . . . ," he glanced briefly at Andi, "something else?"

Andi knew. It was her chance, finally, to say what she had tried to tell him on the swing Wednesday night; what she intended to share in the Superstitions on Friday; what she might have said last night. She leaned forward happily. "You know because everything good comes from the same source, Greg. Isn't the feeling you have reading the scriptures similar to the one you had watching the sunset?"

"In a way . . . "

"Both were gifts from the Holy Ghost to help you recognize him."

"Like at the fireside," Clytie added, "and the temple."

"And even at Enos' game," Andi said, "when you went out of your way to be nice to all those people. You felt bad when you first came, remember? But after you gave of yourself to others, you felt better."

"Well, yeah, I guess."

"That's what the Spirit is, Greg," Andi continued, "and that's what it's like to have the Holy Ghost with you all the time. It isn't like he tells you things in so many words, usually. It's more like he says 'that's right' when you recognize truth for yourself."

Elder Pratt had been listening, for a change, and felt the Spirit's promptings himself. Maybe it wasn't too late to lose the statue idea and try to gain something of a more lasting worth. "You said you've been feeling happier and more hopeful since you've read the Book of Mormon," he began. "That's probably the strongest testimony you can receive. Jesus said, 'Learn of me, and listen to my words; walk in the meekness of my Spirit, and you shall have peace in me.'"

Greg noted the new tone in the zealous young man's words and smiled. "Thank you, Elders. I think I've learned something today."

"I think I have, too," Elder Pratt said, returning the smile. "Could we, uh, start this lesson over? I think I may have missed a point or two you'd be interested in."

Andi smiled at the honeyed sun slanting in through the bay window. She'd known all along that this was going to be a perfect day.

CHAPTER 30

When Andi came back downstairs from changing for the Young Adult home evening, Greg was seated on the floor by the end table, pencil in hand, explaining an algebraic concept to Clytie. Francie sat on his lap reciting her ark book and Enos had climbed up his broad back, trying to get him back outdoors for another game of catch. She cleared her throat purposefully and flushed at Greg's appreciative look. She knew that even in her favorite silk shirt and best-fitting jeans, she didn't look much like a fashion model, but the way he gazed at her made her feel like one. "Any chance you could spare Greg? We have a date."

"We do?" he asked hopefully as he handed Clytie her pencil. He sat Francie carefully on the table and swung Enos into his lap for a quick tickle. "A real date?"

"Well, maybe not a real date, but . . . "

"I knew it sounded too good to be true. Do I at least get to buy you dinner before the next lesson?"

"Yes, we can eat."

Greg winked at Clytie as he gathered Enos under one arm. "That's what she says now. Last time your sister invited me to dinner, I didn't get two bites."

"That wasn't my fault," Andi protested. "You're the one who ran off."

"True enough." Greg deposited Enos on the couch on his way to her side. He flicked the brim of the Cubs cap she had pulled impulsively over her curls with his thumb. "Nice hat. It just happens to be my favorite team."

"Hey!" Enos cried. He jumped up from the sofa and ran to Andi, his hand waving in the air. "That's my hat! You didn't ask."

Andi removed the cap reluctantly. "I saw it in the hallway, Enos. May I wear it, please?"

"No! It's my best one. You can wear my Diamondbacks hat."

"Not with me, she can't," Greg grinned. "But give Enos back his hat, Andi. I have one in the car you can have for keeps."

Andi set the cap on her little brother's head. "Thanks, anyway. See you later, alligators." She led Greg out the door and practically skipped to his car. There she sank blissfully into the seat and ran her hand over the buttery-soft leather as he started the engine. "So, where's my hat?"

Greg reached under the seat and produced a well-worn All-Star cap with his name and number embroidered between the seams. He looked it over and grimaced. "Uh, never mind, Andi. I think it's seen one wearing too many."

She extended her hand and wiggled the fingers. "Hand it over, Howland. You promised me that hat."

"Give me until tomorrow and I'll get you a new one."

"Uh uh. It's that one or the Diamondbacks." She reached playfully for the door handle.

Greg dropped the hat in her lap with a shrug and backed out of the driveway. "Suit yourself. Do you like Chinese?"

"People, policy, or food?" Andi knew she was being silly, but felt so good she was almost giddy.

Greg cast her a sideways glance. "Food."

"I love it!" She pulled on his cap and leaned back in the seat, savoring the wind on her face and the feeling that she loved everything today.

"Good. I know a great take-out."

"I promised you time to eat," she teased. "You don't have to take your food with you."

"I'm not taking any chances. It's no wonder Mormons serve food at all their meetings. It's the only chance you people have to eat."

She glanced over at him uneasily. "You don't have to go to this meeting tonight, Greg."

"It's not a complaint," he said quickly. "It's an observation. In the six days I've known you, you've been to at least five church meetings, if you count the Friday night social and the missionary lesson today. Plus, Brad and the girls went to meetings Wednesday night and your mother had a meeting Thursday. Clytie said there were three hours of church on Sunday before the two she took me to that night. That's a lot of religious training."

"You've 'observed' pretty carefully," Andi said slowly.

The sudden appearance of his lopsided grin was all the assurance she needed. "With all that teaching going on, Andi, I can't help but worry about how much there is to learn."

Andi pulled his worn Book of Mormon from between the seats. "You seem to be a pretty quick study. Hang around another fifty years or so and you might get the gist of it."

A stoplight gave Greg the chance to look carefully into her face. "Is that an invitation?"

Andi colored, but recovered quickly. "It's an observation."

"You don't spend enough time here?" Andi asked as Greg parked in the back lot of HoHoKam Park after procuring cartons of lemon chicken, moo goo gai pan, and egg rolls.

"I thought it was about time I had the home field advantage," he said, swinging open her door. "Besides, you'll never see the inside of a stadium any other way."

Andi looked up at the high gates as he opened the trunk. "Do you have your own key?"

"No, but someone's bound to be here cleaning up after the game." He pulled out a duffel bag, then slapped the trunk closed as a worker rounded the corner. "Yes! Hey, Chuck!"

A thick-set young man, concentrating on the task of collecting stray paper, looked up at the sound of his name. His jaw dropped. "Mr. H-Howland?"

"Hi, Chuck. It's great to see you again. This is Andi; Andi, this is Chuck. He and I work together."

The young man shook his head slowly. "We don't work together. You pitch and I clean up."

"Oh, sure," Greg said with a grin, "go ahead and point out which one of us does the real work. If you don't mind, Chuck, I'm trying to impress this girl."

"You know my name?"

"You know mine and I see you almost every day. Besides," Greg added honestly, "it helps to have it there on the front of your shirt. Anyway, is there any chance you could let us in the gate? I don't want to get you in any trouble, but Andi's never been in the stadium. I hoped maybe we could have a picnic dinner in the stands."

"Oh, yeah, sure." Chuck fumbled at his waist for the keys. "It's no problem, Mr. Howland. Anything you want." He unlocked the gate with alacrity and beamed when Greg put down the duffel to clasp him on the shoulder.

"Really, Chuck, thanks. I owe you one."

As Greg led the way down the stairs toward the field, Andi glanced back at the admiring custodian and asked, "Is there anyone in the world who doesn't like you?"

"Besides your father?"

"He . . . "

"Sterling Channing?"

"I mean . . . "

"Joe Sills."

"Who?"

"A guy I struck out to end a 50-game hitting streak. I still feel bad about it." Greg found the spot he wanted, in the front row along the first base line, and deposited the cartons on top of the Cubs' dugout. "Is there anyone who doesn't like you?" When she didn't respond right away, he zipped open the duffel. "That's what I thought."

Andi watched in astonishment as he pulled a snowy cloth from his bag and draped it over the concrete. Then he unwrapped two crystal goblets from linen napkins and filled them from a bottle of apple juice. Finally, he produced a cut-glass vase and a tissue cone containing a single, long-stemmed rose.

"This is beautiful," Andi murmured, settling into her seat and admiring the small china dish and silver utensils he placed in front of her.

"Well, everyone was supposed to bring their own plate, but I covered for you."

"Where did you get all this?"

"Would you believe I found that thrift store you were talking about? Unfortunately, someone beat me to the pie tins, so I had to settle for this stuff." Greg shrugged at her smile and spooned food onto her plate. "I can read. I can shop. I can recite the infield fly rule. What more could anyone want in an American male?"

Andi ducked her head and the question. "Playing baseball's pretty complicated, isn't it?"

"The fly rule aside, it depends on who you ask." He turned her toward the left. "See that little triangle down there? That's home plate. It's my job to get there when I'm at bat and throw well enough to keep everyone on the other team from getting there the rest of the time."

"That's all?"

"Yep. You know what they say: baseball's six and a half minutes of excitement crammed into three and a half hours of game."

"Why do they say that?"

"Because . . . " Smiling, Greg shook his head. "Never mind, Andi. I suspect that baseball isn't something we have in common."

Andi raised questioning, bronze-rimmed eyes to his. "Do we have anything in common, Greg?"

He looked down at her for a moment, then passed the egg rolls. "Sure. We both like Chinese food. We both love alligators." He paused. "We're both Homo sapiens. I think that's enough to start an eternal relationship, don't you?"

Andi bit into her egg roll and Greg looked politely away. He knew that ploy. When she finished chewing, enough time would have passed for her to safely change the subject.

"It must be exciting," she sighed finally, gazing at the sea of green seats rippling out from the field.

"What?"

"To be out there in front of thousands of people who pay money to see you play." Her eyes returned to his face with almost a sense of wonder. "You know, Greg, I keep forgetting who you are."

"Andi, pitching baseballs is what I *do*. You're one of very few people who know who I *am*."

"Still," she insisted, "it's impressive. You're the very best."

"The best what?"

"Pitcher, of course. You're not the only one who can read, you know."

"I hope you don't believe everything you read about me." He looked out over the field reflectively. "You know, I think I'd like to retire to a Little League field before much longer."

"Retire? How old are you?"

He raised an eyebrow. "Sixty. I have good genes." When she didn't laugh, he said, "I'm twenty-four, Andi. That's just the term."

"But what would you do?"

"I don't know. Sell shoes?"

"Don't you already do that?"

"I meant at Sears." Greg stabbed a piece of chicken as Andi frowned.

"But that seems backwards. Doesn't every boy who becomes a shoe salesman dream of playing in the World Series?"

"I don't know."

"Didn't you?"

"I guess so. But mostly, Andi, I just wanted out of Peosta. The only raw materials I had were lots of spare time, a good arm, and a whole lot of rocks. I was lucky." He shifted in the plastic chair. "Maybe I was blessed."

"Maybe?"

Greg returned her smile. "At any rate, it got me to the same place. For the first dozen years of my life I was dirt-poor and told every single day that I was stupid and worthless. Now, in the last dozen years, just because I learned to throw a baseball, I'm some kind of golden boy who's worth millions. Strange deal, huh? I think it's about time I figure out for myself who I am—away from the field of public opinion."

Andi's eyes had grown soft and a little sad. Greg reached for his duffel. "But that's another lesson, right?" Rummaging inside the bag, he said, "You know, I've felt bad since Thursday night that I didn't have anything for you when I sent the stuff for your family."

"You brought me flowers," Andi pointed out, "and now you've given me your hat." She adjusted the bill. "I love it."

"I'm glad. I hope you'll love this, too." He withdrew a long, velvet case and placed it in Andi's hand. Her fingers caressed the soft, burgundy sides but made no attempt to open it. After a minute or two, Greg said, "Uh, Andi, the gift part is on the inside."

Still, she hesitated until finally Greg's long fingers covered hers and gently lifted the lid. "It's to thank you for listening to me and giving me hope. I don't know how to tell you what you . . . your friendship . . . means to me." His worried eyes searched her face as she stared down at the gold filigree bracelet. He had spent the better part of an hour at the jewelers, trying to choose a gift so appropriate and personal that she couldn't refuse.

He watched her pink and white nail lightly touch one of the miniature charms. Impatient, he reached over again to pull the bracelet from the case. His fingers felt thick as he looped it around her slender wrist and fumbled with the clasp.

There were five charms: a tiny alligator with detailed, prickly scales; a golden spool of silver thread; a heart; a crystal and gold angel; and a twinkling, silver candy kiss.

Andi glanced up quickly. She was especially touched that Greg had remembered the story of Ariadne and Theseus, and the spool of thread she had given him to help him find his way out of the maze. "Thank you, Greg," she sighed. "It's beautiful."

"Thank *you*, Andi. Last Monday I left this field feeling like it was the end of the world. Today, because of you, it feels much more like the beginning."

A reasonable person wouldn't accept this gift, the responsible little voice in Andi's head began to lecture. A reasonable person would calmly eat her meal, not move it aside to lean toward this man. A reasonable person would certainly never kiss him . . . Suddenly, Andi couldn't hear the voice of reason, or even the tinkling of glass as she upset her goblet. She was listening, instead, to the accelerated beat of her heart.

CHAPTER 31

Greg and Andi arrived at the Park of the Canals just before Justine's lesson. They were a little late because Andi had been giving a short history lesson of her own. If Greg was going to play baseball at HoHoKam Stadium, she reasoned, he ought to at least know where the name had originated.

The thirty acres of mostly barren ground in the northwest corner of Mesa comprised her favorite city park. To her mind, it offered something much more valuable than the acres of grass and trees available all over the nation. This park stood for heritage.

The acreage itself probably hadn't changed much since 300 B.C. when it was part of an intricate canal system dug by Native Americans with only stone tools and an intimate knowledge of the lay of the land. Here, the Hohokam Indians had farmed and flourished for almost seventeen hundred years, then mysteriously disappeared.

After lying abandoned for almost half a millennium, the same canals were cleared in 1878 by Mormon pioneers. In defiance of the naysayers of the time and, seemingly against the law of gravity, this small band of men got water to flow up the bluff, bringing life back to the desert. A century later, however, only a trio of narrow trenches, a National Geographic plaque, and this urban park remained to note the accomplishments of these different, remarkable peoples.

Justine began her lesson on the plan of salvation with a short story, then offered one end of a nylon rope to Sterling and pressed the other end into Greg's hand, instructing them to stretch it to its full length.

When the men stood about fifty feet apart, the rope taut between them, Justine held up a short length of thread. "Let's pretend that this rope stretches both directions forever and ever. That way," she said, motioning toward Sterling, "is where we came from—all the time we lived before we were born. The other way represents where we are going—all the time we will live after we die. Remember, the rope goes on forever." She tied the thread midway. "This represents the time we spend on earth." Justine opened her Book of Mormon to Alma 34 and read:

> *For behold, this life is the time for men to prepare to meet God; yea, behold the day of this life is the day for men to perform their labors. . . . Behold if we do not improve our time while in this life, then cometh the night of darkness wherein there can be no labor performed.*

"The thread illustrates how short life is," she concluded, "and how important it is to make the right choices now."

After the closing prayer, Justine took the coiled rope from Greg and hooked her arm through his with a 100-watt smile. "They're setting up for volleyball now. You can be on my team."

"Uh, thanks," Greg said, "but I'm not very good at volleyball. How about I root for you from the sidelines?"

Sterling smiled pleasantly. "You don't always have to be the best player to enjoy a game, Howland. A sport's supposed to be something people do for fun."

Tell it to Biderman, Greg thought. The Cubs manager would have a conniption if he caught a player risking injury over a volleyball game. Still, he looked from Justine to Andi sheepishly, unable to think of an excuse that wouldn't make him sound like an overpaid prima donna.

He still hadn't responded when Bishop Ferris lay a hand on his shoulder. "I'm sorry to interrupt," the short, sturdy man apologized, "but could I have a word with you?" He nodded at the others. "Go ahead with your game. I won't keep him long."

As he led Greg to a nearby pavilion, he said, "Life's funny, you know? About the time you were born there was a show on TV about a six-million-dollar man. Now here you come along with one arm worth ten times that. Some kind of inflation." Catching a look at the young ballplayer's face, he added quickly, "Don't be embarrassed, Greg. God gave you the gift and put you where you are for a reason."

Greg smiled gratefully as the bishop slid onto a picnic bench and motioned for him to do the same. "Thanks for getting me out of volleyball."

"It's only fair to your employer to protect his assets," Bishop Ferris smiled, "but I'd be dishonest if I didn't confess to an ulterior motive."

Greg ran a finger along one of the parallel grooves in the metal table. "I guess you want to talk about Andi."

The bishop laughed heartily. "Andi Reynolds is a match for anyone. My motives are more ulterior than that." He leaned forward. "You probably get sick of hearing this, so I apologize in advance, but I pitch for the Fraternal Order of Police and—"

"I thought Andi introduced you as a bishop."

"She did, but she apparently didn't explain that our church has a lay ministry. I'm Bishop Ferris to these young adults, Detective Ferris at work, and Fireball Ferris on the mound."

"Fireball Ferris?" Greg grinned. "It doesn't sound like you need my help."

"I'm fast enough for an old guy, but my problem is with control. I've seen you throw smoke right where you want it. How do you keep your speed and still get them over the plate that way? I'm all over the place."

"It's got to be in your mechanics. Show me what you do."

The bishop rose eagerly, then paused. "Darn it, I don't have a ball."

"We don't need a ball," Greg said, untangling his long legs from beneath the bench. "I'll bet that field is full of great throwing rocks."

Andi's performance in the volleyball game was bad, even by her unexacting standards. She spent most of her time on tiptoes or leaning around other players to watch Greg and her bishop pitch rocks into a cardboard box they had set up in the desert. She admired Greg's build when he removed his jacket to throw the stones and smiled when she heard him laugh. She wondered what, besides baseball, they discussed so earnestly. Andi was so distracted, in fact, that she didn't notice the volleyball served to her position. It hit her squarely in the side of the face. Sterling and Justine were immediately at her side.

"Andi! Are you all right?" Sterling asked, as he draped an arm protectively around her shoulder and led her to the side. "Justine, run over to the restroom and bring a cold cloth for her face."

"I'm fine," Andi protested. Her face stung, but from injury or embarrassment it was hard to say. She tried to shrug off Sterling's arm, but it only tightened as he shepherded her over a small footbridge to another part of the park. There he settled with her on a bench near the empty playground. Justine joined them in a few minutes with a dripping paper towel.

"Thanks, Justine," Andi said, wringing it out. She was more grateful for her friend's return than for the wet paper towel. "I'm fine now. Let's go back to the others."

"Rest here a while," Sterling advised firmly. "You can't be too careful with a head injury."

"It isn't a head injury, Sterling. It doesn't even hurt."

"Go find some aspirin, Justine," Sterling suggested. "I'll stay with Andi."

"Aspirin? She just said it doesn't hurt."

Sterling inclined his head with a meaningful, impatient look.

"Oh, aspirin," Justine said. "Yeah, sure, aspirin. I'll be right back."

Andi sighed. From the playground she couldn't see the field where Greg and Bishop Ferris were throwing.

"I'm a convert myself," the bishop continued as he and Greg returned to the pavilion after twenty-some minutes of tossing rocks. Somewhere along the way the talk had veered from baseball to beliefs. "It's been almost thirty years since I joined the Church."

"Then you were young . . . I mean . . . " Greg rubbed his face but the older man was chuckling.

"I was about your age, Greg. I was a military police officer in the army at the time. My partner was the one who told me about the Church."

"And you believed it?"

"It's been three decades and I'm out here during basketball playoffs with a bunch of kids."

"But you probably knew something about God before you read the Book of Mormon," Greg guessed. "I mean, weren't you already going to church and reading the Bible?"

"You don't know much about the army, do you, Greg?"

The younger man smiled. "I don't know much about anything, I guess, especially religion. I've only been inside a church twice in my life." His voice trailed off and he looked down at his laced fingers, wondering what it was about this week that had him telling strangers things he'd never before discussed, even with Jim.

"I've learned over the years, Greg, that if there's one thing that'll get you farther along in life than knowledge, it's faith. You don't need to know much. The gospel of Jesus Christ is really very simple." Bishop Ferris rested his elbows on the metal table and regarded Greg kindly. "Want to tell me about what you've experienced lately?"

Greg noticed that his hands were dry and dusty from the rocks. "I don't know what to tell. I don't know what to think, even. About a week ago, I was . . . depressed, I guess. My brother had died and everything in my life seemed so . . . out of control." He glanced up nervously, but the man's hazel eyes were warm and sympathetic. "So I prayed . . . for the first time in my life, actually. I didn't know what to say, so I asked God for whatever help He thought I needed."

Bishop Ferris nodded and leaned further forward. "And?"

"And within a few minutes I saw Andi and she was so . . . I don't know . . . different from anyone I've ever met. I had to see her again. She invited me to dinner and I met her little brother and sister and . . . everything's gone so fast since then. I've read the Book of Mormon and been to a fireside. Today I had a missionary lesson. And I've tried to keep praying."

"Do you think God is answering your prayers?"

"Well, I thought so."

"But?"

"But last night I realized that I'm, uh, well, attracted to Andi, so I can't help but wonder if that's most of it." Greg let out a breath. "And the really strong feeling that I had when I first prayed about the Book of Mormon on Friday night hasn't come back and I wonder if I imagined it. I just don't know."

"I think I understand, Greg. In the Doctrine and Covenants—"

"The what?"

"Doctrine and Covenants. It's a book of scripture given as revelation for the latter-day church."

"You mean there's another book?"

The older man chuckled. "A couple of them. Our Father has taught His children throughout time and commanded them to keep records. We're fortunate to live in a day when more have been revealed. But you don't have to learn everything all at once, Greg. You can't." When the young pitcher nodded, Bishop Ferris continued, "To get back to your original point, though, there was once a man who felt very much as you do now. He'd received a strong witness that what he'd heard was true, but time passed and the feeling didn't return, so he wasn't as sure anymore. The Lord spoke to him, and the rest of us, in a revelation in the Doctrine and Covenants."

"What did God tell him?"

Bishop Ferris smiled at Greg's willingness to accept him at his word. "He said, 'If you desire a further witness, cast your mind upon the night that you cried unto me in your heart, that you might know concerning the truth of these things. Did I not speak peace to your mind concerning the matter? What greater witness can you have than from God?'"

Greg felt the hair stand at attention along the back of his neck. It was becoming a familiar sensation and he nodded wordlessly. Before he could gather his thoughts to respond, he noticed the timid approach of a young woman who had stood on the perimeter of activities most of the evening. She was, Greg noted, obviously anxious for Bishop Ferris' attention. The ballplayer rose quickly. "Thank you, sir."

The bishop stood with him and circled the table. He pulled a business card from his wallet, a pen from his pocket, and wrote briefly. Then he handed the card to Greg. "My work number's on the front and my home phone's on the back. Please know that you can call me anytime, Greg. Okay?"

"Thanks, uh, Bishop," Greg said with the hesitation of someone speaking a foreign language.

Ferris took Greg's outstretched hand in both of his. "You're going to be fine, son. I can see that. And you can call me Fireball."

"Really, Sterling, I'm fine," Andi insisted. "We ought to get back to the others. Greg will wonder where I am."

Sterling cleared his throat. "I need to talk to you about him. I admire what you're trying to do, missionary-wise and all, but I don't want you to be alone with that man again."

"You don't want—"

"I went by your house tonight to pick you both up, but you had left an hour early. That was poor judgment, Andi."

"Sterling, Greg Howland is a perfect gentleman." *Which is more than I can say for you*, she thought, trying again to wiggle out from under his arm.

"Perfect gentlemen do not frequent the hotel rooms of Hollywood actresses." He waited for Andi to respond. When she didn't even let out her breath, he continued, "You saw today's paper, didn't you?"

She lifted her chin. "I don't read the gossip column."

"You should have read this one. You knew that Howland had a so-called early breakfast with Jacy Grayson on Sunday?"

"No, but it's no sin to eat breakfast, Sterling, even with an actress. Greg said that the press always manages to make something of nothing." She hoped her words carried more conviction than she felt. Greg had also said he didn't know Jacy Grayson.

Sterling's tone was paternal and a little patronizing. "You're so naïve, Andi. Really, what do you know about Greg Howland?"

Andi shook her head, not trusting her voice.

"I know it's disappointing when you had such high hopes to convert him, but we ran into people like that all the time on my mission. They dabble a little with the truth, but never changed their lives." Sterling rubbed her shoulder, trying to massage away the stiffness. "It doesn't matter. Howland's only in town for three more days. This is the end of it anyway, and you'll be blessed for your efforts."

Three days? The words bounced around in Andi's mind when she tried to push them aside so she could think. Last Wednesday Greg had told her he was in town until the end of March and today was the 27th. She must have known he was leaving soon. Certainly *he* knew it. She closed her eyes. Last night and this evening hadn't meant anything to him. She was such a fool to think . . . Andi shook her head to clear it and swallowed the painful lump in her throat. Then she gave Sterling her best imitation of a smile. "Thanks for your concern, Sterling. You're a good friend."

"I'm more than that." He moved to kiss her, his lips brushing her hair as she lowered her face. "Are you sure you're all right?"

"Of course," a voice that sounded like hers responded. "I told you, I'm fine." Andi rose quickly to her feet, hoping to convince Sterling of the truthfulness of her words. As the charms brushed against her wrist, she crushed the paper towel in her hand and wondered what it would take to convince herself.

Greg glanced around the small park in the dim, artificial light. Andi wasn't playing volleyball, or anywhere among the sets of young people clustered together talking animatedly. She must be with Sterling and Justine. He noticed high adobe walls which set off a near-by nature walk and wandered over and through the arch to see if they were there.

A sand-brown gecko started as Greg stepped too close. He watched it streak across the granite path to take refuge in the root of a tall agave plant. Except for himself, and the lizard, the garden was deserted. He paused to read the lighted sign at the base of the unusual vegetation. The tall stalk was also called a century plant, so named because of the infrequency with which it bloomed in harsh desert conditions. As Greg looked up at the clusters of straw-colored blossoms, he heard his name from the other side of the wall. He started to respond, then realized Justine was not talking to him, but about him.

"I can't believe you actually thought Andi would be interested in someone like him," she giggled. "I mean, I'd take him in a half-second, but you just know how high he ranks on that eternal companion checklist of hers."

"But he's gorgeous," an unfamiliar female voice responded, "and he's rich and famous and—"

"And Andi isn't impressed by any of those things. She's always had her heart set on Sterling. He's everything she wants in a man. They're probably making wedding plans right now."

"Sterling isn't jealous?"

"Of course not. He knows Greg Howland is just Andi's latest fellow-shipping project. She's been doing this kind of thing forever, you know."

Greg stood motionless behind the wall, waiting for Justine and her companion to move away. He looked up into the sky, but thick clouds obscured the stars and a cold breeze stung his eyes. He closed them as he lowered his head, thinking of the rope and thread in Justine's lesson. Life, he thought, seemed to stretch on forever. Eternity was incomprehensible.

Andi walked with Sterling across the bridge from the playground, still holding the damp cloth to her cheek. It felt good against the hot flush of her skin. She gnawed her lower lip for composure as Greg strode across the parking lot to meet them.

"Are you okay?" he asked, bending forward for a better look at her face.

"It's nothing. I wasn't paying attention and the volleyball hit me."

"I've taken care of her," Sterling said, tightening a possessive arm around Andi's waist.

Andi flinched, but didn't pull away as her eyes searched Greg's face. The lines around his eyes were deep and his jaw seemed carved from stone. Her heart leapt. Was he jealous? She said, "Excuse us a minute, Sterling."

The young man hesitated.

"I won't keep her long," Greg said quietly. "I was looking for the two of you to tell you I'm leaving."

"I'll be right over there," Sterling said as he gave Andi a reassuring squeeze.

Andi watched him retreat to a nearby bench, then lowered her voice as she turned to Greg. "You're leaving? Do you have another date tonight?"

"Another?" Greg asked sardonically. "As I recall, I didn't have a first one. I seem to have spent all my recent free time with a Sunday school teacher."

"Is that what Jacy Grayson does?"

Greg raised an eyebrow. "Slow news day in Phoenix, huh?"

"I thought you didn't know her."

"I don't. Didn't. My publicist arranged this breakfast thing yesterday . . . "

"You don't owe me an explanation."

"You're right, Andi. I don't." Greg crossed his arms and leaned back against the stone wall of the bridge. "I don't know what I do owe you, though. I've never been anyone's reform project before."

"Reform project? Is that what you think I want? To convert you?"

"Every woman I meet wants something," Greg said levelly. "Money, publicity, something. But you're the first who's actually gone after my soul."

The look of shock and indignation on Andi's face gave Greg a moment's hope. Maybe Justine was wrong. Could Andi possibly have come to love him, too? His voice softened and his face became earnest. "That's what this has been to you, hasn't it? What do you call it? Fellowshipping?"

Andi hesitated, her anger swept away by a wave of uncertainty. When she lowered the towel from her cheek, the charm bracelet tinkled gently against her wrist. She covered it with her other hand and lowered her eyes. She couldn't lie to him, and wasn't that exactly what she'd called it, at least at first? What would she call it now? "When we first met I felt sorry for you," she began. "You'd just lost your brother and—"

"Thanks for your pity, Andi, but I don't need it. I do a pretty good job of feeling sorry for myself."

Andi's heart sank. This wasn't coming out right at all. "Greg, you're a nice guy . . . "

"But?"

She shook her head and forced back the tears. *But what about Jacy Grayson?* she thought. *I love you, Greg. But you're leaving me. But . . .*

"Let me help you out here," he said. "As far as eternal-companion material goes, on a scale of one to ten, I'm a negative four." Greg smiled ruefully when she glanced up in surprise, the truthfulness clear on her face. "Don't worry about it, Andi. You can't save the whole world. You go back to Elder Charming over there, and I'll go back to Chicago." He shrugged. "At least the alligators got something out of the deal."

As he turned away, Andi gripped her wrist tighter to keep from reaching after him, pressing the charms deep into her flesh. The marks they would leave, she knew, would fade quickly. Unfortunately, the impression left on her heart by all they represented could well have the staying power of the Hohokam's remarkable canals.

Andi watched Greg walk away before turning back to Sterling. It was for the best, the reasonable voice assured her. It had been right about both men all along. She never should have ignored it to listen to her heart.

CHAPTER 32

Small drops of a light, unpredicted spring shower beaded on the leather seats and speckled the windshield of the convertible as it sped along the city streets. Greg saw the rain reflected in the twin beams of headlight before he felt it on his skin. He reached automatically for the button to raise the top, but returned his hand to the wheel before completing the task. The cold drizzle seemed appropriate as he drove aimlessly and perhaps a little carelessly, with no destination in mind.

The thin whine of the cell phone, almost lost under the volume of the radio, puzzled him at first. Finally, Greg recognized the sound and responded to it, holding it away from his ear at the sudden burst of expletives. "Mr. Biderman?"

"Where are you, Howland?"

Greg slowed as he looked for a street sign, a familiar landmark, anything to get his bearings. "I don't know . . . " He winced at the new stream of profanity and clicked off the blaring radio. "I mean, I'm in my car, sir."

"I want you in my office."

"Tonight?"

"Right now," the manager barked. "Fifteen minutes and no excuses."

"Yes, sir."

The ten minutes it took Greg to make it into the lot at the darkened team complex wasn't time enough to figure out what he might have done to pull down the wrath of the Cubs management. He hadn't been on rotation to pitch since Saturday, but those few innings had been great and his practice stats looked good. He knew they wouldn't care about the Jacy Grayson thing, but maybe they had heard he was at the Children's Hospital and were sore that he hadn't used it for PR. He faced the forbidding building reluctantly as he climbed from the car. Surely they weren't sore enough to dress him down at this time of night.

A security guard swung open the glass door at his approach, and Greg followed him wordlessly to the entrance of Biderman's office. The murderous look on the manager's face reminded Greg, for a moment, of his father, and he took an involuntary step backwards. Then he swallowed hard and entered the office. "Yes, sir?"

"Where have you been all day, Howland?"

"I, uh, ran an errand before the game this morning. Late this afternoon, I had an appointment and—"

"You had an appointment with public relations this morning, but you didn't show."

Sharon. Greg rubbed his forehead. "I'm sorry, sir. I forgot."

The manager's face was mottled with rage. Greg's eyes grew wide. He had a hard time believing this was about one lousy ten-minute meeting. "You forgot? What did you remember to do instead?"

Greg advanced cautiously into the room until he stood by the chair in front of Biderman's desk. He didn't dare sit without an invitation, but grasped the back for support. "I, uh, went shopping."

Biderman was interested. "Shopping? For what?"

Greg's fingers kneaded the back of the chair nervously. He felt foolish. "For, er, dishes. And I bought a bracelet."

"And?"

"And?" He searched his memory. "Uh, well, apple juice."

"Apple juice?"

"Yes . . ."

"Apple juice." Biderman leaned forward, his elbows on the desk. "Drink it at the stadium tonight?"

"Yes, sir," Greg said slowly. This was getting stranger by the moment. It wasn't about the hospital, or the missed appointment, but he still couldn't imagine what it might be about. "I, uh, took a date there for a picnic dinner." Were there rules against that?

"And then you went back for something you left in the locker room."

Greg frowned in confusion. "No, sir. I didn't leave anything I needed in my locker. We never left the stands."

The crash of Biderman's fist onto the desk caused Greg to jump. His fingers dug into the vinyl chair.

"That's it, Howland!" the manager bellowed. "It's over. I know all about you. I've half a mind to throw you off the team tonight."

Now, even without an invitation, Greg pulled the chair back and sank into it. "What? Why?"

Biderman lowered his voice with effort. "It's not so much the drugs, even. It's that you sat right there and lied to me."

"Lied? Drugs?" *This is a nightmare,* Greg realized suddenly. *It's just another one of those screwy dreams I've been having. In a minute I'll wake up and this whole rotten evening will never have happened.* He wondered if there was anything to that notion of pinching yourself awake.

"A guy from the cleaning crew found the stuff in your locker." Biderman was saying. "He turned it over to security and they called me."

Why can't I wake up? "There's some mistake . . . "

Biderman opened his drawer. "So, you're saying you've never seen this before?"

Greg stared at the small cellophane packet in the manager's hand. He couldn't look away or meet Biderman's eye. He'd seen it all right, a week ago to the day. His voice was flat. "That was in my locker?"

"This was in your room." The manager withdrew another packet from the drawer. "This was in your locker."

Now Greg's eyes met Biderman's in surprise. "My room? That's impossible. How could it have . . . ?" His voice trailed off. *Friday night. So that's what Zeke was doing there.* Greg tried to think. He couldn't tell Biderman about Zeke without telling him about Jim as well. It was a no-win situation, no matter what he said. He shook his head and mumbled, for what it was worth, "Mr. Biderman, I've never taken drugs in my life. I give you my word."

"Under the circumstances, Howland, your word isn't worth spit." He rolled back in his chair and regarded Greg contemptuously. "I've got a medical technician waiting for you in the clinic right now. The guard'll take you down for the test."

Greg let out a deep breath, maybe the first he'd taken since he entered the room. *A drug test. Of course.* "That's great."

"I'm telling you, Greg, if there's so much as a trace of baby aspirin in you, you're out of here for good."

Greg needed the support of the chair to stand. "Yes, sir. Thank you, Mr. Biderman."

"Either way, this isn't over. Now get out of my office. I'm sick of looking at you."

The drizzle had become a downpour by the time Greg left the clinic to walk slowly around the complex toward his car. The young pitcher hardly noticed. Nor did he look over when a long, black Lincoln pulled up beside him.

The passenger window hissed slowly down. From within the smoky interior, Zeke removed one hand from the wheel to wave him in. "Need a lift?"

Greg ignored him and kept walking, but the sleek town car matched his pace. Finally he whirled, grabbed the handle, and yanked open the door.

When he was inside, Zeke rolled to a stop. "Hey, Grego. How's tricks? Great deal with Jacy. I told you she's all girl."

"I should strangle you, Zeke. What in the world do you think you're doing?"

Zeke's thin, cashmere-clad shoulders shrugged languidly. "Just taking out a little extra insurance, kid."

"Insurance? You're crazy."

"Crazy like a fox, maybe. You and me need to talk business."

Greg ran the back of his arm over his face and hair to clear the dripping water from his eyes. It did little good. "I know your kind of business and I don't want any part of it."

"You don't know what we're gonna do about the games now that Jim's gone." Zeke smoothed his sideburns. "The way I see it, we can do a little better than predict the scores this season. You know what I mean?"

Greg did. His right hand gripped the handle of the door. Before he could figure out how to unlock it, Zeke reached for the sleeve of his jacket and continued, "You know, kid, this time the white stuff was nice and safe. A little slap on the wrist and it's all over. They aren't gonna ax their precious golden goose." Zeke leaned nearer and Greg turned away. "But next time, Grego, what if it was in your car, or your bag, or even in your pocket? Not so private-like, you know? And what if the cops happened to be the ones to find out about it first? Then your handsome mug wouldn't just be all over the papers. It'd be on the police blotter, too."

Greg watched the rain wash over the dark windshield, distorting the images of everything outside Zeke's warm car. *He can probably do it.* He'd been in his room and even managed to plant the stuff in his locker. Greg took his hand from the door handle and leaned back in the plush seat, willing himself to play it cool. The face he turned to Martoni was more composed than he felt. "What about your golden eggs, Zeke? You willing to give up your cut so easy?"

"It's only money, kid, and I'll always have sources. You're the one with everything to lose here—career, reputation," he paused meaningfully, "freedom. Possession's a crime in all fifty states, Grego." He smiled, satisfied now that he would close his most profitable venture to date.

Greg's gaze settled in his lap as he considered his options and came to rest on the bright, silver band between the knuckles of his little finger. *Why does choosing the right come so natural for a guy like Nephi and so hard for me?* Greg wished for a moment that the Spirit would—what was the word?—'constrain' him to kill this man a la Laban. *No such luck.* Then what *would* the Spirit have him do?

Zeke watched with interest as Greg closed his eyes and lowered his head. Lighting a congratulatory cigar, Zeke inhaled comfortably and breathed out the blue smoke. It had been a while. What was the kid doing, anyway?

Finally, confident now of the promptings of the Spirit, Greg raised his chin. "Let me get this straight, Zeke. You want me to fix games?"

"Just a few, Grego—a couple, even."

Greg nodded his understanding. "I don't think so."

Zeke's eyebrows rose in surprise, the thin French cigar forgotten between his thumb and fingers. "Maybe you don't get me, kid . . ."

"I understand you fine." Greg's voice was even, his gaze level, and there was something in his eyes Zeke had never seen before. "I've had it, Martoni," he said. "I'm finally doing what I should have done the first night I saw you." Greg pushed open the door and swung his feet onto the wet pavement. "Forget the ride. It's such nice weather, I think I'll walk."

Zeke's eyes were slits. "Howland, I'll—"

"Then do it," Greg interrupted. "Take your best shot."

"You'll go to jail, kid."

"That's a heck of a lot better than where I'd end up with you, Zeke."

Martoni flinched at the slam of the door and watched in disbelief as Greg disappeared into the rain. After a few minutes, he stroked his chin and began to consider. What was the kid's game, anyway? Maybe he should have offered him a cut.

It would never occur to Zeke that he couldn't understand Greg. In his book, virtue was nothing but a cardboard cutout that a coward stood behind to hide his lack of opportunity. He took a long pull from the cigar and considered the glowing tip. Even if he'd lost Howland tonight, it was a temporary setback. If he gave the kid time to think, he'd come to his senses soon enough. Every man has a price: greed, fear, something. Zeke hadn't nailed Greg's down yet, but he would.

He blew smoke rings at the ceiling, remembering the redhead in the pictures. He'd call that worthless detective, he decided. Maybe Simpson had found a way to up the ante. Howland wasn't off the hook yet. Not by a long shot.

CHAPTER 33

If not for the rather snide note in the hotel manager's voice, Greg might have ignored his call and told him to send the girl away. She was, after all, a little more than he felt he could face right now.

He consulted the clock on the nightstand and was surprised to see that it was only eight a.m. He would have sworn it was closer to noon. Rubbing a hand across his unshaved cheek, Greg sighed. It had been a long night and promised to be a longer day. He had already spent the hours since dawn flipping from one morning show to the next, wondering how long it would take Zeke to get the tapes he had of Jim on national TV.

Now he tossed down the remote, picked up the phone, and dialed the Eat Inn. He couldn't leave Clytie standing at the front desk all morning. Relieved when Lupe agreed to take Clytie into a private dining room, Greg dressed quickly, grabbed his sunglasses and a hat, and loped across the parking lot to the restaurant.

Lupe met him at the door. "I put her in the Saguaro Room, *mi jo. No está occupado.*"

"If that means it's empty, Lu, thanks. Things are crazy enough right now without a scene."

"You come to my house for dinner tonight," she said, patting his hand. "We're having enchiladas. That will make life better."

They'd have to be some enchiladas, Greg thought, to improve *his* life much right now. He said, "Yeah, well, we'll see, okay? But thanks for taking care of Clytie for me. Are you sure you can get away long enough to drive her home?"

"*No problemo*," Lupe assured him, leading the way to a private banquet hall at the rear of the restaurant.

"I don't know what I'd do without you, Lu."

"This little girl, surely she is not the Mormon you've been seeing?"

"Her sister."

Lupe patted his shoulder as she pulled open the heavy door. "I am ready to go whenever you say. "

Clytie's face lit up when Greg entered the empty room, but the light faded as he strode over to pull up a chair across the table from hers. Any thought of an enthusiastic greeting faded as well. At the look on his face, the most she could manage was a meek, "Hi, Greg."

"Clytie, what do you think you're doing here?"

"I just had to see you before you leave Arizona," she replied, her eyes beginning to mist. "I had to! I'm sorry you're mad, though. I guess you don't want anyone to see you with me."

Greg ran a hand across his face, his annoyance with Clytie all but forgotten in his anger at himself. "No, Clytie. That's not it at all. It's . . . " He reached across the table to take her tiny hand. "Look, I'm sorry. I just said it wrong, okay? I meant to ask how you got here. Did your mother drive you?"

"No. I came on the bus."

"The bus?" Greg couldn't imagine how she could climb the steep stairs.

Her aqua eyes were defiant. "You think I can't take care of myself because I'm a little person."

"No, Clytie," he said, grasping her hand more firmly. "I think you have more courage than I'll ever have."

"I don't care what people think about me," she insisted. "They can whisper and stare all they want. It's what's inside you that counts."

"Is it really possible not to care what anybody thinks?" Greg needed an answer to that question above all else right now and hoped this remarkable young woman could help him.

She lowered her eyes. "I guess not, not really. But everyone's opinion shouldn't count the same. The Savior's counts the most and, after that, the people you love and admire."

"I'm afraid some people I love and admire, people like you, Clytie, are going to be thinking some pretty bad things about me soon, no matter what I do."

"Not me, Greg," she declared loyally, her blonde head shaking vigorously to emphasize her words. "I think you're perfect!"

He released her hand. "I'm a long way from perfect."

"You'll be perfect when you're baptized."

Greg picked up a spoon in the silence that followed. "I thought about that all last night," he said, slowly turning the utensil over in his hand. "I was afraid that my feelings for your sister were what were bringing me toward the Church, but now that I know where I stand with Andi, I can be sure it's more than that." He held up a hand to halt her eager reply and looked away from her bright, hopeful face. "But I can't be baptized, Clytie. I can't have anything to do with the Church, even, unless I can get through this other thing."

"The Lord understands. He'll forgive you."

"I know. But He'll be the only one who does." He tapped the spoon on the tablecloth and avoided her eyes. "Things will at least look bad, and I don't want any of that to reflect on the things I really care about."

"I don't understand."

"I know and I can't explain right now. But try to believe in me, okay? Even when nobody else does? Knowing that you still had faith would help me a whole lot."

"I promise, Greg."

He smiled at her fondly, then consulted his watch. "Should you be in school?"

"Yes, but—"

"Your parents don't know you're here, do they?"

"No, but—"

"Clytie, that was really dumb. Even when you mean well, you still need to think things through before you do them. It isn't safe to run off this way. You could have been hurt. It was unreasonable to—"

"You sound like Andi."

Greg's jaw tightened, but he was determined to finish the lecture. "Listen, Clytie, you don't understand—"

"*You* don't understand," she insisted, raising her chin. "I had to come. I thought you loved Andi."

Greg tossed the spoon away in frustration, his lecture forgotten.

"She says you don't," Clytie continued quickly. "She says she doesn't mean anything to you—that you date dozens of girls at the same time."

"Clytie, despite what your sister may have heard, I haven't dated dozens of girls in my whole life."

"Do you love Andi?"

"That's none of your business."

"It is! It's my fault Andi fell in love with you. And you made her cry all night." Clytie's marine eyes filled with tears themselves and threatened to overflow.

"I . . . ?" Greg tried to ignore Clytie's tears and the sudden tightness in his chest. "Now you're sounding like Darlene," he said quietly. "If Andi's upset, I'm sorry. I probably was kind of rude. But Clytie, I promise you, you're wrong about the other. I'm no answer to your sister's prayers."

"No, you're the answer to mine. For her."

Greg raised an eyebrow. This made no sense.

"Sterling was coming home," Clytie explained between sobs and gulps of air, "and I didn't want Andi to marry him just because of her stupid checklist. I thought she should spend eternity with someone she really loves, so I asked God to please send her a soulmate. He sent you."

"Clytie, I don't know . . . " Greg's thoughts shifted to the bridge at the zoo. When he spoke, it was more to himself. "But I'm the one who prayed."

"I know God answered my prayer, Greg. Did He answer yours?" She looked searchingly into his eyes. "He did! You do love Andi!"

Greg stared back at her in alarm. Within days, if not hours, Zeke would vilify him coast to coast—or worse. He couldn't let any of that touch Andi. "No, Clytie. You're wrong."

"I don't believe you."

"Well, it's true," he lied. "Andi doesn't mean anything to me. I'm going back to Chicago after the game tomorrow."

"But why? Greg, what's wrong?"

"Remember how you were going to trust me, no matter what?"

"But—"

"You promised. We have to leave it, and the thing with Andi, at that. Someday soon, I think you'll understand. Now, the lady who brought you in here is going to drive you home, okay?"

Clytie nodded slowly as Greg rose from the table. *There isn't any more to say*, he thought as he walked away, *but good-bye, and I don't think I can manage that.* At the door he turned, in spite of himself. "Look, Clytie, I don't know how to tell you how special you are to me . . . " Before he could finish, she was out of her chair, running toward him. He knelt to embrace her and kissed the top of her head. "Thanks for coming today, Clytie. Thanks for everything."

The face that stared back at Andi from the polished surface of her vanity mirror resembled dull marble. She reached for a blusher to add color, but the effort seemed too great, so she let the hand fall. It landed atop the blue ball cap in her lap. Greg's hat.

Soulmates, Clytie had called them last night. The idea was romantic . . . and ridiculous. She and Greg Howland had nothing in common. He didn't love her and she . . . what? She wouldn't even think about him, she decided. If only the not thinking wouldn't require so much effort in itself.

Andi heard her father in the hall. She rode with him to the university on Tuesdays and Thursdays, and they always left before nine. It must be later than that now. She tossed the hat under the vanity and picked up her backpack as her dad rapped on the door.

"Okay, Dad. I'm ready."

He opened the door. "Are you feeling well, sweetheart? We missed you at breakfast."

"I'm fine. I overslept, I guess. Sorry I missed scriptures."

"Your mother said not to wake you." He studied her pale face with concern and wanted to cheer her up. "You must have had some time setting Howland straight last night."

"What?"

"Sterling stayed to tell me about it after you went upstairs. He said you sent that young man packing."

"Oh?" Andi wondered what she might have said to Sterling after Greg left her at the park. She could remember agreeing to dinner at his house tonight. Her only other memory was of complaining of a volleyball-induced headache and asking to be brought home.

"He also asked for my blessing."

"Blessing?"

"Ariadne, are you sure you're feeling well? You're not yourself this morning."

"I'm fine, Dad. Go start the car. I'll be right down." When he hesitated, Andi forced a smile. "I'll only be a minute, I promise."

Blessing? she turned to ask the face in the glass as her father left the room. *Marrying Sterling would be a blessing, wouldn't it?* Andi looked away from the haunted green eyes. *Of course it would.* If she had a soulmate, it would have to be Sterling Channing; they were so much alike.

Andi flipped her hair over her shoulder as she left the room. She was fine. She loved Sterling. She'd tell him so tonight at dinner. Planning her wedding would surely put any silly thoughts of a certain ballplayer out of her mind for good.

In the hallway, she approached her grandmother's antique mirror at the head of the stairs. Pausing for just another moment, she put on her most confident look for the marble-faced young woman behind the wavy glass. *This is what I want,* she told her. *Everything is working out just the way I planned.* Anxious to leave the doubtful countenance behind, Andi descended the stairs rapidly. But she was fine, she assured herself. *Just fine, thank you.*

Greg climbed the stairs to his room, turning the conversation with Clytie over in his mind and wondering if he felt better or worse about Andi in light of all she had said. *Soulmates?* That had to be the runaway imagination of a romantic teenager, right? Except why, then, had he loved Andi before even asking her name? *If I prayed,* he thought, *and Clytie prayed . . .* He shook his head impatiently. It was a moot point. He had no future with Ariadne Reynolds. Most likely, he had no future, period.

He heard the phone ring from outside the door, fumbled with the key, and dashed to grab the receiver before Biderman hung up. The high-pitched voice on the line surprised him, and Greg had trouble, for a minute, placing it.

"Bobbie Jo?" His sister-in-law was in the middle of a long dissertation on who-knew-what. Greg interrupted to save himself the trouble of trying to figure it out. "Are the boys okay?"

There was a long pause. "Why do you always ask me that?"

"Then nothing's wrong?"

"Nothing except I saw your mother in town this morning."

Greg gripped the phone as his heart contracted into a hard knot. He had worried that the day would come that his father would turn on her. He couldn't speak.

"She told me," Bobbie Jo continued, "that you called her Monday morning."

"Is that what started it?"

"Started what?" Bobbie Jo's voice rose. "She told me about that girl you think you're in love with."

"What?"

"That girl, Greg. Who is she?"

"Bobbie Jo, is my mother all right?"

"This isn't about your mother. It's about us."

Greg counted slowly to ten, then fifteen, before responding. "My mother's okay, then?"

"Your mother's the same as always, Greg, if that's what you call okay. Now, what about this girl? I'm coming out there."

"There isn't any girl," Greg said, sinking onto the bed in relief, "and I won't be here. I've got a flight to Chicago tomorrow night. I'll call you from there."

"I'll meet you—"

"No, I'll call." He sighed as Bobbie Jo began another soliloquy. Right now, a nice, quiet jail cell somewhere away from her seemed appealing, and he was pretty sure Zeke could arrange it for him. Greg lay on his back and stared at the flecks in the ceiling as Bobbie Jo droned on and on about the difficulties of caring for Jim's two boys and Greg's failures as an uncle. *What don't you like about me?* he asked the faux stars. *Did I cut classes in premortality? Play Frisbee with the halos? What?*

At the first pause, Greg cut his sister-in-law off with another promise to call from Chicago and dropped the receiver onto the cradle. The phone rang again almost immediately. "Look, Bobbie Jo. This has got to stop."

"Howland?"

"Oh, uh, yeah. Sorry." Listening to the manager, Greg was almost surprised to hear the negative results of his drug test. *Zeke must not be omnipotent, after all.* He picked up his keys from the nightstand and headed for the door. He had at least one more day at the ballpark and just twenty minutes to get there.

CHAPTER 34

It was nearing sunset when the Cubs returned from Peoria to the HoHoKam facilities in Mesa, and after eight before Biderman concluded the meetings. Greg had had a long day warming up his arm for tomorrow's closer and signing autographs ad infinitum. As he pulled out of the players' lot, he considered heading straight to his hotel after all. He was tired from too little sleep, too much thinking about Andi, and the constant strain of waiting for the next shoe to drop. Still, he decided, he couldn't face the four generic walls of his room again until he was ready to drop himself.

He would have liked to stop by Lupe's house for the promised enchiladas, but knew it would already be bedtime for a woman whose shift began before five the next day. He opted, instead, for a fast-food burger in a city park. It was dark by now, which should at least insure semi-privacy.

After a quick stop at McDonald's, Greg headed down Main Street and pulled into the front parking area at Pioneer Park, across the street from the temple. It had been in the back of his mind all day. This was the last chance he'd have to look at the pearly walls and decide for sure if the feelings he had had Sunday night were prompted by the spirit of the evening or the Spirit of God.

Greg stepped out of the car and pulled out his bag of food and Book of Mormon. Surveying the park, he chose a spot not far from an outdoor lamp where he could sit anonymously, he hoped, to read the scriptures and ponder the temple through a break in the trees. On his way over, he spit his gum into a napkin and looked for a place to toss it. His arrival at the round, metal receptacle coincided with that of a homeless man.

The old man's shoulders were hunched forward, one gnarled fist shoved into the pocket of twine-belted jeans that were several sizes too large. "These cans is mine," he mumbled, snaking the other thin arm into the open hole and eyeing Greg with hostility.

The young pitcher stepped back awkwardly as the vagrant fished through the trash. He noticed the holes in the man's filthy sweater and speculated on the color it might have been years before. Then he considered the man wearing it. A hoary beard fell in straggly wisps, almost to his waist, from a face that was haggard and wary. Greg's eyes followed the pattern of lines crisscrossing the leathery forehead and cheeks, and wished he could read that particular road map. Surely the deep wrinkles traced a route from childhood through whatever there might once have been of accomplishment, down lonely roads of disappointment and ultimate despair. For the map to lead here, a waystation obviously near the end of mortality, what false signs had there been along the way?

Greg's expression was grim. He had been poor, certainly, but never so poor as this. He couldn't remember the last time he was genuinely hungry—or any night he had slept on the ground without another choice. *Who considers this man's hopes and happiness?* Greg wondered. *Surely everything he wants from life can't be found at the bottom of a trash can.*

Apparently, the old man could scavenge only two pieces of aluminum worth saving. Cursing his luck, he ambled on without a word. Quickly, Greg pulled the bills from his wallet, stuck them in the food bag, and hurried to catch up. "Uh, here. I can't eat this," he said honestly, extending the sack. There was an empty feeling in his stomach, but it wasn't from hunger any longer.

The man's rheumy eyes narrowed suspiciously, but he grabbed the bag with a grunt of acknowledgment and took it unsteadily toward a nearby table. There, Greg observed a younger companion standing guard over their territory. All the worldly possessions the pair had amassed were crammed into a three-wheeled shopping cart. A mangy black dog lifted its head expectantly at the smell of food and beat the grass with a matted tail. The older man lowered himself painfully to the ground and opened the bag. He looked with disbelief at the money then, spurred by the greater immediacy of an empty stomach, stuffed it into his shirt and began to carefully divide his bounty with his two friends. Greg turned away as a park ranger approached.

"You're not supposed to do that," the uniformed man said.

Greg looked down at his feet for a "keep off the grass" sign. "What?"

"Give those homeless guys food."

"Maybe if you posted a 'please don't feed the residents' sign like they do at the zoo . . . "

"Just don't do it. It encourages them."

"That was the general idea."

"Look, smart aleck," the ranger said, poking a finger against Greg's chest, "this is a family park. We don't want them here. Understand?"

"Yeah," Greg said, glad when the man returned to his patrol car. His gaze wandered back to the trio beneath the tree. *Where do we want them?* Shivering, he zipped up his jacket as the soft night air seemed to suddenly turn cool.

"Let's take dessert out to the patio," Andi suggested. Though it was just the two of them, the Channing's spacious dining room seemed close and claustrophobic.

"It's much nicer, inside," Sterling pointed out. "Besides, this dish is crystal." He sank a silver spoon into his chocolate mousse, the grand finale of a dinner it had taken his mother the better part of two days to prepare. "My parents plan to give it to us when we're married. We shouldn't risk breaking it."

Andi shook her head and gazed at her own stemware, her mind replaying pictures of the goblet she'd broken the night before when she'd impulsively kissed Greg. He'd said that piece of crystal didn't matter, and it hadn't seemed to at the time. Nothing had mattered then but the shivering current Greg's lips sent through hers and how perfectly her head fit into the hollow between his shoulder and neck as they gazed out onto the field and spoke softly of nothing.

Suddenly, Andi wished for the broken glass back; it and her fork and the pretty china plate that looked so fragile in Greg's strong hand. She felt the beginning of tears and blinked rapidly. She was being foolish. She loved Sterling.

"Hold my hand," Andi said, stretching her arm across the crocheted-lace tablecloth. Puzzled, Sterling reached for it and she held on tight. "Do you feel anything?"

"Your fingers," he said slowly, with the beginning of a frown. "They're warm."

"No, yours are cold."

"I've been holding this cold glass." Sterling released her hand. "Andi, what is this about?"

"Are you in love with me?"

"I plan to marry you."

"Why?" His eyes, Andi noted, were definitely brown and carried a hint of annoyance.

"Because that's the Lord's plan, isn't it? A year of college, then a mission and temple marriage. If you think it might be more sensible to wait until we've both finished school, I agree. On the other hand, President Kimball taught—"

"But *why*, Sterling?" Andi interrupted. "Why do you want to marry *me*?"

Sterling's displeasure at her nonsense was thinly veiled behind patiently upturned lips. "Because we're alike, Andi. You're from a good family, you're committed to the gospel, and you know what you want. What better reason could there be?"

He was, Andi knew, borrowing from her list. But what had he said about there not being a better reason? Her mind drifted again to the evening before . . . and the cryptic message she had found in her fortune cookie which had haunted her ever since. "'The heart has its reasons that reason knows nothing of,'" she quoted.

"What?"

"That's what my fortune cookie said last night."

"Fortune cookie?" The strained smile disappeared and Sterling frowned in earnest. "What does that silly fortune have to do with us?"

Andi thought it through carefully. *The heart has its reasons that reason knows nothing of.* The eyes she raised to Sterling reflected a light apart from the glow of his mother's candles. "It has nothing to do with us, Sterling," she decided with a smile. "Absolutely nothing."

CHAPTER 35

Greg closed his Book of Mormon, leaned back against the rough bark of the palm tree, and stretched his legs out of the small pool of light onto the grass. It was almost nine o'clock. The traffic on Main Street had thinned, making it easier to see across the street into the glass-fronted visitors' center at the temple. It had been busy there throughout the evening. Each time Greg glanced up from his book, there were people gathered before the velvety blue curtains. He had considered going over himself, to see what was behind the drapery if nothing else, but was dissuaded by the constant crowds.

Now he yawned and rubbed his eyes, deciding finally to call it a night. His career could depend on how well he pitched in tomorrow's game. Well, that and Zeke. Greg pulled up his knees, but before he could rise, a shadow fell across them. He looked up in surprise. The man standing over him was fair, nondescript, and somehow familiar.

"Have we met?" Greg asked.

"We haven't had the pleasure, Mr. Howland."

"You look familiar . . . "

"Probably hundreds of guys around look like me."

Greg nodded slowly. There was something in the man's eyes that belied his harmless appearance. Uneasy, he started to stand but froze as the man reached into his coat. *Great,* Greg thought. *They've only warned me a hundred times about the crazies.*

The man withdrew a manila envelope. "I've got a delivery for you from Mr. Martoni. He said you'll know what it's about. He'll meet you at noon tomorrow in the locker room for your answer."

Greg tore open the envelope and flipped through the pictures in stunned silence. When he finally looked up, minutes later, the man was gone. He stared back into his lap in disbelief. The photos were of him and Clytie: on the temple grounds with his hand on her shoulder; the brief kiss she gave him that night outside her home; riding together in his car; Clytie in front of his hotel this morning; Clytie in his arms. He checked this one closer, but it seemed authentic. Still, he was sure it hadn't happened. He had never . . . then he remembered. When Clytie tripped on the stairs Sunday night, he had caught her before she fell. They had looked this way for two-three seconds, tops. Greg scanned the park, but the man was nowhere in sight. The guy was good.

He dropped the pictures into his lap and tried to swallow, but a dry taste, like that of stale pretzels, had seemed to adhere his tongue to the roof of his mouth. He leaned his head back against the tree and gazed up into the sky. The night was several shades darker now, but the stars had withdrawn. They were distant, cool, and seemingly as artificial as the flecks on his hotel ceiling. Greg leafed through the photos again then, sickened, shoved them back into the envelope. The Book of Mormon slid from his lap, opening to where he had left off reading: "I pray that ye should awake to a remembrance of the awful situation of those that have fallen into transgression . . . "

Then I'm in trouble, Greg thought. *It's damnation with the N this time.*

His gaze traveled back across the street to the visitors' center, and he sat up straighter as the curtains opened, revealing an alabaster statue of Jesus Christ. Even from such a distance, Greg thought he could see the nail prints in the palms of his hands.

Keep the commandments.

Minutes passed as Greg stared fixedly at the Christus. "How?" he demanded aloud. "How?" Doing what Martoni demanded would require him to lie, cheat, and steal—at the very least. But refusing to do so would expose Clytie to national ridicule. Despite the ice creeping slowly into his veins at the prospect, Greg knew he'd take his chances with Zeke before he would ever hurt Clytie.

Keep the commandments.

"I took your advice last night with Zeke, remember?" Greg told the still, small voice. "Look where it got me." He closed the blue paperback impatiently and rose to his feet, grasping the book of scripture firmly with his fingertips. It wouldn't be much of a challenge to pitch it into the garbage can from here. *Maybe that homeless guy will get more out of this than I did.*

Greg had just lifted his arm, when he had a thought. Thumbing through the first few pages of 1 Nephi, he found what he was looking for. The child with the stickers and crayons had boxed it in years before: "I will go and do the things which the Lord has commanded me, for I know that the Lord giveth no commandment unto the children of men, save he prepares a way for them to accomplish the thing which he hath commanded them."

Pressing the book to his chest, Greg gazed intently across the street. "How?" he asked, quietly this time, as he pondered the distant figure of Christ. "Lord, how?" The outstretched arms seemed to beckon and suddenly Greg had an idea.

Another quick scan of the park failed to turn up the transparent messenger, but Greg knew it was a safe call he hadn't gone far. He'd need to execute this next play carefully. He tucked the Book of Mormon and the pictures firmly inside his jacket and walked casually toward the parking lot. There he opened his car door slowly, giving the guy plenty of time to assume they were leaving and get in his own car—wherever the heck it was. Then Greg slammed the door and darted from the empty lot into the street.

At least the last six weeks of wind sprints were good for something, he thought when the first truck missed him narrowly. He raced across the four lanes of traffic and onto the wide lawn in front of the visitors' center. The shadow probably saw him, but he certainly couldn't have followed very discreetly—or very fast.

Greg bounded across the grass, rounded the corner of the building, and leaned for a minute against the pebbled wall to catch his breath. Though the light was on inside, the door was locked and the center was empty. He rapped once on the glass door before turning away in frustration. Of all the times for this to happen, it would have to be on the one day he was in too great of a rush to grab his cell phone.

As Greg considered his rapidly dwindling options, a small group of patrons came down the stairs from the temple grounds to stroll through the gardens on their way to the parking lot. Greg looked up at the white temple walls. Did the House of the Lord ever close?

He forced himself to slow to a walk as he approached the front of the building. A nicely dressed couple carrying garment bags emerged from a revolving door and cast him a disapproving glance. Greg hesitated, looking down at his blue jeans in despair. He couldn't barge into such a holy place dressed like this. Or could he?

This wasn't exactly my idea in the first place, he reasoned. With a quick, uneasy glance over his shoulder, he took the wide steps two at a time and pushed firmly against the door. The tinted glass swung easily inward.

Inside, Greg caught his breath. He was in the House of the Lord. He looked around the quiet reception area in surprise. Except for the large paintings of Christ, it resembled nothing more than the lobby of a small, upscale hotel. *What did you expect?* he asked himself ruefully. *Harp music? Clouds? A throne, maybe?*

A matched pair of men in white suits stood behind the ornate, V-shaped desk. The shorter of the two smiled kindly. "May we help you?"

"Uh, maybe," Greg said, approaching them pessimistically. *What would the Lord need with a telephone, anyway? This was a stupid idea.* He swallowed. "Do you have a phone I could use, please?"

The worker pointed back the way Greg had come in, and the desperate pitcher feared he was being sent away. But when he turned, there was a telephone on the wall near the corner.

"Dial nine first."

"Thanks a lot." Greg picked up the receiver and pulled a card from inside his wallet. Then he took a deep, calming breath. *God, please let this be the right thing.* He pushed the buttons and waited for an answer. *Please, Father.* On the fifth ring, a deep voice responded.

"Hello?" Greg said anxiously. "Hello. This is Greg Howland and I, well, I need help."

CHAPTER 30

"Do you need any help?" Les asked Andi as she sat motionless in the electric cart on Wednesday morning, staring up into the trees along the Tropics Trail and oblivious to their arrival at the alligator exhibit. When she didn't respond, his gaze followed hers into the foliage but found nothing of particular interest to see. "Andi?"

"Hmm?"

"Do you want any help with your stuff?"

Andi looked at him in surprise. "Help?" She took quick stock of the surroundings with a start. "No, Les, I'm fine." Jumping from the cart, she pulled out her waders and a bucket of supplies. "Thanks for the lift."

"You sure you're okay?"

"Yes, of course."

As Les pulled away, Andi turned slowly toward the habitat. She could hear the mated doves burble in the palms and checked their nest on her way across the bridge. It had been a week ago, she reflected, at about this time, that she'd brought Greg here. She'd been herself then: reasonable, unsentimental Ariadne Reynolds—a young woman with a perfect life and a perfect plan to keep it that way. Why, she'd been practically engaged to the man of her dreams. No, she corrected herself. Sterling was the man of her list. The man of her dreams had adopted all these ungrateful alligators, upset their keeper's careful planning, and left her uncertain of the perfection of a life without him.

So, she wondered, *where is that man now?* When she had come home from dinner last night, definitely not engaged to Sterling

Channing, she'd seen Clytie for the first time that day and heard about the visit she'd had with Greg. Clytie had insisted that Greg loved her and Andi had almost believed it. The talk with her sister gave her enough hope, at least, to call Greg at his hotel last night. She'd called until almost midnight, then once again early this morning. After she convinced the reluctant manager that it was an emergency, he sent someone to knock on Greg's door. Then he informed her that Mr. Howland hadn't been in his room all night.

Since then, Andi had created, and rejected, dozens of explanations for his absence. Some were too improbable for her to believe—others too painful. She opened the top of her pail and wrinkled her nose at the strong smell. Admittedly, the only thing she knew for sure about Greg Howland was that she loved him. Unfortunately, despite what Clytie had said, something was still fishy and it was more than what she'd brought these crocodiles for breakfast.

"What do you mean you lost him?" Zeke hissed into the phone. If someone dared to wake him before nine, it ought to be with better news than this.

"I delivered the pictures and your message, just like you said, Mr. Martoni," Simpson explained quickly. "Last night, about nine o'clock."

"You took 'em to his room?"

"No, he didn't go to his room after the game. He went to a park and read that Mormon Bible for about an hour. I had to wait until nobody was around, then told him just what you said."

"And?"

"He opened up the envelope and turned whiter than the paper those pictures were printed on."

This piece of news, at least, was better. "Then what?"

"He stared at the pictures a while and finally went over to his car. I thought he was gonna get in and leave, so I got ready to follow him. But he just bolted on me. Right out into the street. I saw him go, but by the time I got over there myself, he was gone."

Zeke had little patience under the best of circumstances; this, certainly, was not the best. His voice was as brittle, and cold, as ice. "Where'd he disappear to?"

"Around that Mormon temple somewhere. But, Mr. Martoni, I swear, there was no place to go. The center was locked up and they don't let nobody in the temple."

"He went somewhere."

"I watched his car for a couple of hours, but Howland never went back to get it. It was still in the lot this morning. He didn't ever show up at his room, either." There was a long silence. "What do you want me to do now, Mr. Martoni?"

"You've done enough, you idiot. I'll handle it from here."

Zeke slapped down the phone and passed a hand across his brow as he thought over what he had heard. It wasn't as bad as it seemed, he decided finally. The kid had spooked, is all, and that stupid dolt had lost him. It just showed that you get what you pay for. He thought of Greg and smiled. As stewed up as he'd been about that little song-and-dance with his brother, he'd toe the line quick enough for these pictures. Everything was on track. Howland had gone off somewhere to lick his wounds, no doubt, but he'd have to show at the game today. When he did, Zeke would be waiting.

Greg stood at the door of the deserted locker room, waiting for Zeke. He ran the palms of his hands down his thighs as he drew a deep, measured breath in through his nose, the way Coach Trenzle had taught him years ago. There was an uncomfortable pull as his chest expanded, and he adjusted his jersey uneasily, blowing the air out of his mouth as he counted backwards from ten. There was another pull as his lungs deflated. Under the circumstances, this stress-reduction exercise was worse than useless.

What do you think you're doing? Greg asked himself. *This is crazy. If you blow this thing, it's more than your life down the tubes—it's Clytie's.* The muscles in his jaw tightened. He wouldn't blow it, then. He could do this, for her.

The young pitcher leaned cautiously around the corner. *It must be after noon by now. Where is Martoni, anyway?* The pitching coach thought he was doing closing-day PR and Sharon thought he was in the bullpen warming up, but he couldn't stretch this out much longer without somebody noticing. He had a game in less than thirty minutes. They'd certainly miss him if he didn't take the mound.

Martoni must know what I've done, Greg thought anxiously, bending to retie one of his cleated shoes. *I've got to get out of here and find him, tell him I'll do anything if . . .* Greg rose to find Zeke lounging against the wall. *How does he* do *that?* He pulled himself straighter, grateful at the very least for an advantage in height. "Hello, Zeke."

"Hey, Grego."

It was the same old greeting, Greg thought, but was Martoni less exuberant? Wary even? *He does know.* "You wanted to see me?"

"Where've you been, kid?"

If he knew, would he be here? Greg relaxed a fraction of a degree and said, "I've been around. I'm here now."

"So you got my message?"

"You know I did."

A smile played across Zeke's thin lips as he watched Greg twist the small silver ring on his finger. He smoothed his lacquered hair carefully. "Kinda kinky, Grego, you and the little freak."

Greg's features contorted with shock and anger at Clytie's reduction to a single, hateful word and Zeke's sly innuendo. When he felt the nails dig into his palms, he took a deep breath and slowly, deliberately, flexed his fingers. *You can do this,* he told himself firmly. *You have to.* Still, when he could make himself speak, it was through clenched teeth. "What do you want from me, Martoni?"

"I think you know what I want."

Yeah, but just say it, will you? Greg crossed his arms over his chest then reconsidered and dropped them quickly to his sides. "Where'd you get the pictures?"

"You didn't notice that you had a particularly attentive fan?"

"Is he the same guy you got to put the drugs in my locker?"

"You'll learn, kid, that I've got lots of friends in low places. The coke was just a little lesson to teach you there's no end to what I can do."

"But when it didn't pan out, you went after Clytie?"

"Is that her name? Ugly little thing. The tabloids are gonna have a field day figuring the ways you make it with her."

This time, before he thought, Greg's fist lashed into the smirk on Zeke's face. He watched in shock as Martoni's head fell back, then came slowly forward, cold fury hardening his dark features.

"That'll cost you, Howland."

Greg took a step back. "I'm . . . sorry."

"You will be, kid. I promise you that."

Greg ran his tongue along the back of his teeth, hoping to scrape away some of the sawdust that seemed to be thickening it. *You're blowing this big time,* he thought in despair. *Stay calm and try to remember what they told you to say.* "Look, Zeke, I am sorry. You've got the upper hand here. We both know you can name your price for those negatives. But I don't have much time before the game. Just tell me what you want for them, okay?"

"You better listen careful this time, Howland, 'cause it's the last chance you'll ever get to hear it." Zeke stroked the growing welt under his cheek and regarded Greg narrowly. "I call the shots from here on out. Your little Cubbies are gonna start winning the games I tell 'em to. When I say your pitching's off, it's off, see? I'll tell you just how many runs you can give up a game."

"Who tells you?"

The corner of Zeke's mouth twitched, despite the pain. "You finally catching on, Grego? Brains don't exactly run in your family."

"Someone's got to be jerking your chain, Zeke. You've made a fortune off me already. You don't need me to start throwing games just to get you in good with your bookie."

"You hold up your end, kid, and let me worry about my lodge brothers. We won't hafta stew over your precious career, either. They'll want our boy pitching every World Series for the next ten years." Zeke moved to lay a well-manicured hand on Greg's chest and smiled when the young pitcher pressed his back to the wall. "So, kid, have you got me?"

I hope so, Martoni, Greg thought fervently. He studied the self-satisfied expression on the man's narrow face and inclined his head. "Yeah, Zeke, I think I've got you."

CHAPTER 37

The final strains of "The Star Spangled Banner" and the subsequent roar of the crowd packing Phoenix Municipal Stadium was audible across the street in Harmony Farms, which was located in the southwest corner of the Phoenix Zoo. Andi lay down the goat brush she'd been cleaning to turn toward the sound. Was Greg playing there? she wondered. No. Enos had begged to go to the last Cubs game and she'd learned it was in Mesa. Her father, of course, had sent her sulky little brother to school. Andi wished she had taken off work to go to the game herself.

While her mental video camera replayed footage of Monday's date with Greg at HoHoKam Park, Andi's imagination filled its grandstands with people. They looked together toward the center of the field where Greg was on the mound. She could see his kind, handsome face beneath the blue brim of his cap and watched as he pulled back to pitch, the muscles rippling along his strong arm . . .

"Help! It's killing me!"

The little girl's shriek returned Andi to the zoo in a heartbeat. "I'm sorry, honey," she said, scooping the hysterical child into her arms and away from the goat that was contentedly munching her cardboard name tag.

"He wants to eat me!"

"No, sweetheart, just the paper." Andi looked over the remains of name tag dangling from damp, red yarn around the little girl's neck. "Betty?"

"Bethany. I want my mommy!"

Before Andi could comfort her, the wished-for parent appeared and swept her daughter angrily from Andi's arms and out of the pen.

"Now do you see what you've done?" Andi asked the goat. "They won't be back to see you, I bet." Sudden tears pooled in her eyes despite efforts to blink them back. After her thoughtlessness Monday night, Greg would never come back to her, either. "What are we going to do?" she asked, stroking the animal's wiry coat. "Is it too late to say we're sorry?"

The remorseless animal swallowed the last of the tagboard and trotted hopefully away in search of another treat. It didn't even look up with Andi when the loudspeaker across the street announced an early home run.

He'd struck out the first batter, allowed the second to single, and walked the third. Greg pushed the wad of soft gum between his teeth with his tongue, blew a large pink bubble, and waited for the next guy to step up to the plate. His eyes wandered stubbornly to the overflowing stands, but he dragged them back, popping the bubble impatiently with his teeth. He almost never walked a batter. He had to get a grip here.

Nodding briefly at the catcher's signal, Greg dug his fingers into the familiar stitching on the leather ball hidden within his glove. With runners on base, he would throw from the stretch. As he drew his arm up and back, he felt the uncomfortable pull along his chest. There hadn't been time to remove the microphone after his encounter with Zeke, so it was a constant reminder, tugging his mind from the game as surely as it tugged the hair from his skin.

The instant Greg released the ball he knew it would be outside and a little low—another ball. In the split second it would take for it to slap into Riley's glove, Greg's eyes flicked to the designated spot in the crowd. *Where the heck is Ferris?*

A sharp crack of wood surprised him and snapped his attention back to home plate. The bat, he saw with surprise, had just left the batter's hand and was falling sluggishly to the ground, as if in the slow motion of a coaching video. Greg watched Riley begin to rise from the squat, reaching for his mask, his mitt empty. *Where,* Greg wondered now, *is the ball?*

Instantly, there was another crack, louder this time, and he felt himself propelled backward. Small spots of color floated through the sudden darkness—bright stars closer than they had ever been before. Greg reached out to them as he waited for the falling to stop, but the sensation was endless and the stars themselves finally withdrew into the deep velvet blackness that followed.

When Greg opened his eyes, he was standing above home plate. That it was impossible was of little consequence, since it was true. He looked down at the ivory-colored pentagon inches below his feet and wondered why the ump had failed to whisk away the soft brown dirt after the last batter.

When he lifted his gaze, the grass of the outfield was startling in its greenness. Surely he had seen grass before. Why, then, had he never noticed that each blade was a separate little plant, living and unique?

He listened to the birds converse in the tree-lined berm that embraced the back of HoHoKam Park. Their song, and the more distant hum of traffic on Center Street, were the only sounds. Then, from somewhere behind his back, a whisper rose to a murmur and Greg turned his attention at last to the men on the baseball diamond. Players from both teams rushed toward one another, converging in the center of the field. He watched their bobbing hats, bright blue and dusky plum, bend over a shapeless form on the mound.

As he looked on with little interest, the hats parted to admit Biderman, a couple of trainers, and the team physician who had examined his arm. As the group closed behind them, photographers rushed forward and Greg read Jensen's name from the back of his jersey. The outfielder angrily flung one camera away and Greg was about to move closer to help his roommate when the indistinct sound rose again, this time from a murmur to a din.

Curious now, without a thought as to how he did it, Greg rose high above the plate to determine the source of the excitement. A man lay rigid and lifeless on the ground. Only the number on his striped shirt seemed familiar. But as Greg moved closer, he caught a glint of sun off the small, silver band on the man's little finger.

Quick realization struck him with greater force than had the ball. *Oh, God, no!* Greg prayed. *Please don't let me die now. Not here—not this way—in front of all these people.* The last years of his life had been lost to the public. If these were to be the last moments, couldn't they, at least, be his alone?

The newest sound to fill Greg's consciousness was more urgent than the commotion of the crowd. It was a rushing wind, a roar with the power to sweep away all other sound as it pulled him along. The scene on the field began to recede as he felt himself drawn inexorably away. *No!* he cried. *I'm not ready yet! I have to finish. Please, God, I've come so close . . .*

He fell again, this time into a fluid passage, governed by an irresistible force. Without his assent or assistance, he moved through it very quickly, away from everything familiar and toward nothing he knew or understood. Greg perceived others in the passage, not far distant, but lacking now every sense that moments before had seemed so sharp, he could not reach out to help, or be helped by, his fellow travelers. There was no beginning to the unfathomable depths of this darkness and, just when Greg despaired of there ever being an end, there was Light.

CHAPTER 38

Andi squinted into the glare of the afternoon sun striking water as she walked quickly across the bridge from the zoo, relieved that her workday was finally over. Maybe she could get to HoHoKam in time to catch Greg as he left the game. Hopefully, there was an innocent explanation for where he had been last night. Surely, it wouldn't be too late for them, after all. She walked faster.

"Andi!"

Barely turning to acknowledge the sound of her name, she couldn't make herself stop walking. She had to see Greg. She called over her shoulder, "I'm in a hurry, Les."

He ran to catch up. "I just wanted to tell you I'm sorry about Howland."

"Sorry?" Andi asked, suspicious of what gossip might be circulating through the zoo. "Sorry about what?"

"You didn't hear?"

"What?" Andi repeated. She stopped at last to turn her full attention to her friend. At the look on his face, her heart, for some reason, began to pulse in her throat. "What about Greg?"

"He was hit by a ball," Les panted. "He took it to the head—just above his right temple. It's been on the news all afternoon. Howland's at Barrows now. They don't think he'll make it, but they can't turn off the machines until his family gets there."

Les and the trees and the lagoon moved in a slow circle as Andi watched helplessly. She reached for the iron railing as it swept past and shrank against it. Les couldn't be right, she thought. He couldn't. Her lips and tongue formed the word "no" but no sound could escape the awful throbbing in her throat.

"Andi?"

Les' face was concerned but out of focus. She closed her eyes. *Please, Father, please.* Prepared to trade all the prayers she might ever utter for the answer to just this one, Andi could think of no other words, so she repeated these over and over as she gripped the rail along the bridge. *Please, Father, please.*

The wooden bridge was narrow, not very long, and lay almost at Greg's feet. Another step and he would be on it, his decision made and the result irreversible. With the Source of Light just beyond the horizon, Greg yearned to move quickly there. But an unseen hand prevented his progress, allowing him passage only with his eyes.

He stood silently, enraptured at the unbelievable beauty of the pastoral scene before him. The grass was as singular as he had seen at the ball field, but the color had changed and deepened somehow. As Greg pondered the difference, an answer manifested itself: colors here were not products of the reflection of light, but the emanation of it—indescribable and pure.

Tiny, snow-white blossoms, imbued with a life-force of their own, glistened among the blades of grass while the slow-moving water under the bridge shone crystal beneath the ethereal blue of the sky. Greg explored the vastness of the heavens with his eyes, but found no summer sun to shine down upon this meadow. The light, he suddenly knew, was inherently present: warm, illuminating, and living of itself.

Greg marveled at his former reluctance to cross to this magnificent new world. Though he had always gloried in the beauty of the earth, this was beyond everything he had seen and all he could imagine. He felt peaceful, happy, and for the first time in his life, unconditionally accepted and loved. Here, finally was a place he belonged. Not far distant was One to whom he belonged. Greg sank to his knees in gratitude, a timeless psalm forming on his lips: *The Lord is my Shepherd.*

A new wave of longing washed over him. But before he could act on it, or even form a plea in his mind, a small group approached from the far bank. Dressed in white, like the sympathetic man in the temple, they advanced in silence yet, Greg believed, with great anticipation and gladness. He rose eagerly to meet them, certain they had come to escort him the rest of his way. But the little band paused, and a single man stepped up to the bridge.

"Jim!" Greg's heart leapt forward, though his feet remained rooted to the spot. This Jim was the man he remembered, before the pain of disease and self-disgust had etched haggard lines upon his youthful face, and the drugs had dulled the light in his loving eyes. He was smiling as he had in their youth, Greg saw with joy, and appeared to be at peace. He moved to embrace his brother, tears streaming down his cheeks.

"No, Greg," Jim said gently, holding up a hand in greeting and caution. His countenance was tender and full of understanding. "It isn't time. You must help us. You must go back."

"Jim, no!" Greg cried, his reluctance to return to life many times greater than it had been to leave. "I want to stay here with you . . . with Him."

"I know, Greg, but please understand. My mission on earth is over, though I have much yet to learn from it here. Yours has just begun. Many of us are counting on you, brother."

Greg looked toward the others in Jim's group. The luminous faces were hopeful, familiar, and well loved.

"We need you," Jim repeated. "You must return to allow us all to go on together. There isn't another, Greg."

As it had before, revelation flowed into him and Greg envisioned himself in white, kneeling before an altar in the House of the Lord. Jim, and many others, stood nearby, able at last to see, but remaining unseen. Still, he hesitated, remembering the darkness, the falling, and the fear. He sought his brother's encouraging eyes across the still waters. "I can't go back, Jim. I don't know the way."

"And lo, He is with you always," Jim said quietly as he moved slowly back to join the others. "He ever has been, Greg. He will be still."

Her front door was impossibly heavy and Andi wished now she had accepted Les' offer to walk her inside. He had already done so much: driving her to the hospital, then home, leaving her car forgotten in the parking lot at the zoo.

It had been a mistake to go to Barrows. The front lot of the neurological center was a media circus. Breathless reporters rushed to interview every employee and passerby, their portable satellites towering in the darkening sky to broadcast live every exciting detail of the possible death of a celebrity ballplayer.

What had she been thinking? Andi wondered now. She was nobody amid the throng of people gathered at the trauma facility. The doctors would never let her in to see Greg, no matter what she told them. She left quickly then, without reaching the front desk, horrified and sickened.

Even now that she was safely home, a wave of desperation washed over her and she reached out a single palm to steady herself against the hardwood frame. What would she have done, she wondered, if the door hadn't opened then, and her father not stepped out to sweep her into his arms?

"Daddy."

"I know, sweetheart," he said, holding her close. "I've been out looking for you. Come inside."

"Come inside," Greg's father commanded, his face contorted and ugly from an all-day binge. "I've been looking for you."

Greg was skidding through his life, losing his place and sense of time, but gaining perspective and a more important sense of self. It was remarkable what he remembered. He relived none of the important things—landmark events in school and baseball, which he thought had defined his life and given it meaning. He saw instead prosaic moments and found them rife with overlooked revelation.

He was three years old, watching his mother slice her homemade bread very thin, the way she knew he liked it. He was seven and Jim had captured a butterfly in his quick hands and held it ever so carefully for his little brother's inspection, then opened his fingers so they could watch together its soaring escape toward the sun. He was fourteen, leaning into Rusty Trenzle's consoling arms after his first heartbreaking loss. He was twenty-one, self-conscious and lonely, entering Lupe's warm, chaotic kitchen for his first sample of foreign food and unfamiliar family harmony.

Alternately with visions of others, he was alone with himself. He watched his character shift from a scene of a hungry youth filching a candy bar from the corner market to that of a man offering his food and money to a homeless old man in the park.

Some memories filled him with joy and satisfaction, others with unspeakable remorse. But underlying all was a bright new sense of the significant. The sacred moments in life, Greg knew now, came cloaked in the robes of sacrifice, and charity shone bright on the earth each time a person paused at another's sorrow, if only to offer a kind word or silent prayer.

Greg remembered his father.

"Are you deaf or just stupid?" Roy Howland sneered. "I told you to come inside."

Greg steeled himself for the glare of disgust and reproach that always struck first, and with the greatest force, then slowly raised his eyes.

He had never seen this man before. This Roy was a stranger, clearly lost, fraught with self-loathing, and pursued by demons of a sort Greg could little imagine. He felt the weight of the horror of his father's past roll over him and recoiled at a glimpse of his future. The instant Greg spent within his father's soul was time enough and to spare. He withdrew to search his own heart then, explored every corner, and found it whole. His scorn had turned to sorrow and his contempt to compassion. He would never, perhaps, forget, but he could eventually come to forgive.

And he could go back.

CHAPTER 39

"Bishop Ferris is here, Andi," Margaret spoke softly through the door. "He asked to see us together."

Andi rose slowly from her bed. It had been three days since Greg's accident. He was alive, but in a deep coma, according to news reports; the resulting swelling of the brain was proving more dangerous than the initial blow which had fractured his skull. She pulled Greg's cap from under her pillow and followed her mother reluctantly down the stairs.

She was surprised to see her father in the living room with Clytie and their bishop. Trent held office hours on Saturday mornings, and Andi couldn't remember him missing a day of work since Francie was born.

Andi extended her hand to the bishop and allowed him to pull her into a warm hug, then sank onto the love seat next to Clytie. Her sister gripped her fingers, her pretty face pink and swollen from crying. Andi patted the little hand and blinked rapidly herself, surprised that either of them could have tears left to shed.

"I'm sorry I didn't get here sooner," Bishop Ferris began, "but there was more to this thing with Greg than the extortion and drug dealing we originally thought. We ended up with a slew of states involved and had to bring in the FBI. I've barely been home since Wednesday." He tapped the envelope on his lap. "I want to make sure Martoni stays put for a long, long time."

"What are you talking about?" Trent interrupted incredulously. "What all is Howland involved in?"

"I need to start at the beginning," the bishop/detective explained quickly, "but first I want to tell you that I've seen Greg." He smiled gently at Andi. "I snagged a doctor I know at Barrows so we could give him a blessing. He's going to be okay, Andi."

"Can I see him?"

"Ariadne!" Trent slapped his knee. "How can you ask to see Howland after what we've been told?"

"I think I can arrange it, Andi," Ferris said kindly, "but let me tell you all something about him first."

Andi gazed at the charm bracelet on her wrist as her father leaned forward expectantly. *The heart has its reasons that reason knows nothing of.* Could anything the bishop might say change how she felt? She was grateful when Clytie's stubby fingers tightened around her own.

Bishop Ferris passed the envelope of pictures to Andi's parents as he began to tell them in detail about Greg's call from the temple, subsequent overnight interview at the police station, and eventual wiring for a taped conversation with Zeke. "In short," he concluded many minutes later, "Greg Howland was willing to give up his career and reputation for his integrity, but he would have sacrificed his soul, if he had to, for that little lady over there."

Clytie had the pictures by now and held them tightly to her chest to keep the tears from spotting a single precious one.

Trent Reynolds looked sheepishly from his misty-eyed wife to his tearful daughters and cleared his own throat roughly. "Did you say, Bishop, that you could get Andi in to see Greg?"

Bishop Ferris smiled. "I did, indeed."

The sweetish, antiseptic smell and utilitarian look of the ICU cubicle gave Andi gooseflesh. Her mother slipped a sustaining arm around her shoulder and guided her gently into Greg's room. A bank of monitors recorded the young man's heart rate and brain patterns with beeps and flashes, while yards of latex tubing dripped fluids in, then drained them faithfully out from his still body.

Andi couldn't bear to look toward the head of the high bed. She turned away to arrange Francie's handmade card, Enos' glove, and Clytie's teddy bear on a small table near its foot, then added a New Testament. The small book of scripture had been pressed into her hand downstairs by a kind Hispanic woman who, with other members of her congregation, held a prayer vigil for Greg in the lobby.

"Are you Andi?"

The girl jumped at the sound of the timid voice from the semi-darkness. She'd been so intent on avoiding Greg's face that she hadn't noticed the slight form huddled on the far side of the room near his head. "Yes," she said tentatively, moving to where there was more light. "I'm Andi Reynolds. This is my mother, Margaret."

"He told me about you just this week," the old woman said, her hand clasping Greg's for all it was worth. "I asked the doctors to call you. But nobody knew who you were."

The woman raised her eyes and Andi gasped at the unmistakable blueness. "Mrs. Howland?"

She nodded, a single tear trickling down her thin cheek. "Sadie."

She wasn't as old, Andi realized now, as she had seemed at first. But a painful life, and now the loss of both her sons, had taken its toll on her features. Andi was relieved, and grateful, when her mother circled the bed.

Margaret put her arms around Sadie Howland's gaunt shoulders in a comforting embrace. "Andi came as soon as she could," she said gently. "The hospital wouldn't let us in before today."

"They say . . . he could die," Sadie said, her voice barely above a whisper. "I never helped him . . . told him . . . he never knew . . . "

"Greg loved you," Andi said. "He told me so." Realizing what tense they were using, she raised her chin. "He loves you, Mrs. Howland. And he's going to be fine." Her eyes darted to the bed and away. "He has to be."

"I came," Greg's mother said. "You see I came. Roy said let it go—wasn't nothing we could do for Greg—but I packed right up when the doctor called and I came." A battered suitcase lay protected between her worn shoes. "I'd hid the money Greg gave me real good. Roy never even knew I had it." She looked quickly up at Margaret and her voice rose as if expecting a challenge. "I'm not ever going back there."

Margaret's hands still rested on the woman's shoulders. "When did you eat last?"

Sadie shook her head.

"Come with me to the cafeteria for a bite. Andi will stay with Greg."

"My boy—"

"Andi will be here. Greg needs you to be strong for him now, so you must eat a little. It won't take long." Margaret gathered Sadie up gently and gave Andi a reassuring nod. "We'll be right back, dear."

As the two women left the room, Andi pressed her fingers to her lips and turned slowly back toward the bed. The side of Greg's head was bandaged, held motionless by a metal collar and twin bolsters of tightly rolled towels. A hair-thin tube extended from the bandage, draining fluid from the swelling over his brain. He looked serene, Andi thought, but very pale, with spidery blue veins standing out on his eyelids.

She went to him then, her slender fingers reaching toward his face, then pausing in the air above his forehead. A fine sanding of blond beard covered the small cleft in his chin, and Andi ran her fingers lightly down his cheek to touch it tenderly.

I can't bear it, she thought. *Being with you this way is worse than not seeing you at all.* She lay her head on Greg's chest as she closed her eyes and listened to the steady, ever-so-comforting beat of his heart. "I love you, Greg," she said softly. "Please come back to me. Please, Greg. Come home."

Greg had been lost for some time in this place of mist and eternal twilight. With no sun or stars to mark the passage of days, there was little way for him to know if he'd wandered a week, a month, or most of his lifetime.

The monsters are gone, Greg thought. One evil, he felt sure, had been slain before he slipped into this place, and the other—the specter of his father—had faded to mist itself and disappeared. There was nothing left to fear but being lost in this endless maze. Alone. Forever.

Greg.

He turned toward the beloved voice and saw, just beyond his grasp, a shimmering copper thread. He tried to reach through the mists for it, but his hand was too heavy to lift and his arm was unwieldy and impossible to move.

Come back to me.

The thread receded toward an amber dawn. Fearful to be left in the deepening twilight, Greg summoned all the strength and concentration he could command. One finger moved a fraction of an inch toward a lock of Andi's hair that spilled across his chest and onto the bed.

Andi raised her face. "Greg?"

The dawn was nearer now; he could almost see it beyond the twilight. He tried once, twice, then forced his eyes to open.

"Ariadne."

He had finally said her name. The realization brought a hint of movement to the corner of his lip. The radiant face hovering over his was more than a vision this time, and more beautiful than one as well. "So, you really are an angel," he mumbled thickly.

"Greg!" New tears, joyous tears, filled Andi's eyes as she caressed his face, unable to believe that she had somehow lived worthy of such a blessing. "Your mother's here," she told him softly.

"An angel *and* a miracle?" Andi leaned closer, unwilling to miss a single precious syllable. "Then this really must be heaven."

"She chose you, Greg."

As his eyes drifted closed, Andi stiffened in fear. But the fathomless blue appeared a few minutes later and this time she drew in her breath at the illumination she saw. "Oh, Greg . . . "

"I want to tell you, Andi," he said tenderly. "Only you . . . when we go to the temple." His fingers moved slowly to touch a nearby curl. "Will you wait for me?"

The tears that had distilled on Andi's lashes fell finally to her cheeks. "I would have waited my entire life to be with you. Forever, if I needed to."

Greg's lips twitched in a shadow of the lopsided grin for which Andi had fallen so hard that first day at the zoo. "Let's hope it doesn't take me that long." He tried to raise a hand to the side of his head and almost managed to brush the bandage. "I take it my new haircut is worse than ever."

Andi captured his fingers as they fell and cradled them carefully under her chin. "You never looked better in your life. But don't get any ideas, Greg Howland. Your most-eligible-man-in-America days are over."

"Already?" he said with a weary smile. "And I never got to be very good at it."

Despite his best attempts to stay awake to be with Andi, Greg's eyelids began to close. His words grew slower and a little muffled. "Speaking of things I'm supposed to be good at, did the guy who got that last hit make it home?"

"I don't know," Andi whispered, softly kissing his forehead, then his lips. "But you did, Greg, and that's all that matters."

ABOUT THE AUTHOR

Kerry Lynn Blair wrote her first novel when she was eight years old and promised herself that she would do it again when she "grew up." Thirty years and four children later—in addition to serving in several ward and stake auxiliary presidencies—she found time to do it. She lives in Mesa, Arizona, with her husband, Gary, and their children, in addition to numerous family pets.

Kerry enjoys baseball, reading, and teaching Sunday School. This is her first published novel.

Kerry welcomes readers' comments. You can write to her in care of Covenant Communications, Box 416, American Fork, Utah 84003-0416.